T0385307

The Great Return

The Great Return

Why Only a Restoration of Christianity Can Save Western Civilisation

Jamie Franklin

HODDER &
STOUGHTON

First published in Great Britain in 2025 by Hodder & Stoughton
An imprint of John Murray Press

1

Copyright © Jamie Franklin 2025

The right of Jamie Franklin to be identified as the Author of the Work has been
asserted by him in accordance with the Copyright, Designs and Patents Act 1988.

A CIP catalogue record for this title is available from the British Library

Hardback ISBN 978 1 399 81492 8
ebook ISBN 978 1 399 81512 3

Typeset in Sabon MT by Hewer Text UK Ltd, Edinburgh
Printed and bound in Great Britain by Clays Ltd, Elcograf S.p.A.

John Murray Press policy is to use papers that are natural, renewable and
recyclable products and made from wood grown in sustainable forests.
The logging and manufacturing processes are expected to conform
to the environmental regulations of the country of origin.

Carmelite House
50 Victoria Embankment
London EC4Y 0DZ

www.hodderfaith.com

John Murray Press, part of Hodder & Stoughton Limited
An Hachette UK company

The authorised representative in the EEA is Hachette Ireland, 8 Castlecourt Centre,
Castleknock Road, Castleknock, Dublin 15, D15 YF6A, Ireland (email: info@hbgi.ie)

Contents

Introduction: A World Without God?

> When faced with the disastrous consequences of a particular course of action, we must retrace our steps and restore, as much as possible, the conditions that existed prior to our setting out on this course.
>
> Yoram Hazony, *Conservatism: A Rediscovery*

The Argument and Some Objections

This is a book about Christianity and the post-Christian or secular West.* It argues that if we want to rescue our civilisation from a bleak, nihilistic, totalitarian future then we must return to individual and collective belief in Christianity. Indeed, it argues that it may already be too late.

The quotation above from the Jewish political philosopher Yoram Hazony suggests that we in the West have embarked upon an ambitious and momentous experiment: the attempt to recreate both ourselves and our environment using the power of autonomous rationality. This experiment is failing, and we have an opportunity, as we stand upon this precipice, to decide if we want to turn around and retrieve that which has been spurned or to keep on walking in the same direction and fall off the edge.

Readers may think that I am being melodramatic. Everything is essentially okay, they may say, and they will reframe the ostensible problems we face as either positive developments or temporary glitches in an otherwise progressive system.

---

* I will use the terms 'post-Christian West', 'secular West' and 'modernity' interchangeably.

But the problems we face are, at least in theory, extremely serious: the collapse of domestic infrastructure and cultural coherence because of the low birth rate and the scale of mass immigration; the breakdown of international supply chains because of the failure of diplomacy between nations leading to food shortages and power outages; nuclear war between the great powers of West and East. We cannot dismiss these, and a myriad of other, very serious issues. To do so would be naive.

These crises are indicative not simply of bad luck or a few poor strategic political decisions but of an ideological and ethical incoherence (or set of incoherences) that lie at the very heart of our civilisation.

Surely, though, we do not need Christianity to solve any of this. We haven't needed it for some time, and we certainly don't need it now. Our civilisation has been built on technological, scientific and political progress that has freed us from the darkness, ignorance and backwardness of the Christian past. We go forward to solve our problems, not backwards.

Yet this objection relies on a questionable assumption about the Christian past. For how long have we been living in a truly post-Christian society? Depending on how you measure it, you could say as recently as the 1960s. The Canadian philosopher Charles Taylor, for example, offers the decline of belief and observance as one of the definitions of secularism.* In Britain, it was only in the 1960s that this downturn really kicked in. In that decade all the normal indicators of Christian belief and observance began to decline sharply: church attendance, confirmations, infant baptisms, communicants on Easter Sunday, and

---

* The other two are the separation of Church and state and the phenomenological sense of what it is like to live in a society in which religious faith is not the central constituent of the so-called 'social imaginary'. The latter is the automatic way that people within a society imagine reality to be. See Charles Taylor, *A Secular Age* (Cambridge, MA: Harvard University Press, 2007), pp. 1–4.

the like.* This was also the decade in which traditional Christian social morality in various areas began to be rejected and replaced with a form of post-Christian liberalism that prized freedom and equality, and their apparent ethical implications, as its central values.[1] In other words, the decline of Christianity in Britain at least has only really taken place in the last sixty years. It has not been very long in the making.

So whether we say that we have become properly post-Christian since the 1960s or that it started much earlier, the fact remains the same: even though the West has at various points proclaimed its independence from its Christian past, it has never fully rejected the values and assumptions that were bequeathed to it by Christianity. It has striven with all its might to justify some of these values using secular reason, not because secular reason leads to these conclusions but because the secular proponents of the assumptions prefer to live in such a world. A historical example of this is the American Declaration of Independence, significantly influenced by the Enlightenment rationalism of Thomas Jefferson, which claims in its first sentence that it is a 'self-evident' truth that all men are created equal. In other words, the equality of all men (meaning, of course, men and women) is something that is simply obvious and can be obtained by rational enquiry. But many cultures and societies have not found this to be a self-evident truth at all. Aristotle, for example, saw a natural hierarchy that consisted of men at the top and women and slaves far below. And even in the society in which the Declaration of Independence was framed it was not considered self-evident that black people were equal to free white men. Indeed, there was a significant question over whether slaves were even human at all. Since there are exceptions such as these – even within the society that made this claim – in what sense

---

* Those implications would be things such as the cessation of marriage and child-rearing as the normative and honourable way of life for the propagation and continuation of society, the widespread acceptance of divorce and adultery, casual sex, cohabitation, abortion, pornography, recreational drug use, homosexuality, prostitution, and so on.

can we believe in the 'self-evident' equality of all men? The argument of this book is that this claim and others like it are not arrived at through the observation of self-evident realities, nor are they the product of logical deduction from first principles, but they are founded in the historical Christian past.

Nevertheless the West has continued to propagate Christian ideas and has rebadged them claiming that it discovered them using autonomous reason. The idea of the equal value of all people is perhaps the central and most important among them.* When we take a historical perspective, we see that the idea of human equality is transmitted to us from the Christian past and derives ultimately from the Judeo-Christian notion of men and women created in the image of God. There is little reason in nature to think that human beings are equal to one another and many reasons not to reach such a conclusion. Creatures are bequeathed with all sorts of strengths and weaknesses that place them in natural dominance hierarchies. Any alternative that stresses equality among people can only be the result of an overarching philosophy which is not derived from nature itself but imposed upon it. I am arguing that that philosophy is the Christian religion.

We might accept that some of our values come from Christianity but still object that the origin of these values is irrelevant and the fact that we prefer a value such as the equality of human beings is enough to justify its being kept. But I will argue that this is not enough because preference is a very weak basis for such values. After all, preferences change and the preferences of the most powerful may very well be that all people are not treated equally but are subjugated for the benefit of the elite.

---

* The other candidate here is the concept of monotheism, which comes to us first from the Hebrew Scriptures and is transmitted into Western culture more broadly through Christianity. As I will explain in Chapter Four on ethics, the idea of monotheism is inextricably linked with the notion that there is one universal ethical standard which applies to all people at all times. This contrasts with polytheism and atheism, which give us no such basis and imply a relativist ethics.

Further to that, there may be many people who do not prefer Christian values at all. The thinker who is most often mentioned in this context is Friedrich Nietzsche, who articulated himself on this point most clearly in his work *The Joyous Science*, published for the first time in the 1880s. Nietzsche claimed that there was a need to take action given the so-called 'death of God': belief in God has become impossible, he urges, and therefore we must face up to the consequences, whether good or bad. For him, it is fair to say that the death of God was, on balance, desirable, but that there were also momentous consequences, which should not be trivialised. One of his aphorisms, 'New Struggles', captures something of this:

> After the Buddha died, people showed his shadow for centuries afterwards in a cave – a monstrous and unEarthly shadow. God is dead; but given the ways of men, perhaps for millennia to come there will be caves in which His shadow will be shown. And we – we still have to subdue His shadow![2]

In this aphorism, the Buddha and his shadow are a metaphor for God and the effects of Christianity respectively. God has died (that is, belief in God) but the effects of belief in God persist. This may go on for some time in some places. The aphorism ends with an imperative however: we must subdue his shadow! In other words, we must curtail the effects of belief in God in our world here and now. We have to wake up to the presence of the shadow of the Buddha and reject it completely. Only in this way can we truly banish the presence of the Christian God from our new world.

The aphorism 'What Our Cheerfulness Means' considers the enormity of the decline of Christianity:

> The greatest event of recent times – the fact that 'God is dead', that the belief in the Christian God has become untenable – has already begun to cast its first shadows over Europe. For the few at least whose eyes, whose suspicious eyes, are strong enough and

subtle enough for this drama, some sun seems to have set, some ancient and profound confidence has turned into doubt; to these eyes our old world must seem to be becoming more vespertine, distrustful, strange and 'old' with every passing day. In the main, however, we may say that the event itself is much too great, too remote, too far beyond most people's capacity to understand, for us to imagine that even the tidings of it could have reached their ears, let alone that very many people would already know what its actual implications were, or what things would have to collapse, now that this belief has been undermined, because they were built upon it, leaned against it and had become intertwined with it: for example, our entire European morality.[3]

The imagery here is typically Nietzschean: a great sun has set and a confident and antique way of seeing the world has been thrown into doubt and confusion. However, as time goes on, we look back at that old world and see how very strange indeed it all was, how it was not actually that illuminating at all but was in fact gloomy and alien to our human sensibilities. Most people cannot understand this because of its significance: the fact that 'our entire European morality' has been bound up in the existence of this Christian God is precisely the reason that people's eyes are blinded to his death.

Nietzsche is showing us that the death of Christianity inevitably leads to the death of Christian values. The persistence of those values is to some degree unavoidable but ultimately limited. Eventually these beliefs will have to 'collapse', as Nietzsche puts it, as people realise, albeit gradually, that the values they took for granted as a self-evident reality are nothing of the sort. They are, rather, radically contingent upon Christianity and the Christian God.

In his great novel *The Brothers Karamazov*, Fyodor Dostoyevsky explored a similar idea and famously put it into the mouth of the atheistic character Ivan Karamazov, who claims that, without God, anything is permitted. At one point in the story, Ivan's brother, the voluptuary Dmitri, facing conviction for the murder of their father, says to his pious brother Alyosha:

'I am tormented by the question of God. That alone torments me. For what if he does not exist? . . . Then, if he does not exist, man is the boss of the Earth, of creation. Magnificent! Only how will he be virtuous without God? That is the question. I think about it all the time.'⁴

Dostoyevsky provides here a penetrating insight: at first the non-existence of God seems wonderful because 'man is the boss of the Earth'; however, it does raise the rather disconcerting question of how man can be virtuous under his own lights. And this is what Dmitri thinks about all the time.

Nietzsche and Dostoyevsky are inversions of one another. Dostoyevsky's view of atheism is undeniably critical. Even in the mid-nineteenth century Dostoyevsky believed that the breakdown of Christian belief was causing catastrophic tears within the fabric of Russian civilisation. The plot of *The Brothers Karamazov*, for example, concerns the corruption of the institutions of the family and the Orthodox Church, and their terrible and far-ranging consequences.

Nietzsche, on the other hand, was more sanguine. Unlike Dostoyevsky, Nietzsche was an atheist and believed that the death of God was metaphysically justified. Yet, it is important to note that Nietzsche did not see the death of God in the somewhat complacent way of contemporary Western humanist intellectuals such as those of the New Atheist movement. Nietzsche knew that a complete re-evaluation of value was entailed by the end of Christianity and that those values clearly propagated by Christian belief could not persist:

In fact, we philosophers and 'free spirits' experience the news that the 'old God is dead' as if illuminated by a new dawn; our hearts are overflowing with gratitude, astonishment, presentiment and expectation – at last the horizon seems free again, even if it is not bright; at last our ships can set sail again, ready to face every danger; every venture of the knowledge-seeker is permitted again; the sea, our sea, lies open again before us; perhaps there has never been such an 'open sea'.[5]

Nietzsche conjures here the imagery of a fleet of ships, bravely and adventurously setting out upon the empty water. However, the horizon is 'not bright' and there are dangers ahead.[*]

The most famous part of Nietzsche's writing is the Parable of the Madman, which captures a far darker mood than those quoted so far. The story begins with the madman running into the centre of a marketplace and crying out that he seeks God but the people standing around mock him and laugh at him, complacently carrying out their transactions, oblivious to the prophetic significance of his actions. Thence follows an extremely powerful passage of literature:

'Where did God go? I will tell you! We have killed Him – you and I! We are all His murderers! But how did we do this? How were we able to drink up the sea? Who gave us the sponge to wipe away the whole horizon? What did we do when we unchained this Earth from its sun? Where is it heading? Where are we heading? Away from all suns? Are we not constantly falling? Backwards, sidewards, forwards, in all directions? Is there still an above and below? Are we not straying as through an infinite nothingness? Do we not feel the breath of empty space? Has it not become colder? Is night not falling evermore? Mustn't lanterns be lit in

---

[*] Aphorism 124 'In the Horizon of the Infinite' also uses this imagery: 'We have left dry land and put out to sea! We have burned the bridge behind us – what is more, we have burned the land behind us! Well, little ship, look out! Beside you in the ocean. True it does not always roar, and sometimes it is spread out like silk and gold and a gentle reverie, but there will be hours when you realize that it is infinite, and that there is nothing more terrible than infinity' (ibid., p. 133).

the morning? Do we hear nothing yet of the noise of the grave-diggers who are burying God? Do we smell nothing yet of the divine putrefaction? For even gods putrefy! God is dead! God remains dead! And we have killed Him! How shall we, the most murderous of all murderers, ever console ourselves? The holiest and mightiest thing that the world has ever known has bled to death under our knives – who will wash this blood clean from our hands? With what water might we be purified? What lustrations, what sacred games shall we have to invent? Is not the greatness of this deed too great for us? Must we not become gods ourselves, if only to appear worthy of it? There has never been a greater deed – and because of it, whoever is born after us belongs to a higher history than all history hitherto!'[6]

The sheer multiplication of images emphasises the point: the dried up sea, the horizon wiped away, the Earth unchained from its tether, the falling of a perpetual night, the coldness of the new world, the stench of the rotting corpse of God, the immense task that befalls humanity to replace God. Nietzsche wants the reader to understand the sheer vastness of this deed, so vast that it cannot be overstated: God is dead, and we are responsible.

The story continues with an epiphany: the people stare at the madman with blank incomprehension. His lantern falls to the ground and breaks into pieces. 'I have come too early,' he says. The people cannot possibly understand and yet 'they have done it themselves'.[7] Here we have Nietzsche as the unappreciated prophet, one who has arrived, like John the Baptist, as a forerunner to the age to come, too early to be understood. In this he was not wrong for, although he died a penniless and unknown lunatic, his predictions have nevertheless come to pass. He is the greatest prophet of the death of the Christian God. His analysis is far more compelling than the consensus of the modern liberal West, which imagines that it can kill God and yet not smell the stench of his putrefying corpse.

Progress or Degeneration?

I have already quoted the great analyst of secularism Charles Taylor and he remains a profound influence upon me personally. He is somebody for whom I have an immense amount of respect. But one aspect of his outlook I find unconvincing is his view of historical progress. I will quote from Taylor himself to explain what I mean:

> I think that, morally speaking, humanity is evolving. Of course, this evolution is not linear, but if we look at things on the scale of centuries, the human conscience has gained in breadth and depth. Sometimes, it makes considerable leaps. For instance, I'm thinking of what we call the 'first axial revolution', triggered by Buddha, the prophets of Israel, and the Greek philosophers. At that moment, for the first time in the history of mankind, and more or less everywhere simultaneously across the planet, the purposes of existence and social organization changed: many became sensitive to a horizon of meaning that went beyond mere survival and the prosperity of the community. I'm referring to nirvana, eternal life, etc. Human conscience leaped out of tribal partitions and opened up to higher aspirations that were, at the same time, more universal and more personal. Jesus represents a decisive leap, and it's the duty of the church to do what it takes for this leap to drive consciences as far as possible.[8]

Taylor here speaks as a Christian influenced by the philosophy of Hegel. He implies that there is a certain benign spirit animating the historical development of humanity. Taylor justifies this from an empirical perspective looking at the broad sweep of human moral development and saying that, on the whole, things are getting better. The first axial revolution constitutes the movement of humanity away from the status of the brute beasts, who only seek material survival and physical satisfaction, and towards a higher aspiration which includes the search for truth and the ultimate meaning of human life. He also includes the notion that 'tribal partitions' became 'more universal and personal'. He is perhaps driving towards a perspective not dissimilar to that of Buddhism which teaches a universal brotherhood of mankind. The role of Jesus in this is to bring about 'a decisive leap' which the Church promotes to 'drive consciences as far as possible'.[9] This must mean that the emergence of Jesus is a positive step forward in this upward process. The Church is a spur to that process, which is ongoing because of the spirit that animates history and encourages the development of humanity. In a Hegelian understanding, it is this spirit – *Geist* is the proper term for it – which is a kind of divine presence in the world not inappropriately associated with the Holy Spirit.[*]

Taylor's philosophy of history sits uneasily with his Roman Catholic profession. From most traditional Christian perspectives, it is not at all clear that the role of Jesus was to bring about a decisive leap forward within an ongoing moral development of humanity. And an important question is whether Taylor's empirical claim can be taken seriously: is humanity evolving morally? There are many who would agree that it is and that perhaps the Western world is at the zenith of that process. They would say that we are more open, tolerant and equal than any society before us and that we are well on our way to developing a global consensus towards a unified humanity free from war, hunger and pestilence.

This position, however, is unconvincing. The Judeo-Christian tradition, and particularly the emergence of Jesus, was not part of a shared development in universal morality but a complete revolution in morality. The antique world into which Jesus was born was characterised by barbarism, the like of which we can hardly imagine: a world in which infants were routinely exposed (see p.182),

---

* This notion of *Geist* or a world-spirit is also a key concept in the thought of Marx and other variants of Marxism, all of which see history as having a certain inevitable direction which is animated by a particular force. Marx secularises Hegel by insisting that it is an economic dialectic that drives the process. The contemporary Marxist idiom usually invokes an abstract concept such as 'justice'.

children were raped and molested; in which slaves, Christians, and other outsiders were forced to hack each other to death or were torn apart by lions for the amusement of braying crowds. This was a world in which Roman men were the only dignified people in society, who could use almost anyone they chose as objects of their lusts according to their whims; a world in which those men were indeed the patriarchal god-like figures in their own households and to whom children, wives and slaves were beholden as though to a deity. This was a society in which warfare and enslavement were glorified above all and in which violence was the supreme religion. And none of this was particularly dissimilar to the other empires of the ancient world.

The cultural context was positively antithetical to the message Christ brought. If Jesus was simply providing a spur to an ongoing moral development within humanity, why was he eventually crucified by the Roman empire? Rome, the Greek city states, the Persian, Median, Macedonian, Assyrian and Babylonian empires were all typically brutal imperial powers of their times. There is no evidence that they were affected by a positive moral development beginning with the 'axial revolution'. They were violent, savage, bloodthirsty empires built upon the ubiquitous human misery of conquest and slavery. The life and message of Jesus could not have been more revolutionary in such a context. The emergence of Jesus was an interruption within history and not a development of it.

The other implication of Taylor's thought is that life will continue to develop positively even given the decline of Christianity. Presumably this will happen even if the Church fails in its task to 'drive consciences as far as possible'. This raises the question of the uniqueness and importance of the Church and Christianity.

Additionally, it is hard for anyone who knows the history of the twentieth century to believe that humanity has been steadily evolving morally for thousands of years and that this particularly gruesome and nightmarish era of political mass-murder and genocide represents the zenith of that inevitable development. It is very difficult to think of these events as a mere flash of madness in an otherwise positive trajectory. One of the central assumptions of liberal political and moral thought is that humanity can improve itself through the operation of autonomous reason, independent of traditional authorities such as Christianity. But doesn't the Holocaust and the various other genocides of the twentieth century call this into question in a decisive manner?

We do not live at the zenith of moral development but on the other side of the Christian revolution which bequeathed to the world a vision of humankind as made in the image of God and destined for transcendent glory. This vision brought about belief in a moral universe that was reflected in the great cultural, artistic and architectural achievements of medieval Europe. We warm ourselves now on the dying embers of that revolution and, as David Bentley Hart has pointed out, its decline has meant a diminishment of our greatness and an embrace of banality:

> When one looks . . . at the crepuscular wasteland of modern Europe – with its aging millions milling among the glorious remnants of an artistic and architectural legacy that no modern people could hope to rival, acting out the hideously prolonged satyr play at the end of the tragic cycle of European history – it is hard to supress a feeling of morbid despair . . . When the aspiring ape ceases to think himself a fallen angel, perhaps he will inevitably resign himself to being an ape, and then become contented with his lot, and ultimately even rejoice that the universe demands little more from him than an ape's contentment.[10]

So, I demur from Taylor's optimism. The decline of Christianity means the decline of humanity as we know it. And this includes not only our moral sense but also our ability to make cognitive sense of the world and to act wisely within it, as our recent history has demonstrated only too well.

Covid-19: Time to Wake Up

I grew up in a Christian household, but I did not embrace the Christian faith until I was nineteen. I was baptised in a swimming pool and was for many years part of an evangelical movement of churches. Later on, in a turn of events that was surprising to me at the time, I returned to my public school roots and became an Anglican, eventually being ordained as a priest in the Church of England.

Some years before that time, I came across Richard Dawkins' *The God Delusion*. I had taken A-Level philosophy and enjoyed engaging with the components involving religion. But I was largely ignorant of the tradition of debate between atheistic thinkers and Christians. Dawkins' book was somewhat worrying. What would I find if I looked inside? Would it shake the newfound faith that I had acquired? Would I soon have to leave the church I loved and be distant from the friends I had made?

But Dawkins' book did not bring about such a re-evaluation. I do not remember my response in detail, but it did not result in my renouncing the faith. In fact, I came across a literature of Christian responses to Dawkins which seemed to me adequate and intellectually robust. I now think that Dawkins struggles to engage well with the Christian tradition because he is not as familiar with it as he could be. He is quick to point out when people misrepresent aspects of evolution, but is not so quick to grasp diligently, for example, the Five Ways of Thomas Aquinas before critiquing them. Further, he is often not familiar with the tradition of thought that goes along with the points he is critiquing. In the case of Aquinas, for example, he shows no awareness of any of the medieval commentators, Neo-Thomists such as Réginald Garrigou-Lagrange, the proponents of Nouvelle Théologie, such as Henri de Lubac and those sympathetic to their views such as David Bentley Hart, or Anglican thinkers such as E.L. Mascall, Hans Boersma and John Milbank.

At the time of writing, it seems that the influence of Dawkins and the other 'New Atheists' is waning. But people like Dawkins do represent a modern example of a tradition of atheistic attacks upon Christianity. Before Dawkins, perhaps the most well-known atheist of this sort was the philosopher Bertrand Russell. Just as Dawkins is now, Russell was a convinced believer in the project of modernity and of the resources of contemporary thought to furnish humanity with answers to the deepest questions.

To the criticisms of modern atheists, Christians have often provided apologetic answers: that is, responses to direct attacks upon Christianity that demonstrate the fallaciousness of the criticisms. While apologetics are an important part of the Christian intellectual tradition, Christian thinkers need to do more than simply respond to the objections of atheists and formulate counter arguments as to the existence of God, the resurrection of Christ, and so on.

Moreover, I believe that we need something else: a conversation about what Christianity really means to our world and what the loss of it would truly entail. My aim is to demonstrate that Christianity largely created the world that we take for granted and that, as Christianity declines, significant parts of that world will change in ways that will be deeply undesirable and worse. It might be the case that the reader, like Nietzsche, will hope for a new world of opportunity and discovery while also recognising the significant loss of Christianity. Or it might be that the reader will, like me, see that the true implication of the loss of Christianity is the loss of our present world and all that we love about it.

This book is for everyone who is interested in the subject matter, but I address it specifically to the many who have felt in recent times a sense of encroaching darkness and even evil in our culture. For many years, as a believing and practising Christian, I was very keen to share my faith with other people. But I was aware that there was a hardness and indifference towards Christianity. I have lived in wealthy cities such as Canterbury, Winchester and Oxford, and perhaps this affluence can serve to exacerbate such a lack of interest and complacency. In general (and without trying to sound too much like Karl Marx) it seems that economic conditions do insulate us from the need for Christianity: comfort, wealth, luxury, distractions are all easily co-opted into a mindset which thinks of God and the Bible as so much unnecessary persiflage. These things can be dismissed as eccentric hobbies and mere community activities for the lonely. Churches are hard to grow because there are not many Christians, and not many people convert from secular indifference. And this is to some degree because they are materially comfortable.

But something changed. It began in March 2020 with the onset of Covid-19. From the beginning, I was very disturbed by the situation. It was not so much the existence of the virus that worried me but that it seemed to me from quite early on that the severity of the situation was being exaggerated. There was a reluctance at the level of national government and international governance to take a more optimistic outlook. It appeared that these bodies rushed to imprison hundreds of millions of people in their homes – that perhaps they even wanted to do it. And, even stranger, that many people desired to be locked away. This was done in the hope (for that is all it was) that these actions would prevent infection and death.* And this was the most disturbing aspect: that we had all of a sudden arrived at an unquestionable consensus that the only thing that could possibly be done was to

---

* In Britain, we were told initially that the purpose of the lockdown was not to reduce overall infections and deaths from Covid-19 but to ease pressure upon the NHS so that the health service itself did not collapse and cease treating people who were in need of medical assistance for other illnesses. Boris Johnson's famous line was that we needed to 'squash the sombrero', referring to the curvature of the predictive graph of infections and deaths. To some this did not seem particularly coherent because the destruction of the national economy would result in the breakdown of the NHS anyway. Additionally, during this period, the NHS was essentially turned into a Covid-only service resulting in, for example, millions of missed cancer diagnoses.

shut people away in their homes at the behest of the government and hope that fewer people would be infected with the virus. No consideration was given to all that would cease in order to do this: social life, sports, business, religious observances, hospital, hospice and care home visits, family get-togethers – the list could continue. We were told that the only hope we had was that the pharmaceutical companies would produce a vaccine eventually and that, until then, we had to live in this way, prioritising this particular virus and our war against it above literally everything else.

I sensed that something was badly wrong. And I was not alone. Across the nation and across the world millions of people began to believe that they were being manipulated and lied to, that faceless elements in the structure of national and international governance were twisting this situation for their own ends to the detriment of humanity as a whole. This was merely an instinct at first, but it became a much clearer reality as information became more available and the fallout from this disaster more apparent. If the aim of governments around the world was truly to promote the well-being of their citizens, then their actions made little sense. It seemed to many that our governments had chosen to attack their people, to isolate them, to control them, to take away their God-given liberty and to impoverish them financially and emotionally, perhaps so that they would be more docile and easily manipulated.

Whatever was really going on, a new mood prevailed. Such a turn of events was unimaginable beforehand. The Chinese Communist Party invented the concept of lockdowns, and we would not previously have thought possible the importation of such a draconian idea into Western countries. Indeed, this was even admitted to publicly by one of lockdown's chief proponents, Professor Neil Ferguson.[11] And yet that is exactly what happened. Millions of people were profoundly shaken, and they sensed not just a moral but a spiritual darkness.

At first, sceptics of the narrative seemed few in number. To take a snapshot of public opinion from social media or from the corporate news was to have this intuition confirmed. But I knew at least a few other people who had the same reaction as I did. I remember seeing one of them share a news item on social media to the effect that the Swedish government had not implemented a lockdown and that there were not bodies piled in the streets of that Scandinavian nation. As time went on, more people became sceptical, and sceptical people found each other, mostly it would seem, through the internet.

I was working as a curate at the time and had only been in post some seven or eight months. I did not live in the parish in which I worked and my young family and I were quite isolated. Like many people, I had a sense that I wanted to do something about the situation. So, along with a like-minded curate friend, I started a podcast. After a few abortive attempts, my friend Thomas Pelham and I released the first episode of 'Irreverend: Faith and Current Affairs'. We really had no expectations as to what would happen next. But the first messages and emails started coming in from week one. As we became better known and the audience grew, we sensed that we were tapping into something significant.

The Church of England, along with every other major Christian denomination in Britain, had acquiesced to the Covid orthodoxy. It had even gone further in closing down all of its church buildings and the Archbishop of Canterbury had forbidden parish priests from going into their buildings alone in order to say prayers and celebrate Holy Communion (although they were allowed to go in to clean, flush the toilets and run food banks). We were told that we had to set a good example by staying at home like everyone else. This was the first time for 800 years that churches in England had been forcibly closed. Back at the beginning of the thirteenth century, it was the result of a squabble between King John and Pope Innocent III over the succession of Stephen Langton to the Archbishopric of Canterbury. But in 2020 the bells of the Church of England were silent on Easter morning for a quite different reason:

because the government had told us that we were not to gather together to worship the risen Christ in case we infected each other with Covid-19.

The significance of the podcast dawned on us as we continued to receive similar feedback and registered the disappointment vast swathes of people felt with the Church. There were, and continue to be, different takes on what the Church should have done as a response to the situation. These takes range from total defiance and rejection of the dictates of the secular authorities to a sadness that the Church did not bring even the gentlest challenge to the power of the state and its narrative. But what all of these responses had in common was the view that the Church's response was weak and lacking in something vital. To many, its response revealed something significant about the outlook of its leadership: a lack of genuine faith in the reality of the Christian religion. Whether or not this criticism is fair, it was certainly the perception. And even the perception has been very damaging.

One cannot remove the sense that the Church had a great opportunity at the time. Here was a nation – a world – shaken to its foundations by fear and uncertainty. For a moment the affluence and prosperity of our economy could not shield its citizens from the twin realities of suffering and death. In this context, we had an opportunity to have a voice, to be a real sign of hope, and to preach the message of the gospel to a perishing culture: Death is a fearsome thing, but God is real and he has redeemed those who will put their trust in him through the life, death and resurrection of his Son Jesus Christ.

But that is not what the Church said. Instead, what was said was in effect a parroting of the government's messages: propagandist slogans, carefully constructed, alliterative rhetorical maxims designed for effective memorisation and repetition. In some videos, the Archbishop of Canterbury and other bishops were literally repeating these slogans verbatim, sighing as though exasperated at the need to remind their recalcitrant clergy of the simplicity and urgency of the message: stay home, protect the NHS, save lives.*

And this is why, I believe, our podcast found the audience that it did. Among other things, we were questioning the shutdown of the churches. There was a principle at stake, which was the right of the government forcibly to deny Christians the liberty to gather together to worship God and to celebrate the sacraments. But the whole response appeared to be dramatically unnecessary: an overreaction to the threat that was posed by the virus. Was it really necessary to forbid worship in this way? Why couldn't the people who were especially vulnerable be informed of the risk and allowed to make their own decisions? Why were healthy people who were clearly not vulnerable banned from going to church? And there were many other questions beside these that simply were not being asked by any senior authority within the Church. People were desperate for leadership and they were not getting it. I believe that, in our grassroots podcast, they found a pale echo of what should have been.

Tom and I added a third sceptical vicar to our team, Daniel French, and we continued for some months, growing and hearing similar feedback all the time. In April 2021 we became, for the first time, the number one Christian podcast in the UK according to the chartable.com website. At the time of writing, every episode we release goes to the top of the episodes chart for Christian podcasts in Great Britain.

In addition to the Christians who were contacting us, we received correspondence from people who were either not Christians or who had some experience of Christianity – a lot of the time from

---

* Cf. Church of England, 'A Message from the Archbishop Justin Welby, on the need to keep church buildings closed', accessed 29.01.2024, [https://www.youtube.com/watch?v=QY44A6FlhkI]. As well as repeating the Dominic Cummings propaganda line, the Archbishop also makes the strange argument that shutting the churches and 'meeting' online constitutes a return to the earliest days of the Church when people gathered together in their homes.

childhood – but who were finding solace in listening. People were saying frequently that they were deeply disturbed by a tangible sense of evil, often for the first time, and that they were now seeking spiritual light and illumination. We heard from many, many people who became Christians during this time because they had trodden upon a similar path. They realised that the philosophical outlook and lifestyle they had followed was not equal to the darkness they were facing, and they knew they had to seek a spiritual light.

Thinking back to that time, it is as though people found themselves, all of a sudden, in a very different and disturbing world. Many were beset by an atmosphere of political hypocrisy and immorality and a desire on the part of the national and international elite to use this crisis to extend their powers over ordinary human lives. The beauty of life was crushed underneath the ugly weight of the so-called 'measures'. Many found, for example, the mass adoption and imposition of facemasks extremely disturbing, not least women who had been raped, whose mouths had been covered as they had been assaulted, or autistic children, who rely upon face-to-face recognition for reassurance from their parents and those who care for them. Laura Dodsworth and others have now demonstrated the significant amount of evidence that exists to show that facemasks in the UK were imposed by law for political and psychological reasons and not because there was real belief that they provided protection against Covid-19 infection.[*]

---

[*] Laura Dodsworth, *A State of Fear: How the UK Government Weaponised Fear During the Covid-19 Pandemic* (London: Pinter & Martin 2021), pp. 110–13. Dodsworth makes a number of substantiated points, not least her observation that both England's Chief Medical Officer, Chris Whitty, and the top US science lead on Covid, Anthony Fauci, said early on in the Covid crisis that masks do not reduce infection, only for this view to be completely reversed for no apparent reason some months later. Dodsworth observes that Robert Dingwall, a professor of sociology and advisor to the government, told her that he 'was convinced that masks had been introduced partly because they are "a symbolic reminder that people are dangerous, the world is dangerous, and you might feel safer at home"' (ibid., p. 113).

Another source of concern was the growing sense that the public were being intentionally manipulated and gaslighted during the now notorious daily press conferences in which endless graphs were produced to prove that hundreds of thousands would die unless complete obedience to the regime was adhered to. These graphs were produced by computer modellers, and it was never explained that the outcome of a model is entirely dependent upon the data and assumptions that are put into it.[*] The models were also conveniently forgotten when their predictions failed (which they always did) and the proponents simply continued to produce further models like Jehovah's Witnesses tweaking their predictions for the end of the world. We were told that we were planning for the 'reasonable worst-case scenario' but what we were really doing was assuming the worst possible scenario and, crucially, not paying attention to the catastrophic damage that these measures were going to do to our world and the people in it.[†]

I am not saying that our podcast was a perfect riposte, or that

---

[*] To take a single instance of why this is important, Neil Ferguson's early model, which was used to justify the first lockdown in March 2020 and predicted the deaths of hundreds of thousands of people unless the Chinese Communist Party's mitigations were adhered to, assumed that there was literally no prior immunity to Covid-19 in the population of the UK. It also assumed that the mitigation strategy would be successful. My point is not that these assumptions were wrong – although there are plenty of reasons to believe that they were – but that other assumptions could have been made: that there was a certain amount of prior immunity in the population, that lockdowns had never been tested and therefore couldn't be assumed to be effective, and that this uncertainty should be weighed, however speculatively, against the damage they would cause, and so on.

[†] One of the vastly underreported aspects of this catastrophe is the effect that this course of action has had on the poor both domestically and internationally. It is difficult to summarise the appalling damage done to poorer nations, but Toby Green, who is a left-leaning academic at King's College London, has done a heroic job in trying. For this, see Toby Green, *The Covid Consensus: The New Politics of Global Inequality* (London: Hurst & Company, 2021).

it was even particularly good. But I think it brought a measure of comfort to some people and perhaps articulated a number of their concerns. The fact that we were clergymen – even junior clergymen in the case of Tom and me – was significant. The fact that we were among only a few public Christian voices calling any of this out was probably even more so. I believe that we were trying to do what the Church should have been doing all along. Perhaps we did not do it well or in the right way. But we were trying, and there were not many others.

This book presents me with an opportunity to expand on some of the themes that we have been exploring over the past few years. It also picks up many of the issues I have been thinking about personally and in the course of my academic work.

What became clear to many at the time of the Covid crisis was that the Church is not doing a great job of preaching an authentic Christian message. The problem underlying this appears to me to be that it has largely been colonised by a kind of atheistic, left-leaning secularism that is apparently invisible to bishops and clergy. Understanding this and taking steps to challenge it is, to my mind, the greatest and most important task that faces thinkers in the Church.

Covid was a manifestation of this ecclesial secularism: we should close the churches and ban worship in order to save people from dying of a virus, and this is because people's physical health is important. But what about all the other aspects of Christianity that ought to have been considered? What about the supernatural components? Miracles, the preaching of the gospel, the grace of the sacraments, eternal life, and so on? If there existed a more robust and genuinely Christian outlook within the Church, surely we would really be wrestling with these sorts of questions.

Hence what I propose here: post-Christian secularism will result not only in the death of the West but in the death of the Church too. We have to realise that we cannot have traditional Western values and culture without Christianity, at least not for long. That change is already before our eyes in many ways. The

Church cannot acquiesce to this – and it certainly should not allow itself to be infiltrated by it. It must call the prodigal culture home before it is too late.

The Great Return

This may sound somewhat vague so let me be clear: our civilisation is changing to its great detriment because it has abandoned collective and (largely speaking) individual belief in Christianity. If we want to avert a full-scale civilisational crisis then we must return to both. It is by no means evident to me that the crisis is avoidable at this point but the great return of which I speak is the only option. This theme can be applied to various important and broad topics such as history, science, aesthetics, ethics, and the Church.

On history: in the West we tell ourselves a self-congratulatory story about the origin of the modern world. This story has various permutations but is essentially a secularisation of the main historical idea of the Protestant Reformation: that the world was held in darkness until a great light emerged which brought illumination to humanity.* In the Protestant Reformation story, that light was held to be the rediscovery of the gospel through a return to a faithful reading of the Bible. In the modern Western story, that light is the light of scientific discovery and political liberation from ecclesiastical domination. On this view, the modern world stands in almost total discontinuity from the Christian past. It is in antagonism to it and is its contrast. The modern Western story bears very little resemblance to the historical record, however, and is based upon a mythical view of the spontaneous emergence of

---

* The Protestant Reformed view of which I speak here was more typical of the continental Reformation, associated with figures such as Martin Luther, Ulrich Zwingli and John Calvin, than it was of the Church of England and Anglicanism, which had a much more ambivalent view of the medieval period and sought to reform the Church in continuity with Catholic principles such as that of the historic episcopate.

the contemporary world. Something does not come from nothing, and the modern world did not invent itself but rather sprung directly out of the Christian medieval age that preceded it. Thus, we are not to be congratulated for inventing ideas which underpin our deepest political and intellectual convictions – such as the dignity of the individual or the basic presuppositions underlying the scientific worldview – because these came to us not from our intuitive faculty of reason but from Christianity.

Following on from this, belief in 'science' constitutes the intellectual justification for the modern secular outlook, a justification that is simply nonsensical when examined closely. The view that modern science can give us a comprehensive picture of reality is flawed in multiple ways. One of the most basic problems with it is that it relies upon Christianity for its metaphysical backdrop and cannot possibly justify its own assumption of an ordered and explicable universe. There is no point of total discontinuity between the medieval period and the early modern one. Empiricism was not invented in the seventeenth century; neither was the application of reason to scientific questions. The idea that it was is simply a myth. Thus, the whole notion of a 'scientific revolution' which began a brave new world of progress and discovery is highly questionable. The significance of the seventeenth century was the beginning of a shift in outlook from Christianity to atheistic materialism – that is, from a picture of the world that assumed the existence of God and the supernatural to one that did not. The development of the scientific method did not justify this move, although it is assumed to have done so. One of the most obvious problems with the resultant materialist scientific worldview is that its ethical implication is nihilism: there is no objectively existing ethical framework but only preference. Neither can a materialist view explain the fundamental problem of Being: why does anything exist at all? The answers that have been proposed to this conundrum range from unquestioning faith – 'it just does' – to the irrational – 'nothing created something'. Because the modern atheistic and materialist scientific project is founded upon such assumptions and incoherent beliefs, it must guard itself by enforcing dogmatic presuppositions. These include the belief I have just alluded to: that everything that exists popped into existence out of nothing. Science will continue to recede into dogmatism so long as it rejects Christianity and cleaves to materialism. It will become less and less preoccupied with a disinterested quest for truth and will resemble any other institution that is captured by the politically and financially powerful. For science to address this it must have the humility to abandon its hubristic claim to be a comprehensive view of reality and take its proper place as one of many other disciplines within the range of human knowledge.

One of the great downfalls of the materialistic worldview is that it jettisons the aesthetic realm and denies people access to transcendence. There are at least two points of importance here. First, the materialist worldview cannot give an account of art or beauty that does not diminish them to the point of emptiness. Second, the materialist worldview denies the possibility that any sense of transcendence – whether through art, natural beauty, religion or human experience more generally – is necessarily illusory. And yet, in spite of the prevalence of this worldview, we continue to seek the transcendent in various artistic, aesthetic or sensuous pleasures, or we ally ourselves to secular political trends with quasi-religious sensibilities. But all this activity does not dispel the lingering sense that there is a tragic element to the secular life, which, without a horizon beyond this world, is ultimately powerless to contend with the terror of death.

Further, because science has been exalted to such heights, we are left with a serious problem in the domain of ethics. We assume that science can answer every question. And yet science provides no ethical principles at all. If we look to science for ethics, we will get nihilism; that is, a belief in no transcendent or objectively existing standards. Built upon these premises, modernity cannot justify its own dearly held assumptions such as belief in the dignity and equal value of individual human beings.

It is historically demonstrable that belief in inherent human dignity came from Christianity. This belief was outworked in political developments during the second millennium such as greater levels of democratic participation, human rights, protection of children from arbitrary death and exploitation, the abolition of slavery, and many other endeavours. These were all justified because of the Christian assumption that human beings are made in the image of God, possess dignity and equal value, and should be treated with respect and honour. If we abandon the Christian belief in humanity's origin in God, then we will inevitably abandon the conclusion that was drawn from that belief. We will begin to treat people as though they are not human, and this because our whole concept of humanity will have been lost. I will demonstrate that various practices with which we have been, and are becoming, familiar have more in common with the pre-Christian forebears of the Greco-Roman world than with our more recent past.

Another example of the ethical drift arising from the decline of Christianity is the re-emergence of Marxism in the form of woke ideologies such as so-called 'anti-racism'. These ideologies reject the notion that human beings are dignified individuals who have a significant capacity to live harmoniously with one another in spite of differences, and instead divide society into hermetically sealed and inherently antagonistic groups. The transhumanist movement, promoted by organisations such as the World Economic Forum, constitutes yet another post-Christian power-crazed ideology that seeks to improve the human race through the fusion of men and women with machines. And the incipient transgender ideology that seeks to disrupt the binary between men and women is providing an opportunity for the emergence of a post-Christian patriarchy. The conclusion of this ethically disastrous descent into nihilism will be a Nietzschean reality in which the strong rule over the weak and use them for their own purposes. I will argue that we can only truly oppose these developments by returning to the bulwark that kept such forces at bay.

The principles of democracy, the rule of law and the liberty of the individual are part of our Christian inheritance, all of which are being jettisoned as alternative political ideologies replace them. Here we see two principal political concerns which are deeply connected to one another. The first is that of the post-democratic globalist technocracy which seeks to diminish and ultimately remove democratic, nation-based decision-making in favour of an increasingly centralised international body of apolitical experts who believe that they can implement an improved society based upon axiomatic principles and subject-specific knowledge. The co-opting of science into this globalist agenda is one of its most pernicious features and has served to deceive hundreds of millions that the globalist technocratic elite are simply proceeding according to neutral scientific principles when in reality they are cynically exploiting events such as the Covid-19 situation and ostensibly man-made climate change in order to further their command-and-control agenda.

The globalist agenda is closely tied to the neo-Marxist movement which is commonly referred to as 'woke'. Far from being a novel political agenda with its own ideas, the woke movement is simply a revivification of various Marxist ideas such as the division of society into oppressors and oppressed, the false consciousness of the oppressors, the deconstruction of traditional society and rejection of tradition as a legitimate category, the delegitimisation of alternative viewpoints, the need for centralised redistribution based upon inequality, and other things of this sort. Its aggressive incursion into almost every sector of public life has caught many by surprise, but it is important to recognise that this is a symptom of the failure of post-Christian liberal democracy to make good on its promises.

Put simply, liberalism's two central values are freedom and equality. And yet these values contradict one another because freedom necessarily entails inequality and equality necessarily entails restriction. If people are truly free to pursue their own goals, based upon their own desires, using their own talents and opportunities, there will be some winners and some losers. Some will be rich and some will be poor. There will be freedom but there will also be inequality. To have complete equality, therefore, the freedom of the privileged and the gifted will have to be curtailed so that they are not allowed to accrue more wealth and power than others. Advocates of a more classical form of liberalism might attempt to avoid this conundrum by insisting that equality does not mean so-called equality of outcome (where everybody ends up with the same amount of money or similar-quality housing, for example), but equality before the law and equality of opportunity. Yet it seems that the turn to neo-Marxist wokeism is because of a dissatisfaction with the failure of secular liberalism to produce what is considered to be a fair society. In this way, liberalism has given birth to neo-Marxism. We have moved from one set of post-Christian political ideas to another.

The disastrous political trends that we witness before us are therefore the direct result of our jettisoning of the Christian past. Although this book is not primarily about politics, it is nevertheless my conviction that the only way we can counter these trends is to revive a Christian political vision that was common prior to the turn to secular liberalism during the twentieth century. This would emphasise, among other things, empirical wisdom from the past, national religion including respect for and knowledge of the Bible, the nation state as the guardian of a particular land and culture, limited executive power, individual freedom, and equality before the law. The alternatives to this vision are being played out before our eyes. And the consequences are disastrous.

If this is the return that is to be sought in political life, then we must seek a similar one within the Church itself. The Church must rediscover its confidence in Christianity as the pervasive influence that has shaped our civilisation for millennia. We cannot allow ourselves to be dictated to by the forces of post-democratic globalist totalitarianism or divisive neo-Marxism, but we must instead rediscover our orthodox and intellectually robust theological tradition. We are witnessing a tragic attempt by the Church of England to imitate the very trends that seek to oppose and destroy Christianity while we scratch our heads and wonder why attendance and income are falling. We should take heart from enormously popular thinkers such as Jordan Peterson whose ethical outlook clearly owes so much to a fading Christian inheritance, but we must go beyond even this and insist that any such outlook ultimately finds its fulfilment in an objective and transcendent good to which all are called to orientate their lives.

Strange as it might seem, orthodox Christianity is the key to renewal: by placing science in its proper metaphysical context and purging it of both dogmatic materialism and pretensions to political power; by grounding ethics in both a vision of the transcendent good and a Christian anthropology that insists on the dignity of all human beings made in the image of God; and by grounding our political vision upon a similar Christian sensibility.

Perhaps this is all hopelessly ambitious. I do not pretend to have the academic expertise to engage adequately with all the subjects that follow. I hope I know enough to say at least something of interest though. And I hope, further, that people who are much more qualified than I am will take up these themes and work towards a vision of a renewed Church and society, of a great return to individual and collective Christianity, to head off the disaster that is quickly coming upon us.

I have believed in something like the central argument of this book for a long time. My doctoral thesis (later published as a book entitled *Charles Taylor and Anglican Theology: Aesthetic Ecclesiology*) closed with a plea to the Church to take seriously the beauty and the glory of Jesus Christ in its proclamation and witness to the world.[12] I still trust in that message, but I am sad to say that, in the years since I wrote those words, I have come to believe that the world and the Church are in a far darker place. It has not been my intention to turn into a religious curmudgeon (and, indeed, I hope this is not what has happened), but the accelerating rush towards civilisational suicide is not something that can escape my notice without deep concern. The great return of which I speak is necessary to reverse the course of recent developments, and it holds out great hope: that we can recover, and that a new and better world can emerge as a result.

I

History: The Myth of Enlightenment

'I am pride. I disdain to have any parents.'

Christopher Marlowe, Doctor Faustus

The founding myth of secular modernity tells us a story in which science and reason displaced religion, by which is meant, more specifically, Christianity.* That displacement, so we are told, created the conditions for the civilised and prosperous world we know today. The benefits we enjoy – technology, medicine, education, democratic political systems, and so on – are the result of the shift away from a religious worldview and towards a scientific and rational one.

This secular myth, in its essentials, is false. It is a shoddy and ironically pseudo-religious basis upon which to build the intellectual fabric of a civilisation. The patchwork quilt of anecdotes that undergirds this narrative is more similar in character to a fable or fairy tale than to historical reality. And this is because these anecdotes promote a mythical view of the emergence of science and reason from the darkness of the religious past. Where there is a grain of truth to them they are invariably presented in the worst possible light for Christianity, and key details are either embellished or omitted to that end. In addition, this mythology intentionally plays down the profound continuity between the Christian medieval period and the modern period which is thought to have begun with the so-called 'Scientific Revolution'.

---

* By the word 'myth' I do not mean the positive sense when used of certain stories in, for example, Plato's dialogues. In that context, a myth is a knowingly constructed fable given to illustrate an important truth. The type of myth I am critiquing is a made-up story that masquerades as fact and claims to be able to explain significant features of the present.

It is taken as a fact that modern science was 'discovered' around the turn of the seventeenth century. But was this discovery genuinely new or was it simply a continuation of the progress made in cathedral schools, early universities and monasteries for hundreds of years previously?

The truth is that the modern, secular West did not invent science, nor did it invent rationality, nor did it invent empirical research. When one considers it, the most profound intellectual invention of the West is not any one of these but is, in fact, atheism and the rejection of the Christian religion.*

This is important because so many people believe the unexamined proposition, undergirding their lives, that somehow science has given us the key to the doors of reality, that now the world can be understood properly and comprehensively, that somehow we have become ethical as a result of a scientific worldview and learned how to live peacefully with one another – and that there is no need for that strange phenomenon, religion, which ignorant people of the past used to think so important. Religious people today are very strange, very odd and eccentric. Why would anyone need to be religious these days since we have a scientific and rational way of understanding the world – a much better way than the dark approaches of the past?

---

* Was there atheism in the West before the modern period? Michael J. Buckley argues that the intellectual possibility of atheism could only have arisen within a heretical Christian framework that began within the late medieval period and was channelled through the rationalist philosophy of René Descartes. Descartes attempted to ground belief in God on an indubitable basis and inevitably failed. This created the conditions for a total rejection not only of the existence of God but of the entire transcendent order. Even sceptics in ancient Greece, such as Critias of Athens who ridiculed Socrates' belief in the gods, nevertheless did not disbelieve in the transcendent realm and in the existence of the gods in general. Buckley's persuasive thesis is that atheism relies upon Christianity and could not have existed without it. Cf. Michael J. Buckley, S.J., *At the Origins of Modern Atheism* (New Haven: Yale University Press, 1987). For further details, see Franklin, *Ecclesiology*, pp. 27–9.

And yet one of the most famous quotations in all philosophy comes from the mouth of Socrates, who proclaimed, 'The unexamined life is not worth living.' I will adapt this slightly for the purposes of this chapter and say, instead, 'The unexamined history is not worth believing.'

So, let's examine it now.

The Secular Myth Itself

The Canadian philosopher Charles Taylor's greatest work *A Secular Age* begins with a discussion of the different senses of the word 'secular'. 'Secular' often means something to do with the separation of Church and state or it refers to the falling away of religious belief. There is another meaning, however, which concerns the 'background conditions' of secularism. How is it possible that 500 years ago in the West it was not only an option to believe in God and the supernatural world but it was indeed the only option, whereas now belief in God has become not only optional but marginal? How has that happened? We must admit that a seismic change has come upon Western civilisation. The entire order of life and society was orientated around the Christian religion and, somehow, that has been completely fragmented. What unifies society now? Is there anything that unites people? It is very hard to say. But it is certainly not the Christian religion as it was prior to AD 1500.

All human beings live within a story. A lot of the time we are not aware of the power of the stories we believe, and how these stories cause us to orientate ourselves towards the world in a certain way. Many people have never considered seriously the story upon which the modern age is built, even though such people believe this story on a very deep level. But the story in question – the story of the triumph of science and reason over Christianity – is extremely influential. It has found a home in each one of us, even those who are conventionally religious, and it gives us a sense of who we are and what we are about.

Psychologist Mattias Desmet begins his book on political total-itarianism with an argument that implies the truth of this mythi-cal story.* It begins with Galileo Galilei. Galileo was in a church in 1582 listening to a priest recite Scripture. And yet Galileo was not listening but was instead focused on the chandelier swinging above the priest's head. He was wondering why it swung more at some times than at others. And this was surely far more interest-ing than the dry, dusty book read by the priest.

Desmet then gives us the first example of what might be the 'Supersession Narrative'. By 'supersession' I mean the idea that, around the turn of the seventeenth century, an entirely new way of understanding the world was born. Not only did it bear no resemblance to the past, but it was in complete opposition to it. One age superseded another in total contradiction. 'Instead of something that had to be revealed to man by God,' writes Desmet, 'knowledge became something man could come to on his own. All he had to do was observe phenomena with his eyes and think logically.'[1]

We will encounter many such statements which adopt a simi-lar approach. Again, these pronouncements are not argued for, and historical evidence for their truth is rarely offered. They are simply assumed and asserted. Here is Desmet again, mounting such an argument with respect to the sixteenth- and seventeenth-century scientists Copernicus and Galileo:

> Galileo dared – to think . . . Other brilliant thinkers, such as Nicolaus Copernicus and Isaac Newton, also pulled the dogmatic wool from their eyes to register the world around them with an open mind . . . They had the courage to set aside the prejudices and dogmas of the time . . . Science also liberated man from

---

* Desmet's book overall is more nuanced than I imply here. Although he does repeat the science/reason versus religion story, he is certainly not a materialist who believes that science alone can fathom conclusively the mysteries of existence.

his self-incurred immaturity. It broke through rule by religious dogma that, in the public sphere, had largely decayed into coercion and oppression, pretense and hypocrisy, deceit and lies.[2]

Desmet uses these modern scientists as paradigmatic examples of people apparently willing to articulate inconvenient scientific truths and to speak them to the religiously powerful. And, like others who have made brave and noble stands, they were persecuted and martyred for their efforts. They admitted their ignorance and were curious and open to what phenomena have to say for themselves. This 'not knowing' gave birth to a new knowledge, a new knowledge for which they would do anything, for which they were willing to give up their freedom, sometimes even their lives.[3] The great early Church Father Tertullian once said the blood of the martyrs is the seed of the Church.[4] In Desmet's rendering, the tradition of martyrdom has been adapted so that these modern-day protagonists die not for their Christian profession but for the cause of science.

The science-conquering-religion story has a shape, a narrative arc. It suggests that in the Greco-Roman age (roughly from the middle of the fourth century BC to the end of the fourth century AD) civilisation was developing positively. It was the coming of Christianity (beginning, of course, in the first century AD, but developing further influence over the next two centuries and, eventually, gaining imperial power with Constantine's Edict of Milan in AD 313 and the full Christianisation of the Roman empire about a decade later) that halted progress. This, it is said, was because Christianity was and is fundamentally irrational, relying upon revelations from God as opposed to using the tools of reason and observation. Given that Christianity is this way, so the story goes, it makes sense that the gatekeepers of the Christian religion would need to use their authority to discourage people from rational and empirical enquiry. They are said to have done this in many ways: inquisitions, threats of hellfire, social ostracisation, and so on. Christianity, therefore, is said to have ushered in a period of intellectual and social darkness. And that is why the Christian age, which spans the long period from the end of the Roman empire to the turn of the seventeenth century, is often called the 'Dark Ages'.* The story suggests that this was an age of superstition, backwardness, intolerance, and intellectual and societal stagnation. And the last four centuries are supposed to have turned us away from that dark chapter towards a new dawn of knowledge, truth and liberation. That is why it is called the 'Enlightenment'. We believe now that we have switched on the light after centuries of darkness and that we can 'see' again.

To describe this myth further, we can look at three apparently seismic transitions from one age to the next: from irrationality to rationality, from ignorance to knowledge, and from war to tolerance.

From Irrationality to Rationality

To begin with, the story tells us that Christianity opposed the use of reason and has only ever seen it as antagonistic to revelation. The ancient Greeks and Romans were philosophers and early pioneers of the scientific method but the rise of Christianity is supposed to have put a stop to all of that. From the Christian age onwards, we are told, it was the authority of the Church and its holy books alone that could legitimately be relied upon for human knowledge. Because of this narrowness of outlook, Christians are said to have set about systematically destroying the work of pagan antiquity, which included the murder of the pagan Alexandrian proto-feminist philosopher and mathematician Hypatia in AD 415 and the destruction in AD 391 of the 1,300-year-old intellectual treasure-house, the Library of Alexandria. Roving bands of violent Christian zealots, with ostensible hatred for human advancement, are blamed for these terrible crimes.

Because of these alleged religious lunatics, this was not an age

---

* We will see, of course, the deeply problematic nature of the use of the term 'Dark Ages' as we continue.

that afforded the stability and leisure necessary for the conduct of fruitful scientific observation and rational enquiry. So the story tells us that it was only at the beginning of the seventeenth century, with the emergence of the scientific method, that the tide began to turn.

Perhaps the most important name in the story of the beginning of the Scientific Revolution is that of the famous lawyer, politician and philosopher in the court of Elizabeth Tudor, Francis Bacon (1561–1626). Often called the father of empiricism, Bacon was indeed a proponent of the inductive method. Induction is a way of learning about the world through observation and experience which seeks to document instances of correlation between phenomena and their causes and to draw general laws from these correlations.* For example, Bacon did experiments to find both where heat was present (the sun's rays, in flames, in boiling liquids) and where it was not present (in the rays of the moon and stars, in natural liquids); he then sought to draw conclusions about the nature of heat based upon these observations. Now, the story tells us that Bacon was unique in using the inductive method and we will examine below whether this is really true.†

The broader philosophical tradition of empiricism is associated with philosophers such as Thomas Hobbes (1588–1679), John Locke (1632–1704) and David Hume (1711–76). Empiricism stresses that knowledge comes to us primarily through our sense

---

* This in contrast to the method that was common in ancient Greece of developing general theoretical frameworks and interpreting natural events in light of them.

† Where Bacon was in fact truly revolutionary was in his strong emphasis upon the utility of nature for serving people's needs. Nature, so Bacon said, ought to be tortured and put on the rack to force her to yield up her secrets to us. Only by the careful observation of (and experiment upon) the natural world will we be able to understand it and utilise it more fully for our advantage or, in the words of Bacon himself, 'for the relief of man's estate'. This was a seminal change in outlook from the medieval view of the cosmos as the theatre of the glory of God.

experience – what we see, touch, hear, and so on. We are not born with any innate knowledge and all that we can know about the world is what the world chooses to disclose to us. This is important for the myth because it tells us that people like these empiricist scientists and philosophers were responsible for freeing us from reliance upon holy books and revelation and for giving us the philosophical tools to find things out for ourselves.

From Ignorance to Knowledge

The use of reason and observation in the pursuit of knowledge is intrinsically linked to the most important part of this story, which involves the purported discovery of 'science'. Again, the story runs, whereas the Christian Church had for a millennium told the world that the operations of nature were dependent upon the will of God and that the Bible should not be contradicted, the early scientists of the sixteenth and seventeenth centuries gradually broke free of this hold upon people's minds and began to observe and experiment with the natural world. This was apparently somewhat controversial because the scientists found that their observations and those of Scripture were often opposed to one another.

And so we come to the key concept of this specious war between science and religion. The conflict is epitomised by the struggle over the position of the Earth relative to the sun. Before Galileo Galilei's (1564–1642) epic showdown with the Catholic Church, the astronomer Nicolaus Copernicus (1473–1543) had first dared to put the sun at the centre of his cosmological model. The Earth is not, so he argued, set upon firm foundations and unmovable, as Psalm 104:4–5 says, but in fact goes around the sun. Galileo agreed and he wasn't afraid to say so. The Catholic Church, unable to stomach such an unbiblical supposition, had Galileo investigated and tortured by the Spanish Inquisition, condemned as a heretic, threatened with death and consigned to house arrest for the remainder of his miserable life. All for saying that the Earth moves around the sun. Almost none of this story is true but it still retains an immense hold upon the popular imagination.

At every turn, science is presumed to have met with opposition. Among its other supposed crimes, the Christian Church is said to have banned autopsies on human cadavers in the name of human sanctity, opposed smallpox vaccination and, of course, contradicted Charles Darwin's theory of evolution because it did not cohere with the first chapters of the book of Genesis.

Together with Galileo, Darwin is held to be another paradigmatic example of the putative distaste of Christianity for scientific truth. Darwin, the Victorian natural scientist, having once thought himself a future clergyman, is said to have gradually abandoned his faith in God. And this apparently because he discovered the laws of evolution and concluded that the creation of the world as described in Scripture was egregiously transgressive of the empirical evidence. According to this story, Darwin concluded that there is nothing in nature that is not, in principle, explainable by his theoretical evolutionary framework, and so all apparently reasonable people have agreed ever since. And, of course, the account always adds the vital detail – regardless of whether or not it is true – that the Church and Christianity ineluctably opposed Darwin and his findings.

Thus, the story goes. Science won the war. After these repeated bruisings, what could religion do but retreat into the ever-decreasing spaces that science left for it? And now, as our knowledge of the world increases, so too, we are told, the need to resort to God is further diminished. The story insists therefore that we have progressed from an age of irrationality and faith to one of reason and science. We are told that the modern age is a revolutionary and complete change from what went before.

From War to Tolerance
Even the most diehard proponent of the story of Enlightenment will find it difficult to argue that the post-Christian age has been one of peace. But the principal difference is said to be that the

modern age has rid the civilised world of specifically religious warfare. There are still wars, of course, but we are told that they are now conducted for much better reasons.

The (highly misleading) story is as follows: the Reformation brought a split within Christendom between Catholics and Protestants. In Europe, some princes and emperors were one and some were the other, so they fought with each other for dominance. And that dominance was sought in the name of correct doctrine. Tens of thousands of people were slaughtered and died in manifest agony over the differences between two factions of Christianity, over the question of whether or not the bread and the wine turn into the body and blood of Christ, over the question of the authority of the Pope relative to the Bible, over the question of whether the Mass should be in Latin or the vernacular. For these matters, the whole continent was torn apart by the Wars of Religion. This madness continued until people had had enough and discovered that it was much better to live together while tolerating religious disagreements. What could be more obvious now, we wonder. But it was apparently not obvious then. Only with the newly discovered value of religious tolerance could Europe return to a peaceful state. The Peace of Westphalia was a treaty signed in October 1648 by the principal factions in these long religious wars thus securing a lasting cessation of violence in the name of God.

Modern liberalism is often traced back to this moment. We are told that liberalism sets people free from religious control and from oppressive family, cultural and social expectations.* Echoing key themes of the mythical story of Enlightenment, the political theorist Judith Shklar puts it this way:

---

* We will see that liberalism may, in some sense, 'free' people from obligations to family, religion and other associations, but it also creates the possibility of the individual and society becoming dominated by the oppressive civic or state authorities.

... liberalism ... was born out of the cruelties of the religious civil wars ... If faith was to survive at all, it would do so privately. The alternative then set, and still before us, is not one between classical virtue and liberal self-indulgence, but between cruel military and moral repression and violence, and a self-restraining tolerance that fences in the powerful to protect the freedom and safety of every citizen.[5]

So people are said to have been liberated from the restrictive power of the Church both in mind and body. The repressive morality of Christianity was ostensibly done away with as we discovered superior values. The liberal political tradition is associated with thinkers such as John Locke (1632–1704), Immanuel Kant (1724–1804) and John Stuart Mill (1806–73) who are upheld as having used human reason (as opposed to religious revelation and presuppositions) in a unique way to construct a more humane way of living. We are also told that key concepts of equality before the law and maximal freedom for the individual come from this form of political thought. Upon this apparently novel view, no human being is to be treated any differently before the law: no divinely mandated kings nor Spanish Inquisitions, just simple equality and fairness.

The story of liberalism is deceptively simple: it begins by securing freedom of conscience with regard to religion and then applies this principle to other areas where people have conflicting ideas about how best to live one's life and how to order society. It tells us that it seeks not to judge between these conflicts but only to create a neutral framework which allows individuals to pursue their self-chosen goals. We are told that it is only liberalism that can create a context in which we can pursue our own ideas about happiness and meaning. It is not for the government or for clerics or for anyone else to tell us what we should value, who we should love, what we should aim at, or where we should go. For those are decisions that should be made by the individual and by the individual alone. Again, so the story goes.

Because of this self-congratulatory story of liberal freedom, the liberal state is able to say about religion that it is an essentially private matter. People can believe whatever metaphysical propositions they like but religion is value-laden and has the potential to be oppressive, so it must be kept out of the public sphere. The story justifies this move.

The Power of the Secular Myth

The secular myth is powerful largely because it is simple. It is a movement from darkness to light, from irrationality to rationality, from ignorance to knowledge, from useless revelation to fruitful reason, from religion to science, from slavery to freedom, from arbitrary violence to toleration and decency. There are heroes (Isaac Newton, Francis Bacon, John Locke), there are martyrs (Galileo) and there are villains (the Spanish Inquisition, the Catholic Church).

But the myth is also powerful because it tells us that we are living at the highest point in human history when so much has been discovered, so much has been gained. Not only are we greater than what went before but we are far greater. We are told that we invented ourselves out of the mess of ignorance that preceded us. There is, undoubtedly, a powerful psychological pull in believing such a story. Sometimes it is very difficult to disentangle our desire to believe something from the evidence of its truth or falsity and this is certainly a good example.

Two Serious Problems with the Secular Myth

The myth of the secular is a story through which we make sense of ourselves as modern people. There are authorities that we can rely upon ('science') and there are authorities whose time is past ('religion'). Again, religion must be tolerated (albeit begrudgingly) because not to tolerate it would be illiberal; it is not something that should be taken particularly seriously though. Very sadly, this way of thinking has been largely accepted by the Christian Church itself, which has been unable to muster the intellectual resources to mount a defence. Some public religious figures such as the bishops of the Church of England are now regarded by some as more comical than serious. And the bishops themselves are more likely to defer to science as a higher authority than to their own traditional sources of revelation.[*]

So why would anyone cavil? There is one simple answer to this question: the myth is a fantasy. It is not true, and in almost every significant detail it is misleading at best. There are two broad points to make: first, the myth is based on historical inaccuracies. And, second, the myth ignores to the point of criminality the astonishing achievements of the Middle Ages and the continuity these achievements have with the modern period.

The Secular Myth is Historically Inaccurate

Within the broader story of the triumph of reason and science over Christianity, there is a litany of lesser and greater legends that exemplify the supposed conflict. Some of these are well known, others less so but still influential. These stories are either totally false or so misleading that they might as well be. Some of them are very simply disproved by stating simple historical facts and some of them require slightly more space. We start with the most famous.

---

[*] An example would be the Bishop of Worcester's 2023 epistle in which he set out his reasons for same-sex marriages in church. His first major point was that scientists now believe that being gay is not a choice. He draws an analogy between this and the Church's (ostensible) volte-face on the issue of creation and evolution in light of another scientific authority, Charles Darwin. Cf. Right Reverend John Inge, 'An open letter from Bishop John', Diocese of Worcester, 09.01.2023, [https://www.cofe-worcester.org.uk/an-open-letter-from-bishop-john.php#_edn19].

'Galileo Was Persecuted by the
Catholic Church for Heliocentrism'

The archetypal persecuted saint of the science-versus-religion myth is, of course, Galileo Galilei. His story has a powerful ability to move us. The symbolism at its core is paramount: foolish and ignorant Christians who believed that the world literally revolved around them because their holy book told them so, until men like Nicolaus Copernicus and Galileo dared to venture another theory, a theory with the potential to change everything: the planets and the sun do not in fact revolve around the Earth but the Earth revolves around the sun. Such an idea was tantamount to blasphemy. Not only did it contradict the Scriptures, but it also relegated the Earth to the status of merely another planet and thereby undermined the importance of human beings. At the very centre of the universe was not a lush green and blue planet, specially created by God for us to enjoy, but a fiery ball of burning gas, relentless and unfeeling. As has already been noted, the Catholic Church is said to have been so threatened by this that it tortured and condemned Galileo as a heretic before proceeding to lock him up indefinitely. But, of course, the heliocentric truth could not be hidden and would emerge eventually.

This story does contain an element of truth: Galileo was indeed banned from teaching heliocentrism by the Spanish Inquisition in 1616. He defied this ban and was put on trial and consigned to house arrest in 1632. But the major elements of the story – elements that change the whole complexion of the narrative – are almost always underreported or simply omitted altogether.

To begin with, Galileo was a devout and orthodox Catholic who held to the view that the Holy Scriptures, though inspired and truthful, ought not to be held up as a compendium of scientific description. He appealed specifically to St Augustine in this regard, but he would have been well aware that he sat within a venerable tradition of Christian thought that took in many of the Church Fathers and great scholastic thinkers such as Thomas Aquinas. Admittedly, the Catholic Church was notably touchy about such notions during this particular period, probably as a result of the insecurity caused by the Protestant Reformation. It was a reactionary attitude, therefore, and it did not characterise Christian attitudes more generally.

Moreover, many cardinals and bishops supported Galileo even after he had essentially come out as a heliocentrist, including the Dominican Tommaso Campanella and the Carmelite Paolo Antonio Foscarini, both of whom were influential and important men of the Roman Catholic Church. They agreed with Galileo's scriptural principles and wrote in his favour. Also on the list of his backers was Cardinal Maffeo Barberini, who was to become Pope Urban VIII (the Pope under whom Galileo was supposedly tortured and condemned). This latter relationship was so positive that Barberini had even been known to take up the pen and compose poetry in praise of Galileo's achievements.

So Galileo had support within the Catholic Church in the context of an ongoing internal dialogue around the proper interpretation of Scripture. In addition, it is important to note that, outside of the Church, there were in fact detractors of heliocentrism – mainly secular philosophers who disliked it because it contradicted Aristotle's geocentric cosmology which had a rich millennia-old pedigree. This indicates that the reason why many were geocentrists was not, in the main, because they got it from the Bible but because they got it from pagan sources such as Ptolemy and Aristotle.

This relates to another often misunderstood but crucial point about the wider context. The mythic hagiographical story implies that, up until the time of Galileo, people believed that, as well the sun going around the Earth, the Earth was the centre of the universe, and that this centrality was somehow crucial to the metaphysical and religious presuppositions of Christianity. But nothing could be further from the truth. The fact is that medieval people, drawing upon cosmological models of the past, believed that the Earth was simply one point in relationship to the rest of the universe. C.S. Lewis, who was an expert in this subject owing to his mastery of medieval and Renaissance literature, coined the phrase 'the anthroperipheral universe' to describe this phenomenon. Quoting Lewis, Jason Baxter summarises Lewis's view in this way:

> . . . humankind is at the periphery of everything that really matters. This 'geocentric universe [was] not in the least anthropocentric,' because it 'made man a marginal – almost . . . a suburban-creature.' It was not only that 'everyone' knew 'the Earth is infinitesimally small by cosmic standards' but also that the Earth was made out of the dregs, after the purer bodies of stars had been made . . . Everything interesting, festive, fiery, light, clean, and harmonious was way out there, while we, poor fools, dwell at 'the lowest point' of the universe, 'plunged . . . in unending cold'; the Earth was 'in fact the "offscouring of creation," the cosmic dust-bin.'[6]

To return to the Galileo story itself, then, we could add to the common omissions the fact that the Church never called into question Galileo's scientific observations. In fact, Galileo's legend as a leading luminary is somewhat overblown, partly because of Galileo's own habit of self-promotion. Galileo would claim that he had invented things which he hadn't, such as the telescope, and that he had conducted empirical research, such as the famous example of his dropping weights from the Tower of Pisa, which, again, he hadn't. Further, he could not substantiate his claim to have verified heliocentrism. His results were incomplete, and his deductions were incorrect. The evidence for heliocentrism was not in place for another two centuries. Galileo majorly overstated his case.

This brings us to the nub of the matter, which is what really happened between Galileo and the Roman Catholic Church. Much of this concerns Galileo's own personality defects: his arrogance and vindictiveness, his absolute insistence that his theories be recognised and confirmed by the Church. The latter is the only reason for the consultation of 1616 which ended because Galileo failed to produce any evidence for the Copernican model he claimed to be able to substantiate. Galileo was, at that point, put under a mild injunction by the Church to stop teaching that particular viewpoint.

The more important confrontation came about in 1632. This was, however, in the words of Arthur Koestler, nothing to do with 'a fatal collision between opposite philosophies of existence' but instead 'a clash of individual temperaments',[7] the temperaments in question being those of Galileo and his former admirer and poetic praise writer Pope Urban VIII. It began with Pope Urban VIII asking Galileo to include in any of his publications a disclaimer to the effect that definitive scientific conclusions could not be reached with absolute certainty because the omnipotence of God could produce natural phenomena in different ways. This might sound a strange thing to say but it was as much a political statement as a theological one. It was a way of evading the, for the time, controversial question of the limits of science vis-à-vis biblical interpretation and, ironically, it was also a way of limiting the Church's interference in such questions by leaving many possibilities open. If Galileo had simply included this disclaimer, it is highly probable that nothing further would have happened to him and that he would have been allowed to pursue his investigations without interruption. But that is not, in fact, what happened. Galileo did include the requested disclaimer, but he put it into the mouth of one of three speakers in his 1632 *Dialogue Concerning the Two Chief World Systems* and that speaker's name was Simplicio which, in layman's terms, means 'idiot'. In the same dialogue, Simplicio defends geocentric cosmology and is presented as an object of ridicule. The Pope took offence at such a move, and this led to the denouement which was the trial of the same year. That said, Galileo was never tortured or imprisoned, and Pope Urban VIII used his power to protect Galileo from a worse punishment. His real fate ultimately included his living first at a friend's house and then at his own house and continuing his scientific work, which included the publishing of an important treatise on motion, *Two New Sciences*, in 1638, a full six years after the confrontation with the Roman Catholic Church after which he was supposedly tortured and jailed.

The irony of Galileo's attitude must be commented upon. Speaking of the extremely complex and palpably ludicrous Copernican model that Galileo chose to promote, David Bentley Hart comments:

> Galileo elected . . . to propound a theory whose truth he had not demonstrated, while needlessly mocking a powerful man who had treated him with honour and indulgence. And the irony is, strange to say, that it was the church that was demanding proof, and Galileo who was demanding blind assent – to a model that was wrong. None of which exculpates the Catholic hierarchy of its foolish decision or its authoritarian meddling. But it is rather ridiculous to treat Urban VIII as a man driven by religious fanaticism . . . or Galileo as the blameless defender of scientific empiricism.[8]

The story of Galileo is, in the end, nothing to do with the general philosophical conflict between science and Christianity but with the specific details of the historical context and personalities of the players involved. Had this controversy really concerned the conflict between science and Christianity, then some of the other scientists at large in Europe, and especially in Italy, would have been persecuted in similar ways to Galileo. But they weren't. They were allowed to go about their business unmolested, and the only reasonable conclusion here is that Galileo largely brought upon himself the problems he encountered.

Rodney Stark notes that the only more general conclusion we can draw from the whole instance is that dominant groups will often abuse their power to impose their beliefs as may be expedient for them. But this is hardly unique to Christianity: the communist regime outlawed Mendelian genetics because of the doctrinaire Marxist belief that all characteristics are caused by environmental factors, for example. It is, in other words, not a reflex of religious belief but primarily of power.[9]

'Christians Believed that the Earth was Flat'

This again is a story that is based on a small shred of truth. The small shred is that there were two obscure early Christian thinkers who, citing certain passages from Psalm 104,* argued that the Earth is flat and not round. Their names were Lactantius and Cosmas. Set against the views of these two individuals are 'tens of thousands of Christian theologians, poets, artists, and scientists [who] took the spherical view throughout the early, Medieval, and modern church'.[10] The Oxford historian of science Allan Chapman comments on this as follows:

> . . . no Medieval scholar of any worth thought that the Earth was flat . . . One needs only to read the astronomical literature of the Middle Ages to realise that the spherical nature of the Earth, about 6,000 or 8,000 miles across, was standard knowledge, and taught to university students from Salamanca to Prague.[11]

Indeed, if one acquaints oneself with the most important works of literature from the Middle Ages, this is quite obvious. Dante's *Divine Comedy*, for example, written in the early fourteenth century, treats the Earth as a globe, as does Chaucer's *Canterbury Tales*.

The fact is that these two obscure thinkers, Lanctantius and Cosmas, were chosen not because they were true representatives of pre-modern Christian thought but because their views fit the science-versus-religion narrative.

Among all the dishonesty on display, we can also cite the American author Washington Irving who made up a story about

---

* For example, Psalm 104:5, speaking of the Earth: 'Thou didst set the Earth on its foundations, so that it should never be shaken' (RSV).

Christopher Columbus being persecuted by the Catholic Church for believing that the Earth is round (a story still believed by many people and which is, again, entirely fabricated).

'Hypatia Was Killed by a Christian Mob'

The story of Hypatia is perhaps not the most famous of this genre, but it is still well known enough to merit comment. It is, moreover, a good example of the way these stories tend to take something with an element of truth and to exaggerate it out of all proportion. In his masterful deconstruction of this story, David Bentley Hart observes its recent depiction in the 2010 Alejandro Amenábar motion picture *Agora*, starring Rachel Weisz as Hypatia. Hypatia herself is depicted as a young, beautiful, brilliant mathematician and philosopher native to Alexandria whose murder (coupled with the destruction of the Great Library of Alexandria) ushered in the Dark Ages. So brilliant was this great proto-feminist intellectual that she is even depicted suggesting the heliocentric cosmological model about a thousand years before Copernicus and in complete contradiction to her (actual) commitment to neo-Platonism and the Aristotelian-Ptolemaic system.[12]

It is not only Hollywood that has exaggerated this legend though. The *Guardian* newspaper went so far as to put Hypatia alongside Pythagoras, Euler and Gauss as one of the '10 Best' mathematicians of all time. And this, in spite of the fact that Hypatia has not one single notable contribution to mathematics to her name, that only a small fragment of her mathematical work remains, and that there were other contemporary scholars of the subject whose work is superior to hers.[13]

Hypatia's murder (and she was indeed murdered) became a basis upon which to exaggerate her legend. The story that emerged epitomises the way the Christian faith is supposed to have opposed everything that enlightened modern people stand for: scholarly progress, scientific endeavour, free enquiry, women's liberation, equality under the law, and so on. But

Hypatia's murder cannot be understood in this way because she was not murdered for any of these reasons. To start with, it is true that she was killed by a Christian mob. But, again as Hart notes, 'in the lower city [of Alexandria] . . . religious allegiance was often no more than a matter of tribal identity, and various tribes [including not only Christians but also pagans and Jews] often slaughtered one another with gay abandon'.[14] We don't know for certain why she was killed but it was definitely not because she was a female intellectual or a scientist. It was very likely the result of a political squabble between the city's imperial prefect and the city's patriarch Cyril. So, although we don't know precisely what happened, we can say for sure that she was not killed for the reasons she is commonly said to have been.

There are other significant facts that mitigate against the anti-Christian interpretation. For a start, there were many female intellectuals in the Eastern empire at the time and the scientific and philosophical class in Alexandria was populated fairly evenly by Christians, Jews and pagans. The historical evidence tells us that there is no sense in which Christians were uniquely prejudiced against the disciplines of mathematics and philosophy or, indeed, that there was any prejudice at all. Further to this, pagans, Christians and Jews studied together and actually collaborated intellectually. Of Hypatia herself, the records we have are from a Christian source, Socrates Scholasticus, who praises Hypatia for her learning. Some of her devoted students were Christians and scholarship in Alexandria continued long after her death. And, again, this scholarly enquiry was at least partly carried out by Christians such as John Philoponus.

'A Christian Mob Burnt Down the Great Library of Alexandria'

The murder of Hypatia was not the first time an anti-intellectual Christian mob is said to have struck with venomous abandon in the city of Alexandria. About twenty-five years earlier, in AD 391, they had destroyed the City of Alexandria's Great Library, destroying tens of thousands of scrolls compiled over centuries and ushering in a bleak age of ignorance. They did this, so the story goes, because they hated knowledge gained through scholarship and would only stand for those things that God had revealed in holy books.

Again, none of this is true and appears to have been fabricated by the Enlightenment historian Edward Gibbon, who misread a sentence from the Christian historian Orosius and used that as the basis of the tale. The Great Library of Alexandria didn't even exist by AD 391 and was spoken of as early as AD 23 by the Greek intellectual Strabo as a legendary place from the past. Other sources say that Julius Caesar destroyed it in whole or in part in 47 or 48 BC, while others that part of it was still in existence in the Brucheium in AD 272. The Brucheium was the royal quarter of Alexandria and was destroyed in that same year during the Aurelian wars when whatever remained of the Great Library would also have perished. This was over a hundred years before a Christian mob supposedly attacked and destroyed it.

The only potential shred of truth to this whole story is that there may have a been a daughter library in the grounds of the Serapeum temple complex which was destroyed in AD 391 because a number of Christian hostages had been executed inside it. This was ordered by the Christian Emperor Theodosius but there is no suggestion in any of the accounts that an important collection of books existed in the complex at the time, nor was it anything to do with Christian anti-intellectualism.

'The Church Opposed Autopsy, Pain Relief in Childbirth and Inoculation'

Before we come to the greatest myth of all, we will here briefly face the accusation that the Church has at various points opposed autopsy, pain relief in childbirth and the development of the technology of inoculation. Again, the Church is said to have opposed these things simply because it has always opposed scientific advancement generally and, in the case of childbirth, that the pain involved is a punishment visited upon women for the sin of Eve in the Garden of Eden. Therefore, its relief would mitigate against God's just dealings with woman. We need not dwell long upon these accusations which are all highly misleading.

First, the ancient Greeks and Romans had a taboo on autopsies and dissection: '. . . it was simply the position of nearly everyone nearly all the time across the ancient world that dead bodies were not to be messed with. This view was a constant, regardless of religion, language, mythology and level of scientific sophistication.'[15] Dissection only appears in an exclusively Christian context in the twelfth and thirteenth centuries in the medieval schools and universities of Christendom. So, far from banning this practice, the Christian Church was instrumental to the overturning of the ancient world's taboo on it.

Second, the hostility to pain relief during childbirth is taken from a story about a nineteenth-century Scottish obstetrician named Simpson who erroneously believed that he needed to write a pamphlet to defend his use of chloroform in the face of religious zealotry. The pamphlet turned out to be unnecessary because he was never attacked in the way he had feared he would be. Rather, there was a concern at the time about the medical implications of giving pain relief to women in labour because doctors weren't sure how it would affect the mother's ability to push at the right times. Without evidence to the contrary, this was a legitimate medical concern. But it clearly had nothing to do with the sin of Eve. It was ultimately Simpson's arguments that demonstrated that the concern was unnecessary and pain relief has been used in this context ever since.

Finally, inoculation was never uniformly opposed by the Church or by Christianity. Like every new and developing medical technology, there have always been controversies over aspects of vaccination. There may have been the occasional sermon denouncing it for all anybody knows, but there is no historical reality to the idea that it was opposed in the name of Christianity for a reason internal to the logic of the faith itself. Hutchings and Ungureanu tell the story of the landmark case of Boston in the 1720s, which was hit by a wave of smallpox. At that time, it was in fact Christian clergy, including one Revd Cotton Mather, who said that caution should be thrown to the wind and the technology implemented at that time of crisis. Physicians for the most part opposed this view, perhaps because the longer-term effects of the treatment weren't known. Whoever comes out of this story with more praise or blame, however, it has again nothing to do with some inherent bias against medicine and progress on the part of Christianity in general.[16]

Opposition to Darwin

This part of the book would be incomplete without at least a mention of Charles Darwin. In the popular narrative, Darwin's theory of evolution destroyed the plausibility of the Judeo-Christian idea that animals and human beings were, as we know them now, specially created by God. There are, of course, famous proponents of Darwinism, such as Richard Dawkins, who possess such a fanatical regard for the subject that they consider it to have the capacity to explain literally everything about the nature of the universe. But it is unclear, even on a conceptual level, how such an explanation would proceed. Apart from anything else, Dawkins and those like him almost always ignore the metaphysical question of Being itself and imagine that, if they can explain the origin of physical phenomena such as organisms or even planets and solar systems, then that will constitute an explanation of everything. In fact, all it would do is to trace the development of those phenomena over time. It says nothing at all about the fact of existence itself. It does not answer the crucial philosophical question, 'Why is there something rather than nothing?'

That is all a bit of a sideshow. The real point is that Darwin is often thought of as a more up-to-date version of Galileo, whose theories contradicted the Christian view and who was then, as a result, rejected and persecuted by the Church.

What should be said is that the issue of Darwinism illustrates exactly what I have been arguing thus far: not that there has never been a conflict between scientific theories (or 'natural philosophy' in the Middle Ages) and the teaching of the Church, but that the relationship between these two is complex and requires deep thought, theological reasoning and examination of the scientific claims in question. As Samuel Klumpenhouwer, in his paper 'Early Catholic Responses to Darwin's Theory of Evolution', puts it 'there are no simple conclusions to be drawn when exploring the historical relationships between religion and science. Those that present either a straightforward conflict or a perfectly harmonious collaboration run contrary to the evidence of history.'[17] And he then goes on to illustrate this with an array of differing responses to Darwin's theory of evolution by individual Roman Catholics and bodies within the Catholic Church. John Henry Newman, a cardinal in the Roman Church and one of the most important theologians and intellectuals of the nineteenth century, did not think that Darwin's theory was incompatible with divine design. On the other hand, an influential journal directed by Jesuits in Rome, *La Civilta Cattolica*, was firmly opposed to the theory and published this opinion consistently. Additionally, there were enemies of Christianity, such as Thomas Henry Huxley, who saw in the theory of evolution an opportunity to attack Christianity and the Roman Catholic Church by stating that the theory most certainly is a contradiction to the teaching of the latter and its Scriptures.

It is sufficient to note here that the Roman Church did not issue a formal ruling on the compatibility or otherwise of the theory of evolution with the faith and that this created the situation in which disagreement could arise. In Protestant denominations (which are diverse owing to the very nature of Protestantism) there have always been different views about evolution. The Roman Church today is much more sympathetic towards it[18] while diversities of views prevail within Protestantism. But Darwin could never be said to have been persecuted or even formally contradicted by the Christian Church. And his reception is certainly not proof of some ongoing and absolute antagonism between religious faith and scientific fact.

The Wars of Religion

One of the most insidious falsities of the imperious Enlightenment narrative concerns the so-called 'Wars of Religion' which raged in Europe from the mid-sixteenth century onwards and were the result of Catholics and Protestants fighting with each other for dominance over the continent of Europe. These wars are believed to have ended because of the discovery of religious tolerance.

Although this narrative is misleading, to put it mildly, the reason for its success is, again, that it is simple: at one time, everybody in Europe was Catholic and so there was little reason to fight over religion; when many people became Protestant, the two factions battled each other in the name of their differing creeds, tens of thousands were killed pointlessly, and religious toleration was discovered to put an end to the madness. That, as I say, is facile, but the truth is more complicated and difficult.

We have to go back to the world before the Reformation. In the medieval period there were believed to be two great powers in society – the Church and the civil authorities. Unlike today, there was not a sense in which the Church was held to have a proper 'spiritual' domain which it must stick to, whereas the civil authorities controlled everything else. Rather, the two powers vied with each other for dominance of society and, by the time of the Reformation, they had been doing so for some centuries. Generally speaking, however, the church hierarchy was considered superior to the civil authority. This was emphatically established in 1073 when Pope Hildebrand challenged the right of the Holy Roman Emperor Henry IV to appoint bishops in the Church.

The fallout ended with the Pope excommunicating and deposing the Holy Roman Emperor from his political position and the latter being forced to do humiliating penance at Canossa, after which he was restored but with his authority very much checked. Nobody at the time thought that it was in principle strange for the Church to wield temporal power. This temporal power was embodied in church courts and Canon Law, the vestiges of which we still have today in the Church of England and in the Roman Catholic Church.

What happened after the Reformation was not really about doctrine. The civil and secular powers used the opportunity afforded by the weakening of the Roman Catholic Church to assert complete control and to subvert the Church's dominance. This can be seen in the moves made by, for example, the Holy Roman Emperor Charles V and the Queen of France Catherine de Medici.

The struggle for power in France between the Protestant Huguenots and Catholic noble factions is a good example. The mythical, anti-Christian view argues that the civil war in France, including the notorious St Bartholomew's Day Massacre of 1572, was the direct result of doctrinal disputes between Protestantism and Catholicism. These could easily have been avoided if people had not been so silly. The reality is that the French monarchy had been accruing power to itself over the Roman Catholic Church for much of the early part of the sixteenth century. During the Reformation period, Protestant Calvinistic factions started to grow up in France and to challenge the centralised power of the French monarchy. These Calvinists joined with the Huguenots and strengthened their cause. But, again, this Protestant challenge was not about doctrine but about the challenge to the secular authority of the monarchy.

The theologian and political theorist William Cavanaugh comments: 'For the main instigators of the carnage, doctrinal loyalties were at best secondary to their stake in the defeat of the centralized State.'[19] Catherine de Medici (the Queen Mother at this point), under the power of the crown, attempted to create a state church which was a mixture of Catholic and Protestant beliefs. This failed for obvious reasons and so she developed another scheme to assert royal dominance: she used the Catholic faction to wipe out the Protestant Huguenot threat. And that is what caused the St Bartholomew's Day Massacre. So naive about theology was Catherine de Medici, and so little did she care about it, that, in her attempt to create a Protestant-Catholic state church, she overlooked the fundamental differences that divided Western Christendom. Indeed, she indicated personally that she was completely uninterested in them. This was not about doctrine but about the power of the crown and the centralised civil authorities over the Church.

A similar power-grab happened in England. Henry VIII wanted to marry again but could not obtain permission for divorce from the Pope and so he simply declared himself the Emperor of England and the head of the state Church of England. Not only did that mean he could regulate the Church (and so obtain his divorce) but it meant that the Pope and the Catholic Church had no further political power in these lands. This was a textbook case of a secular prince declaring himself the absolute head of the Church and asserting temporal power over it. As is well known, Henry asserted his supremacy through countless acts of judicial murder visited upon those who would not acknowledge him, the most famous of which are the murders of Sir Thomas More and the Carthusian Martyrs of London Charterhouse who were hanged, drawn and quartered for their recalcitrance.

In addition, the so-called 'Wars of Religion' often involved alliances between Catholics and Protestants and, indeed, Catholics fighting other Catholics and Protestants other Protestants. These facts do not fit the anti-Christian Enlightenment narrative and so they are conveniently overlooked.

William Cavanaugh argues persuasively (and he is not alone) that the whole concept of 'religion' as we now understand it arose at the time to subordinate the Church to the power of the state. Previously there was no concept of 'religion' in the way that we have come to understand it today. There was simply a dominant theological worldview that was held to be a comprehensive framework for understanding the nature of reality. That theological worldview was Christianity and everything else – including politics and the role of the civil powers – had to be understood in light of it. 'Religion', as a private and non-political matter, was invented in order to claim that the Church had no right to interfere in the running of state and that 'religion' should not be granted a place in the public square. Rather 'religion', so it was claimed, is a spiritual and internal matter and should be kept private. In other words, the Church can regulate internal matters such as belief and worship, but the state controls everything else. To use an anachronism, this is a classic example of the Orwellian manipulation of language devised to alter people's concepts of reality. So deeply ingrained in us now is the notion that 'religion' is separate to 'politics' that we can't possibly imagine how the Church could ever have thought that it should wield temporal power of any sort. It seems totally outrageous. We take it as a given that the secular state should be in charge of everything. But this is a purely modern assumption that could not exist without the reductive definition of 'religion' that began to be developed around the beginning of the Reformation. The idea of religious toleration, so celebrated today, was born, therefore, not as a genuine humanistic insight into what makes for societal peace, but as the result of the creation of 'religion' as a private set of apolitical beliefs that should not affect the running of the state. It was a political move to separate theoretically the power of the Church from the civil powers and therefore decide future conflict in favour of the state.*

---

* I am not trying to draw the reader to any conclusion about the ideal distribution of political power in modern society. That is a very complex question. My point here is only to note the complete victory of civic power over ecclesiastical power through the manipulation of language and the propagation of fake stories about the past.

The creation of 'religion' as private belief is an idea that persists today. The secular state masquerades as religiously neutral and as uninterested in the questions that religion seeks to answer. This is all a mirage that was formulated by political theorists such as Jean Bodin, Thomas Hobbes, Jean-Jacques Rousseau and John Locke in the seventeenth and eighteenth centuries. The purpose was to subordinate the Church and direct individual loyalty to the state.

The state is not neutral in matters of religion, however, and never has been. It has its own interests in maintaining control and, in our time as much as any other, it has its own ideological agenda which is best understood as a competing religious agenda with its own post-Christian ethical and metaphysical commitments (however vaguely defined).

In addition, the falsity of the Enlightenment narrative comes across most clearly when we consider what happened after the Wars of Religion: did warfare and conflict cease across the continent of Europe? Were we treated to 300 years of international halcyon brotherhood? Of course not. Immediately after this period, Europe was once again wracked by wars such as the War of Spanish Succession and the War of Austrian Succession, both of which were simultaneously mirrored in the colonies of North America. In the nineteenth century, Europe was torn apart by the Napoleonic Wars. And we hardly need mention the twentieth century, such were the horrors suffered by tens of millions as the advent of mechanised warfare came to fruition. Louis XIV, Napoleon, Hitler and Stalin (to name only a few) were not motivated by religion but by power. The ultimate argument against the notion that religion was the motivating factor behind the so-called 'Wars of Religion' is that warfare in Europe continued and got ever more destructive after 'religion' had been dramatically reduced in status. This is because it was never about religion in the first place.

The historical story of the state bringing peace after the days of religious warfare, therefore, is a tale told in retrospect by the victors to justify their absolute control . . . and we can see that it is utterly false.

The Modern World Unfairly Denigrates the Christian Middle Ages

I have already commented on the 'shape' of the secular myth. Its view of the past is that the modern Enlightenment period arose out of a 'Dark Age' which was itself an eclipse of the age of relative progress that preceded it. The latter was the Greco-Roman age in which significant advancements were made which were then apparently halted by the advent of Christianity. For this myth to make sense, therefore, the Dark Ages must be just that: an age of intellectual, social and scientific stagnation in which no significant human achievements were advanced, and, indeed, in which civilisation moved backward instead of forward. Thus apologists for this view, such as Anthony Grayling, speak of 'the near total destruction of intellectual culture in the "Dark Ages"'.* Grayling

---

* A.C. Grayling, *The Age of Genius: The Seventeenth Century and the Birth of the Modern Mind* (London: Bloomsbury, 2016), p. 122. Grayling offers as proof of this outrageous statement the fact that certain engineering skills were lost that had originally enabled the building of the Basilica of Maxentius and the Hagia Sophia. These techniques were recovered during the Renaissance in the construction of Brunelleschi's dome on Florence Cathedral: 'That single fact – just one of very many – speaks volumes' (ibid., p. 328). This is nonsense on multiple levels. For a start, the Hagia Sophia and Florence Cathedral were built as *Christian* churches so this example can hardly be put forward as an example of Christianity's antipathy to sophisticated engineering and architectural achievements. In addition, the loss of a particular form of engineering skill could be accounted for in many ways, such as the general decline in cultural forms and the inherent instability produced by the fall of the Roman empire. And it certainly doesn't justify the statement that there was 'a near total destruction of intellectual culture'. Indeed, as will I demonstrate, the architectural advances of the Middle Ages are perhaps among the greatest cultural achievements in the history of humanity.

and those like him take the view that it took a total rebirth – a renaissance – to retrieve the arts which had been lost and to prepare the world for an even greater leap forward which was still to come.

Happily, this aspect of the mythical narrative has fallen out of favour and most modern scholarship refrains from using the term 'Dark Ages' because it is so obviously polemical and erroneous. There are countless examples of scientific achievement and societal progress that come to us from the so-called Dark Ages. So much so that I will just give a précis of the most significant here. And I repeat an important point: we see in these examples that there was continuity between the (more helpfully described) Middle Ages and the modern period, not a complete change.

Science in the Middle Ages

Let's begin with a quotation from Rodney Stark:

> Just as there were no Dark Ages, there was no Scientific Revolution. Rather, the notion of a Scientific Revolution was invented to discredit the Medieval Church by claiming that science burst forth in full bloom (thus owing no debts to prior Scholastic scholars) only when a weakened Christianity could no longer suppress it. But . . . the great scientific achievements of the sixteenth and seventeenth centuries were produced by a group of scholars notable for their piety, who were based in Christian universities, and whose brilliant achievements were carefully built upon an invaluable legacy of centuries of brilliant Scholastic scholarship.[20]

The phrase 'Copernican Revolution' referred originally to the story of Nicolaus Copernicus's discovery that the Earth moves around the sun. Proponents of the Enlightenment myth emphasise the unique nature of this discovery as though nothing else of any astronomical significance had ever happened up to that point and this discovery is often taken to mark the beginning of the Scientific Revolution. In the myth, Copernicus stands like a sentinel at the beginning of the modern age, throwing off the dark hand of the past through the new light of reason. 'Copernican Revolution' now stands for any similar example of a total change in thought that overturns some great and longstanding error justified through erroneous authority.

But, once again, we find that the story is completely misleading because it does not take into consideration the context of Copernicus's life and work. The reality was that Copernicus stood in a long line of intellectual succession that made it possible for his (actually quite limited) contribution to take place. The intellectual and scientific predecessors of Copernicus were men of the Middle Ages. In this, they were religiously devout, and they saw no contradiction between their scientific endeavours and their religious faith.

Robert Grosseteste (1168–1253) was a Norman English polymath of the highest intellectual calibre who carefully distinguished astronomy from astrology and thereby clarified the dimensions of the discipline. He was also an early and crucial developer of the scientific method (about which, more below). With Grosseteste we have astronomy as a discipline, clearly distinguished from other fields, around the turn of the thirteenth century. William of Ockham (1295–1349) was an Englishman who first studied at Oxford and subsequently at early universities on the continent. Among other things, Ockham argued against the idea that the heavenly bodies in space either moved themselves (through some kind of inner soul) or were moved by something else. He theorised that space was a frictionless vacuum in which the heavenly bodies could move in perpetuity. God may have given them the push, as it were, to start them off, but nothing further was needed to keep them going because there was no friction in space. In the fourteenth century, Nicole Oresme (1325–82) speculated that the Earth turned on its axis. He reasoned that our observations would be the same whether the Earth turned or the heavenly bodies revolved around it. But he argued that it was a far more economical explanation to say that the Earth turned than that all of the heavenly bodies moved around the Earth. Nicholas of Cusa (1401–64) said that, wherever a person stood in the heavens – whether on Earth, on the moon or on the sun – it would appear to the observer that he was motionless, the point being that such observations would not prove that the position of the observer was fixed.

It was only once all these building blocks were in place – the universe as a vacuum, the heavenly bodies moving through a frictionless vacuum, the Earth spinning on its axis – that we came to Copernicus.

But, before we consider his contribution, notice something about the myth of the Enlightenment. It claims that we used to think the Earth was flat and that it was at the centre of the universe until 'science', against opposition from religious believers, said that the Earth was round and revolved around the sun. Consider the ludicrousness of Washington Irving's story (invented in the nineteenth century) about Christopher Columbus that, at the time of his adventures, people believed the world was flat, and Columbus might sail off the edge. Columbus lived in the fifteenth century when all educated knowledge about astronomy would have completely contradicted such a view. Nobody of any education believed that the world was flat. But, even more importantly than this, nobody was bothered about the Earth being the centre of anything nor about its being stationary. Nicole Oresme's assertion that the Earth rotated on its axis was not controversial. Medieval people had no problem believing that the Earth was simply one of the heavenly bodies (and the one upon which humanity happened to live). Even more than this, as we have already seen, the 'anthroperipheral' view was that the Earth was a kind of cosmic outlier, a fallen planet far out upon the edge of space, a spectator of, but not a participant in, the dance of the heavenly bodies.

And so we come to Copernicus – the man who put the sun

in the middle of the solar system with the Earth circling around it as simply one of the planets. He was a mathematician and a geometrist who attempted, and failed, to calculate the future positions of the heavenly bodies. Rodney Stark notes that Copernicus in the sixteenth century was no more accurate in his predictions than was Ptolemy in the second.[21] This was because Copernicus didn't realise that the orbits in the solar system are not circular but elliptical. He therefore underestimated the length of the planetary orbits and speculated that they underwent 'loops' on their journeys around the sun. These loops he imagined as circular detours so that the length of the planetary orbits matched the predictions of his theory. Thus, the only point in Copernicus's *On the Revolution of the Heavenly Spheres* which is accurate is that the sun is the centre of the solar system. All his other calculations are wrong, and it was only with Johannes Kepler (1571–1630), a German Protestant, that this changed because Kepler substituted Copernicus's circles for ellipses. The explanation as to why the planets did not simply fly off into space awaited Isaac Newton's (1642–1727) gravitational theory.

And so, at what point in all this did the Scientific Revolution actually take place? Was there anything particularly outrageous or remarkable about Copernicus placing the sun at the centre of the solar system? There was not. Copernicus was right about that one thing while being wrong about pretty much everything else. And there was nothing particularly revolutionary about any of it. It stood in a long line of astronomical speculation and was completely congruent with it. It did not go against a tide but with one. Copernican revolution is really Copernican continuity.

Having said this, it is not as though science in the Middle Ages was exactly the same as what it was to become in the modern period or today. Nor were there 'scientists' as such, the term being invented in the nineteenth century to describe an emerging professional class who dedicated their time to the subject and its sub-disciplines. Nor did the medieval world have internationally recognised qualifications, standardised methodologies or laboratory conditions. But, as the historian of science Seb Falk argues:

> . . . science today did evolve from knowledge-gathering activities stretching back to the Middle Ages and much earlier, and those activities investigated natural phenomena very similar to what scientists investigate today. Medieval people sought to build understanding of why things in nature behave as they do and used their understanding to make future predictions.[22]

The fundamental science of the Middle Ages was astronomy, which was the first type of science to be based upon mathematics. It is easy in our day to take for granted that we simply know the time and date based on all manner of digital and analogue devices. But, in the Middle Ages, these inventions were yet to be conceived and so astronomy was of paramount practical importance to relevant disciplines such as time-keeping, date-keeping, navigation, geography and medicine. Seb Falk's book on medieval science goes into great detail about the ingenious instruments that were invented in the Middle Ages, which saw the birth, for example, of the first clocks, painstakingly developed in monasteries and cathedral schools. In addition, the medievals invented prototypical 'computers' in the forms of astrolabes and the mysterious equatorium, described in the Equatorie of the Planetis, once thought to have been written about by Chaucer.

In light of this, it is hard to understand individuals such as the popular historian Dan Snow, who is noted by Seb Falk to have tweeted the view that the medievals 'lack(3d) the most basic understanding of the scientific method'.[23] To the contrary, this was precisely the age in which the groundwork for the scientific method – in terms of empirical research and the development of mathematics for astronomical observation – was being developed. If they hadn't done that then the advances of the seventeenth century and beyond would have taken far longer and probably occurred much later. This is why Falk ultimately concludes that the denigration of the Middle Ages as a time of darkness and bigotry must be re-evaluated. As he says, 'The Medieval reality . . . is a Light Age of scientific interest and inquiry.'[24]

Reason in the Middle Ages

One of the basic ideas underlying the mythical Enlightenment narrative is that faith is opposed to reason. Faith claims to reveal but reason investigates and thinks and discovers. Faith is a kind of blind trust in God to tell us something about reality. Reason is the proactive use of a faculty of humans to test assertions and hypotheses. To illustrate this, the two ages are often pitted against each other as the age of faith against the age of reason.

Once again, there is only the tiniest grain of truth in this antithesis; it is, in the main, another catastrophically misleading travesty. For not only were the Christian Middle Ages not opposed to reason, but it is actually the case that our modern understanding of reason and its application were invented in the late Middle Ages, developing from about the eleventh century onwards.

After the fall of the Western Roman empire,* Europe was understandably plunged into a period of fragmentation and turmoil which lasted from around the sixth century to the tenth. It was during this time that the disarray and disorganisation in fields of human knowledge such as law and theology needed to be codified. And it was precisely this unstable situation in which a new understanding of reason emerged.[25] All societies use reason in one way or another. But what was different about the emerging awareness of reason in Europe in these centuries was, as the historian Edward Grant puts it, 'a new self-conscious emphasis on reason' and 'the application of reason to societal activities'[26] beginning with the areas of law and theology in the period after the fall of the Roman empire.

---

* Traditionally dated at AD 476 when the last Western Roman Emperor, Romulus Augustulus, was deposed by a barbarian king, the Germanic Odoacer.

It was indeed in the eleventh century onwards that reason was self-consciously utilised across all academic disciplines and more widely in society. This was because of the development of education that sprang up from Charlemagne's early attempts and evolved into cathedral schools and, from there, the early universities of Europe, which were, of course, thoroughly Christian institutions. As Edward Grant writes:

> . . . it was in the esoteric domain of university scholasticism that reason was most highly developed and perhaps ultimately most influential. Indeed, it was permanently institutionalized in the universities of Europe. Reason was interwoven with the very fabric of a European-wide Medieval curriculum and thus played its most significant role in preparing the way for the establishment of a deep-rooted scientific temperament that was an indispensable prerequisite for the emergence of early modern science. Reason in the university context was not intended for the acquisition of power over others, or to improve the material well-being of the general populace. Its primary purpose was to elucidate the natural and supernatural worlds. In all the history of human civilization, reason had never been accorded such a central role, one that involved so many people over such a wide area for such an extended period.[27]

This ubiquitous belief in reason and its application in medieval Christian Europe can be contrasted with an age such as that of the ancient Greeks who, though they had their champions of reason, such as the Platonists and the Aristotelians, nevertheless were beset by the schools of the sophists and the sceptics who questioned the notion of rationality. It was finally within the Christian context of belief in an objectively ordered cosmos that the widespread and intentional use of reason could emerge more fully.

As Edward Grant implies, the use of reason was bound up with the development of the discipline of Theology. Rodney Stark argues that it was precisely Christianity's emphasis upon the use of reason in theological development that laid the groundwork for its wider adoption in society. In contrast even to Jewish and Islamic approaches to the subject, Christianity uniquely emphasised the need for the application of reason to theological questions; indeed, the possibility of progress and development in Christian understanding due to the application of reason was fully acknowledged. On this, he says, 'The most important of these victories occurred within Christianity. While the other world religions emphasized mystery and intuition, Christianity alone embraced reason and logic as the primary guide to religious truth.'[28] And he goes on to explain as follows:

> . . . from early days, the church fathers taught that reason was the supreme gift from God and the means to progressively increase their understanding of scripture and revelation. Consequently, Christianity was oriented to the future, while the other major religions asserted the superiority of the past. At least in principle, if not always in fact, Christian doctrines could always be modified in the name of progress as demonstrated by reason. Encouraged by the Scholastics and embodied in the great medieval universities founded by the church, faith in the power of reason infused Western culture, stimulating the pursuit of science and the evolution of democratic theory and practice. The rise of capitalism was also a victory for church-inspired reason, since capitalism is in essence the systematic and sustained application of reason to commerce – something that first took place within the great monastic estates.[29]

Stark also notes that the application of reason to commerce formed the basis for the development of capitalism, observing that capitalism developed uniquely in Christian medieval Europe:

> The material conditions needed for capitalism existed in many civilizations in various eras, including China, Islam, India,

Byzantium, and probably ancient Rome and Greece as well. But none of these societies broke through and developed capitalism, as none evolved ethical visions compatible with this dynamic economic system. Instead, leading religions outside the West called for asceticism and denounced profits, while wealth was exacted from peasants and merchants by rapacious elites dedicated to display and consumption. Why did things turn out differently in Europe? Because of the Christian commitment to rational theology.[30]

As has already been stated, the medieval and modern understandings of reason are not identical. In the medieval understanding, reason had two roles, which were to bring clarity to what had been revealed to humanity by God and to probe the workings of the cosmos and the natural world. Again, we can see in the latter role a clear preliminary to the use of reason in modern-day science. As Grant notes,

> Because Christians wisely avoided Christianizing, or theologizing, natural philosophy, natural philosophers pursued knowledge about the universe in a remarkably secular and rationalistic manner with little interference from the Church and its theologians, who were themselves often engaged in the same activity: trying to understand the workings of the physical world.[31]

Without this historical ancestor in medieval Christendom, 'the seventeenth-century version of the Age of Reason could not have occurred'.[32]

But there was a crucial difference which must be noted: the use of reason in the Middle Ages did not allow those who wielded this tool to reach conclusions that contradicted truths that had been revealed by God. This point raises significant philosophical questions. Does it contradict what I have been arguing: that the Middle Ages were an age not of blind faith but of reason? I believe not. What this in fact demonstrates is not that there was an absolute change between the Middle Ages and the modern period, but that there was a difference. The Christian medieval period was an age of faith – an age of faith in Christianity, surprisingly enough, an age in which people believed that God had revealed himself to the world in the person of Jesus Christ, through the Scriptures and the teaching of the Church. It was also an age of reason, however. And it was an age of reason because reason was applied to the Christian worldview, which was believed to be inherently rational and coherent. And, as has already been said, that rationality was used to probe the mysteries of nature and of the cosmos. There were limits which were laid down in advance because of the religious presuppositions of the time, but this does not change the fact that the widespread use of reason came about uniquely in Europe during this historical period. We might even say that it was the Christian metaphysical backdrop that made this possible. To quote Seb Falk again:

> Belief in God never prevented people from seeking to understand the world around them. Loyalty to texts and traditions never meant the rejection of new ideas. Channelling money and creative energies into religious art and architecture never restricted the range of Medieval people's interests. The relationship between faith and the study of nature was – and remains – a complex one . . . Disputed ideas have occasionally caused conflict, of course. But to imagine 'science' and 'religion' as two separate, inevitably antagonistic opponents, or to suggest that such closed-mindedness as does exist has always been on the side of religion, is far too simplistic.[33]

There is a further point: although modern-day science is conducted in a secular context, there are nevertheless limits placed upon it because of the metaphysical presuppositions of the scientific establishment. For example, it is governed by a strong materialistic paradigm, which does not allow for the existence of phenomena that cannot be easily explained outside the context of material and efficient causation. Thinkers such as the Cambridge botanist Rupert Sheldrake have attempted to challenge this paradigm but have been met with institutional scorn as a result.* My point is not that the modern-day paradigm is wrong, but that there is always some kind of metaphysical framework or background which determines the limits of reason. It may be that discoveries using reason challenge that framework, which can ultimately be overturned through a paradigm shift, but, even if this does occur, some other framework necessarily must replace that which has been rejected.

To summarise, reason as we understand the term today is really an ancestor of reason as it was developed in Christian medieval Europe. It is true that reason today is secularised – and many may see this as an improvement – but it is nevertheless a travesty of the historical record to suggest that the modern age invented reason in contrast to the irrational approach of the Christian age that preceded it. The modern age took reason from Christianity and, as I argue in various ways in this book, it is in fact the modern age that is now descending into irrationality as it takes leave of its rational Christian presuppositions.

Underrated Areas of Medieval Achievement

In addition to these observations, we should also add that the medieval period was not a time of intellectual and social stagnation, technological backwardness, and low standards in sanitation. A comprehensive overview is beyond the scope of this book but to make the point is fairly straightforward and it can be put like this: the medieval period passed on to us significant achievements in areas such as science, education, law, literature and other

---

* The case of Sheldrake will be mentioned in more detail in Chapter Two on science. Here I would point the reader in the direction of Sheldrake's *The Science Delusion* for more information on his outlook and its reception by the establishment: Rupert Sheldrake, *The Science Delusion: Freeing the Spirit of Enquiry* (London: Coronet, 2012).

arts such as music, architecture, farming technology, and military and industrial technology. Many historians have made the point that, in contrast to the myth of the burning of the Library of Alexandria, it was in fact Christian monks of the Middle Ages who preserved the literature of Greek and Roman antiquity through the painstaking and laborious copying of manuscripts. The latter occurred in the shadow of the fall of the Roman empire, which makes it all the more remarkable when one considers the instability and transitional nature of that period. And the achievement of Christian monasteries in this regard is of immense significance for the Western world, for it was through the preservation of this learning that the Christian medieval synthesis and subsequent Renaissance rediscovery of ancient humanism was made possible.

Moreover, slavery, though ubiquitous at the time of the fall of the Roman empire, had disappeared almost entirely by the time of the High Middle Ages, only to be revived once again in early modernity, at the onset of the secular nation state and concurrently with the ostensible discovery of science and the invention of the civilised world. This is another area in which the mainstream narrative of the modern day is incredibly misleading. It is rarely mentioned, for example, that all the major empires of the world, prior to the advent of Christianity and during the Christian millennium, were economically dependent upon the mass enslavement of great swathes of their populations. The historical fact that slavery essentially died out in that same millennium uniquely in Christian civilisation is almost never raised. Why did it die out? Specifically, because of the Christian idea that human beings are made in the image of God and possess their own moral agency which should be respected. The implications of these doctrines took some time for Christian theologians to work out in detail, but it is to be emphasised that the overturning of slavery was of world-changing significance and therefore conceptually demanding. But overturn slavery Christianity most certainly did, and this was, once again, a unique achievement in world history. Practically, slavery ended in medieval Europe because the Christian Church extended its sacraments to slaves and then banned the enslavement of Christians. Rodney Stark notes: 'Within the context of medieval Europe, that prohibition was effectively a rule of universal abolition.'[34] Stark quotes Bishop Agobard of Lyons (c. 779–840), saying, 'All men are brothers, all invoke one same Father, God: the slave and the master, the poor man and the rich man, the ignorant and the learned, the weak and the strong . . . none has been raised above the other . . . and there is no . . . slave or free, but in all things and always there is only Christ.'[35] Again, slavery was tragically revived at the onset of modernity and it is certainly the case that many Christians were involved in this revival. This is, of course, lamentable on the part of everyone who was involved. However, it is also the case that slavery was abolished in the modern period at first because of Christians such as William Wilberforce (1759–1833) and the Evangelicals of the Clapham Sect. It is not an exaggeration to say, therefore, that the modern, Western attitude towards slavery is entirely an inheritance of Christianity which emerges historically from the medieval period.

The Christian medieval period was a time of immense progress in many other ways also, some of them perhaps too mundane to be noted regularly. There was, for example, the invention and widespread use of the watermill from the ninth century onwards. Medieval societies began to use water and wind power to replace the slave labour that had enriched and empowered the Roman empire. An astonishing achievement of the early medieval period was the utilisation of windmills in the uncovering of huge tracts of land that eventually became large parts of Belgium and the Netherlands. These countries occupy areas that used to be almost entirely under water but were made habitable by the widescale deployment of windmills which pumped out millions of gallons of sea water. Dams were also invented, with an early significant example being that of the dam built at Toulouse around 1120.

In agriculture, we see the shift to a three-field system in which one field per year was left unplanted but continued to be cultivated, which resulted in far greater levels of crop production. We see also the inventions of the heavy plough and the nailed horseshoe and horse collar which enabled the use of horses rather than oxen in ploughing. We also see the selective breeding of plants which began in medieval monasteries. This all amounted to an agricultural revolution. In addition to the excess materials that were being generated through mills, which in turn contributed to greater levels of economic growth, the amount of food being produced skyrocketed, meaning that a much larger population could be fed. All this contributed to the growth of larger urban populations and led to larger towns and cities.

We could also add to the list the invention of chimneys and eye-glasses. In military technology, there were the inventions of the stirrup and proper high-backed saddles, enabling the deployment of heavy cavalry for the first time. Whereas mounted Roman troops had only been able to use bows or swords due to the instability of sitting on a horse with no proper saddle and no stirrup, in the medieval period, mounted troops could ride over their opponents on enormous horses, wielding lances. This is what happened when the Franks defeated the emerging Islamic forces at the Battle of Tours in 732 and again, four centuries later, at the time of the Crusades. It was the Christian armies at both points that had mounted cavalry able to decimate their Islamic opponents because the latter had no equivalent military technology. Although the Islamic armies had been destroyed at Tours, they had failed, even four centuries later, to mimic the Christian military technology in their defence of the Holy Land.

Again, Romans used slave power in their naval activities. These were galleys powered by oars. The European Christians invented proper sailing ships with cannons. Gunpowder was invented in China, but it was church bell manufacturers in Christian Europe who first used their skills to cast cannons, which in turn transformed the nature of naval warfare from the crude Roman techniques of ramming other ships and engaging in hand-to-hand combat to something far more sophisticated.[36]

One final matter must be mentioned, and that is the invention of Gothic architecture. This was dependent upon the development of the pointed arch which may have first been used internally in Durham Cathedral but is most famously associated with Abbot Suger (c. 1081–1151) and the Abbey Church at St Denis.[37] This simple innovation in architecture led to the transformation of churches, cathedrals and other buildings from that point onwards. The load-bearing capacity of pointed arches meant that walls could be thinner and contain larger amounts of glass and that ceilings could be much higher than hitherto. Structures of immense lightness, beauty and size began to emerge all over Europe. These buildings still astonish and captivate modern people. Even though technological capabilities are far more advanced in the contemporary world, we have lost the imaginative and spiritual capability to produce architectural wonders of this type. When one enters a great medieval cathedral such as Chartres, one is transported to an alternative world of light, beauty, power and immensity that the grandness of a modern skyscraper simply cannot replicate. These buildings alone should be enough to debunk thoroughly the myth of the 'Dark Ages' and of the cultural stagnation of the medieval period. If we were to judge by architecture alone, we would conclude that, far from being inferior, the civilisation that produced these buildings was infinitely superior to our own.

Where the Secular Myth Came From

If the story of the 'Dark Ages' and Enlightenment is as baseless as all this, one would be forgiven for asking where it came from in the first place. And an explanation is, indeed, needful. We have noted that the story has elements of truth to it. Within the grander picture, some narratives are more fanciful than others, but they tend to take a kernel of truth and leave out contextual features that would otherwise change the meaning entirely:

Galileo's relationship with Pope Urban VIII is a classic example of this.

The fact is that a wider interpretative grid, fundamentally ideological in nature, was laid over the top of the historical narrative. That ideological purpose was to denigrate the Middle Ages and to promote the age of Enlightenment as part of a broader anti-Christian agenda. And this ideological inclination is still very much with us. Today, the word 'medieval' is not often intended as a compliment, although it very much ought to be. Rather, to be called medieval is to be insulted as backward, ignorant and cruel. The propagandists have indeed done their job well. Who were they?

The mythical Enlightenment narrative came not from the seventeenth century (the ostensible starting date of the Scientific Revolution), but from the eighteenth and nineteenth centuries. In other words, this narrative is a backwards projection of anti-Christian, Enlightenment beliefs onto the seventeenth century. Almost none of the Enlightenment thinkers was a scientist; rather they were historians, philosophers and literary types. Edward Gibbon (1737–94) who wrote *The Decline and Fall of the Roman Empire* is perhaps the most significant in this regard. But we could also name the anti-Christian polemicist Voltaire (1694–1778), the historian and philosopher David Hume (1711–76) and the political theorist Jean-Jacques Rousseau (1712–78). They tended to portray the seventeenth century as a time of growing scepticism about religious belief in the face of scientific and cultural advance.

But one of the strangest things about the Enlightenment take on the seventeenth century is that it claims as its heroes those who in fact held the very Christian beliefs its proponents were attacking. The scientists and thinkers who these later writers claim as proto-secular revolutionaries were, in fact, mostly either conventional or devout Christians. To confirm this, Rodney Stark identified the main scientific stars of the era – Copernicus, Robert Boyle, Isaac Newton, Johannes Kepler, and many others – and analysed their religious outlooks. Stark found that 60 per cent of those scientists could be classified as devout religious believers, with 25 per cent of them being clergymen. And 38 per cent could be classified as conventional believers, while just 2 per cent could be classified as sceptical of religious belief. The latter constituted only one person, Edmund Halley, who was rejected for a professorship at Oxford because of his so-called 'atheism'.[38] Stark concludes: 'Clearly, the superb scientific achievements of the sixteenth and seventeenth centuries were not the work of sceptics, but of very Christian men.'[39] It was not, therefore, the great scientists of the early modern period who invented the myth of the Enlightenment but pamphleteers, political theorists, philosophers, and historians of the eighteenth century who used the scientific achievements of others as a vehicle for their own anti-Christian agenda. They were the ones who invented this myth.

The myth was then popularised to a huge extent by two extremely influential Victorian authors who have been largely forgotten today: John Mark Draper (1811–82) and Andrew Dickson White (1832–1918). Draper wrote a book called *A History of the Conflict of Science and Religion* and White wrote *A History of the Warfare of Science with Theology in Christendom*. These two books brought to the wider public what is now quite commonly known as the 'conflict thesis', the idea that there is a contradiction between a scientific view of the world and a Christian one. Thus, a human being can choose between either rationality and scientific progress or superstition and religious ignorance. Many of the myths surrounding the relationship of science and Christianity were either invented or elaborated upon by these two men.

Even with this explanation as to the origin of the mythical story, it is still quite hard to understand how it has taken such a powerful and ubiquitous hold over the minds of so many in the modern-day West. There is, of course, something inherently attractive about believing a story that puts me as an individual, and us as a society, at the apex of history. So perhaps the psychological pull goes some way towards providing an explanation. David Hutchings and James C. Ungureanu's already-quoted work on Draper and White, *Of Popes and Unicorns: Science, Christianity and How the Conflict Thesis Fooled the World*, explains how the latter two authors in particular used their literary abilities to tell a story that would captivate so many. But it remains astonishing how such a blatantly false narrative serves as the principal historical backdrop for the world that we live in today.

Conclusion: The Secular Myth is a Christian Heresy

One of the central ironies of the myth of Enlightenment is that it is a fundamentally Christian story. This might sound surprising since it is told to justify a materialist or atheistic worldview but it is nevertheless true. To understand this, we need to go back to the Protestant Reformation in the sixteenth century.

The view of the Reformers was that the Roman Catholic Church had fatally erred in departing from a scriptural understanding of the Christian faith. The Church had become corrupted through doctrines not taken from Scripture but invented by man. One of the issues that particularly exercised perhaps the greatest Reformer, Martin Luther, was the sale of indulgences for the purpose of enriching the Church. A Dominican preacher, Johann Tetzel, is reputed to have composed the couplet 'As soon as a coin in the coffer rings, the soul from purgatory springs'. Which neatly sums up the problem: the Church was saying that people could pay for their relatives to be released from purgatory by purchasing indulgences from . . . the Church.

Another practice to come under fire was that of simony, which is the buying or selling of ecclesiastical positions. Added to that, the Reformers were also deeply critical of the Church's insistence on the use of Latin for the Scriptures. The Bible was only available in the language of Jerome's second-century Latin translation – the Vulgate. The common folk could not read it and thus were not able to educate themselves in the knowledge of God nor hear the Scriptures read aloud in their own language.*

The Reformers claimed to have rediscovered the heart of God's message to humanity in Jesus Christ, summarised in the doctrine of justification by faith. We are justified in the sight of God, so the Reformers argued, not by works of merit nor by purchasing indulgences nor by working off our sin in purgatory, but by faith in Christ alone. Christ has paid the price for sin and now all we must do to be saved is place our trust in him.

Justification by faith was one of the two main planks of the Reformation. The other was the translation of the Scriptures into the vernacular. In England, this tradition began through the work of the martyr William Tyndale on whose translation the later King James Bible would be based.

These two motifs were like two curtains drawn back to allow sunlight into a dark room. Through the translation of the Scriptures, the common folk could investigate for themselves the truths of the Christian religion and could verify whether the Roman Church was teaching and practising the truth. And, through the doctrine of justification by faith, they were freed from the obligation to spend their lives desperately trying to merit salvation through slavish adherence to the rigorous and costly demands that had been made upon them. Through simple faith in Jesus, through adherence to the word of God, they could live the Christian life, liberated from ignorance and bondage. The watchword of the Reformation *was post tenebras, lux!* – 'after darkness, light!'

The Reformers therefore cast the Roman Catholic Church as the darkness and themselves and their message as the light.

---

* As with every aspect of the Reformation, this claim is contested and controversial. The Roman Catholic historian Eamon Duffy argues, for example, that much more Scripture was available to common folk than is generally appreciated today. Cf. Eamon Duffy, *The Stripping of the Altars: Traditional Religion in England, 1400–1580* (New Haven: Yale University Press, 2022)

But even this move was derivative. For the imagery of darkness and light goes back further to the Scriptures themselves. Even the watchword mentioned above found its origin in the pages of Jerome's Vulgate translation: *Post tenebras, lux* is a paraphrase of Jerome's rendering of Job 17:12: 'After darkness, I hope for light.' If the Reformation cast the Roman Catholic Church as the darkness, it was the Judeo-Christian Scriptures that had first identified darkness as the enemy. It did so, though, in contrast to the Hellenic pagan world and in the more abstract terms of sin, death and the spiritual forces that aligned themselves against God. Speaking of Christ himself, the apostle John would write, 'The light shines in the darkness, and the darkness has not overcome it' (John 1:5), while the apostle Paul would frequently use the same sort of imagery: 'For you were once darkness, but now you are light in the Lord. Live as children of light' (Ephesians 5:8).

The point therefore is that the same imagery is used and reused but directed in different ways. In the Scriptures, the darkness is idolatry, sin, death, and the forces of spiritual evil. In the Reformation, the imagery was transferred onto the Roman Catholic Church. And, in the Enlightenment, it was broadened out to refer to all of Christianity and belief in the supernatural itself. It is one of the great ironies of the Enlightenment that this fact often goes unnoticed.

But there is an even more direct link between the Reformation and the Enlightenment than that. For, as well as attacking the Roman Church on the grounds that it obfuscated the gospel and the Scriptures, the Reformers also attacked aspects of Christianity that implied contact between the natural and the supernatural realms. Prior to the Reformation, it was the general understanding within Christendom that the realm of the natural and the realm of the supernatural were closely intertwined with each other, like two porous spheres that intersected. In the year 1500, it was basically impossible not to believe in God and in all that went along with the Christian view of reality. People simply experienced the world as the realm of the supernatural, an arena in which the spiritual forces of good and evil did battle. This experience of the world was buttressed by the practices of the Church, which was the chief conduit of the supernatural realm. In the Mass, it was held that the bread and wine actually became the body and blood of Christ during the consecration. Prayer for the souls of the dead and invocation of the saints were ubiquitous. The use of enchanted objects in liturgy such as holy water and blessed oils was widespread. For example, salt was used in baptism because it was believed that it had apotropaic properties.* Holy relics abounded and pilgrimage to holy places such as the city of Jerusalem, often in pursuit of pardon or indulgence, was routine.

The Reformers cast scorn upon much of this. Most of them explicitly denied the presence of Christ in the Mass or, at the least, downplayed it significantly. They banned the invocation of the saints and cast prayer for the dead as superstitious. The enchantment of objects such as holy relics was rejected. Pilgrimage was condemned. The theological justification for this was that God is present everywhere in creation and not confined to particular objects or geographical locations. But the overall effect was to separate out the realms of the natural and the supernatural, and therefore to remove the presence of God from his creation entirely, thus creating the possibility of seeing the world as a self-automating machine. Perhaps there was a God who started it off, but it didn't need him any more either to intervene or to explain. From there, it was but a short step to declare that the machine was all there was, and the possibility of modern atheism was born. This process is frequently referred to in the scholarly literature and elsewhere as 'disenchantment', which means simply the loss of a sense of the spiritual realm within the natural world.

The Enlightenment is, then, simply a radicalisation of the disenchanting work of the Reformation, the difference being that while the Reformers claimed that God is not present in the objects

---

* That is, properties that could cast out demonic forces.

of bread and wine, the Enlightenment philosophers said that he is not present in anything because he does not exist. But the latter view would never have been possible if the two realms of the natural and the supernatural had not been prised apart in the first place. This is why it is said that the Enlightenment is a Christian heresy: it takes a set of theological premises and radicalises them to produce atheist materialism.

There is, in fact, a striking similarity between certain forms of extreme Protestantism, influenced by the Reformation, and Enlightenment atheism. They are both individualist and anti-authoritarian, insisting that human beings do not need institutions and authorities to mediate truth as they can access it for themselves. And they are both anti-supernaturalist in the sense that God does not intervene directly in the physical processes of this world.*

Even more generally, the myth of Enlightenment relies on Christianity for its narrative structure. The very shape of the narrative depends upon a secularised version of the Christian story of fall, redemption and salvation. In the Christian story, the fall is brought about by the sin of Adam and Eve; in the Enlightenment story, it is brought about by religious ignorance, superstition and clericalism. In Christianity, redemption is brought into the world through Christ and the gospel; in the Enlightenment, it is won for us through science and reason. In the Christian understanding, only the return of Christ will usher in a new age of eternal peace and joy; in the Enlightenment paradigm, mankind will bring

---

* Admittedly, this varies enormously in the present day according to the kind of Protestant Christianity in question. The Charismatic movement, comprising many hundreds of millions of Christians, is highly supernaturalist in its outlook but in a very different way from Roman Catholicism. And the doctrine of the Church of England as encapsulated in the Book of Common Prayer perfectly balances the need for reform of the superstitious excesses of the Roman Catholic Church and the retention of the supernaturalist worldview of Christianity as mediated through the ministry of the Church.

about his own paradise through the march of progress. The main difference between the two stories is that the central character – the hero – has changed. In Christianity, it is God redeeming the world through Christ; in the Enlightenment, it is man redeeming the world through reason.*

It is interesting to note that there are some Western thinkers who have acknowledged these Christian themes within the Enlightenment paradigm and advocated for their rejection. The twentieth-century German phenomenologist Karl Löwith was wary of utopian thinking because he saw it as continually grasping towards some final state in which the problems of the present time will be banished, a view that encourages discontentment and an unpleasant sense of perpetual striving. Löwith said that pagan cyclical theories of time are much better for facilitating human contentment and happiness because, in a cyclical view in which history repeats itself, there is no utopian final state and there never will be. So we might as well stop trying to bring one about and make the best of the situation here and now. He may have had a point. After all, the idea that humanity is one day going to bring about a utopia of its own making creates an awful lot of pressure.†

The point here is simple: the idea of progress as we see it in the myth of Enlightenment is taken from Christianity. The central difference is that it replaces God with man and puts all the pressure upon the latter to bring about 'heaven' for himself. Without

---

* Even the secular notion of the redemptive power of reason corresponds to the Christian idea of redemption through Christ. This is because Christ has always been associated with reason: for example, he is described in the Gospel of John as Logos, meaning 'word' or 'reason'. Thus, Christ is the principle of reason through which all things in heaven and Earth are ordered. Again, the Enlightenment story sees something of the power of reason but strips it of the supernatural aspect it has in the Christian story.
† We might also mention the fact that utopian thinking led to the mass murder of tens of millions of people in the twentieth century under political regimes ranging from Hitler to Stalin to Chairman Mao and beyond.

Christianity, it does seem rather a strange thing to believe: that mankind is inevitably advancing towards a utopian state, and that not only his technological but also his critical and moral faculties are gradually improving. Thus, the story of the Enlightenment myth itself is a kind of theft, an infringement of the intellectual copyright of Christianity, derived from, and dependent upon, the very story that it claims to reject.

The myth is false in every important way and the anti-Christian history it claims to support is deeply misleading. There were no 'Dark Ages'. The so-called 'Scientific Revolution' was simply a continuation of the utilisation of reason and science that began centuries before. Christians discovered these endeavours and the modern world takes credit for them. Because of this, the modern world believes it does not need to invoke the supernatural to make sense of the natural world and human existence. We will see in the following chapter why this, too, is yet another error.

II

Science: Why It Can't Replace Christianity

'Ah, it is the fault of our science that it wants to explain all; and if it explain not, then it says there is nothing to explain.'

Bram Stoker, *Dracula*

Just as the use of reason did not suddenly appear in Western Europe in the seventeenth century, neither did modern science emerge out of a conflict with medieval Christianity. (This too is a feature of the secular myth.) Rather, science was the product *of* medieval Christianity. And this is not a coincidence because it was Christianity with its belief in a rational creator of all things that provided the metaphysical backdrop for the emergence of science. Christianity dramatically altered the pagan landscape into which it was born which would explain natural phenomena by recourse to the activity of specific gods. The pagan world was thus a chaotic one of competing natural and supernatural forces. But there was no overarching and metaphysical order, no singular God over all, that held them together. It was only Christianity that universalised this idea which it inherited from Judaism. In the Christian worldview, it was God who created everything that exists, and it was by the wisdom and power of God that the cosmos operated. Because God was one singular God and not one of multiple warring deities, the world was thought to operate upon stable rational principles that came from an undivided divine mind. Thus, once again, the idea that Christianity put a break upon scientific endeavour could not be more wrong: it created the conditions and appetite for 'science' in the first place.

Scientific truths in the medieval period had to be understood in the light of the truths revealed by the Christian religion. Were an ostensible scientific discovery deemed to contradict an aspect of revealed truth, it was the discovery that would be considered wrong.* This feature of science has changed today but that change does not alter the fact that science and the widespread use of reason were first birthed in medieval Europe in a Christian culture.

In contrast to the contemporary model of antagonism and warfare, I will offer a better understanding of the relationship between science and Christianity. This is not a history of the 'discovery' of science and the throwing-off of an oppressive religious hierarchy that sought to limit its domain. Rather, the true history shows that science was birthed within the Christian world but eventually came to view itself as a rival and superior religious worldview to Christianity. It hid this fact cleverly by framing itself as an anti-religious outlook, maintaining that reality was purely physical and not supernatural. It called itself 'materialism' or sometimes 'naturalism' and said that this was the obvious fact that it had discovered about the world: only matter exists; only nature is real. To bolster this argument, it pointed to its many achievements in understanding the physical world, claiming to have improved the world through helping people to live longer and better lives with medicine and technology. It promised that one day it would be able to understand literally everything and that, when that day came, the conquest of religion would finally be complete. There would be no need for God or for the supernatural world, for all would be explained. All the mysteries of existence would be solved. The scientists needed a bit more time. But it would come eventually.

---

* This, of course, seems insane to modern people. But it only does so because of the underlying assumption that revealed truths are necessarily false or, at least, extremely questionable. Medieval people held that the revealed truths of the Christian religion were real and valid. Therefore, any scientific theories that appeared to contradict them must be false. This is a simple deployment of logic.

Science had become a way of understanding the world comprehensively. It had become, in other words, a religion – a secular religion without a god, but a religion none the less. And this religion has become the way that people in the Western world see reality. Because of our culture, our technology, our education and the way we are brought up, we inevitably see the world through the glasses of the scientific worldview. Our conditioning makes it seem as though this worldview is the most rational and most likely to be true. Indeed, it makes it *seem* as though this is just the way the world *is*. But the reason for this is that we have been conditioned to see things this way.

Further, because science is now revered as the great revealer of all mysteries, like many religions it has become dogmatic and defensive while its intellectual citadels are patrolled by its high priests who permit certain thoughts and not others. Even worse, those high priests and cardinals have allowed the entire enterprise to become a vessel of corruption: the scientific establishment has been captured by the politically powerful and has been turned towards their frequently nefarious ends. And now there are increasingly significant indicators that the religion of science is losing its grip upon the imagination of man.

Science as Science and Science as Religion

To make this clear, let us first consider what science is and what it is not. The definition of 'science' is contentious, but there are certain things that most people agree on. I'll begin with a definition from the American philosopher of science, Ken Wilbur:

> As for scientific method, general science texts seem to be in agreement: (it is) a method of gaining knowledge whereby *hypotheses* are tested (instrumentally or experimentally) by reference to *experience* ('data') that is potentially *public*, or open to *repetition* (confirmation of refutation) by peers. In bare essentials,

it means that the scientific method involves those knowledge-claims open to *experiential* validation or refutation.[1]

The key words in italics concern hypotheses, testing, experience (or data) and the public nature of science. A hypothesis is a supposition or, more crudely, an educated 'guess' about some aspect of the physical world. That 'guess' is then tested through experiment. The experiment gives us some data or information which tells us whether the original hypothesis is likely to be correct or not. This process is, in theory, accessible to anybody who would like to confirm it. Obviously not everybody can confirm scientific experiments because most people lack the training, means or intellectual capacity to do so. But, in theory and given the right conditions, anybody would be able to re-run the experiment and check the results.

This definition is quite reasonable but it leaves a lot out. On the one hand, there are many who would say that the definition is too broad and could include other areas that are not scientific. Wilbur himself points out that religious experience could be subject to these kinds of tests. Perhaps music, art and social sciences could also make use of them. So perhaps it is too vague and could be more specific.

On the other hand, there are areas that most would consider 'science' but which miss out some aspects of this description. For example, astronomers and palaeontologists do not do experiments as such but work through empirical observation. If we were strict about it, the theory of evolution would not be scientific because it can't be tested experimentally or confirmed by repeated experiment. But most would want to say that all these disciplines are scientific.

Within the scientific field, we also have general theories. General theories are more abstract and concern the explanation of knowledge gained through science under some broader theory. Again, general theories of science are not necessarily contained within our definition because they are arrived at using abstract reasoning and not through hypothesis and experiment.

So the definition of science is not absolutely clear. But most people mean by 'science' something that concerns hypothesis, experiment, data and public verifiability. Some would say that is too broad; others would say it is too narrow. And the debate, within the corridors of academic philosophy faculties throughout the world, continues.

What, therefore, is the difference between scientific accounts of the world and religious or metaphysical accounts? The difference is that scientific accounts deal with aspects of the physical world: biologists study organisms, chemists study chemicals, physicists study laws of nature, and so on. Religious and metaphysical accounts may touch on areas that are related to some of these *but* they are not fundamentally about them. The religious or metaphysical question is about developing a comprehensive account of the nature of reality.

Scientific knowledge changes as time goes on. Old scientific paradigms are overturned by new ones. Experimental knowledge is reframed and understood differently. Technological development brings about new possibilities. The scientific enterprise is shifting and dynamic; it does not yield total results about the nature of reality, but about aspects of the natural world. Religion and metaphysics, in contrast, seek a more comprehensive and stable view of how things are in their totality.

What is the difference between 'religion' and 'metaphysics'? To put it simply, religion goes about obtaining its understanding through revelation. That is, God reveals himself in some way to human beings. Metaphysics uses reason to describe the order of reality and does not rely upon revelation. These two things can come together – as they frequently do in Christianity and other religions – but they are not exactly the same.

My point here is that there is a fundamental difference between science as a tool for understanding the physical world and religion or metaphysics as a means of obtaining a comprehensive understanding of reality. It doesn't matter how many scientific experiments you do or how successful they are, they will never add up to a comprehensive picture of reality in themselves.

Nevertheless, there are clearly many who do think that they add up to such a picture: that somehow the success of science in developing medicine and technology and advancing human knowledge implies that the physical world is all that exists and that there is no God. But this argument is based upon nothing logical or reasonable. It is a commitment based on blind faith, and it should become very clear why science properly understood should not lead us to this conclusion.

The Modern 'Social Imaginary'

To understand this further, we have to begin with how we got to this point. How is it that many people believe that science can deliver to us answers to all the mysteries of existence? How did we come to live in a world in which science has become the dominant religious paradigm? It is clearly not the case that each individual person weighs up all the arguments in a completely rational way and decides that, on the basis of the evidence, science is true and religion is false, that there is no God and that science will tell us everything about the nature of reality. What really happens is that we are conditioned to see the world in a certain way and this is largely because of intellectual and societal factors that shift and change over long periods of time. Those factors are transmitted to us through our parents, education, advertising, government, arts, the media, and through a whole host of other features of what we broadly call 'culture'. The majority of people have only a very dimly held understanding of how conditioned they really are.

We have all been conditioned to see the world in the so-called 'scientific' way: namely, that the physical world is what really exists and that the spiritual world and God do not. This goes for everyone in the Western world including religious people. We can't live in this society without being conditioned in this way. Through spiritual practices such as prayer, meditation, and so on, it seems that we can train ourselves out of this phenomenological habit to an extent, but it is extremely difficult.* It really concerns the way we feel about things: what seems true, what seems real, and so on. It operates within us on a subconscious and pre-rational level such that most people never examine these impulses or even realise that they have them.

Religious people have to battle against this conditioning in order to pursue the spiritual life. Atheists and materialists have their own battle, which is against the nagging feeling that there may indeed be a God and that in denying him they may be misinterpreting the nature and purpose of existence. Because of a mixture of views in our culture, all people within it face a kind of pressure that pushes them in one direction or another.²

The central point is that we do not see things as they really are but, rather, we see the world as we imagine it to be. This is not to say that we see it in a false way, but we are limited and see only partially from a given perspective. So we see certain things and not others. And what we do see are the things that we pay attention to, both as individuals and as a culture. The things that we pay attention to are the things that come to seem real to us. To put it slightly crudely: if we pay attention only to material reality, it will seem reasonable to us that only material reality exists. And that is what I believe has happened to us as a culture: a long and sustained focus upon material reality to the detriment of spiritual reality has conditioned us to believe that only the material realm is real. As such, it has come to seem that religious ideas are not plausible, that there may be a God but it's not particularly important if there is or not. Further, if there is one, he is probably nice and is not too bothered about our apathy towards his existence and desires. What matters for us is the physical: physical comfort, physical health, physical pleasure, and physical longevity.

---

* 'Phenomenological' and 'phenomenology' simply mean experience without reference to abstract theory. A 'phenomenological habit' is a habit of seeing the world in a certain way without coming to that conclusion through rational reflection.

This, to use Charles Taylor's term, is our 'social imaginary' – the way that we, in our shared, social existence, imagine the world to be. It is not the way that academic philosophers or religious mystics come to understand the world, but the way that ordinary people generally experience it, in this case, as matter, as nature, as devoid of the presence of God. But this was not always so and it has happened for bad reasons. To understand what those bad reasons are, we have to say something more about the history of the materialist worldview.

From Cosmos to Universe

The shift in outlook began in the early modern period, starting roughly around the time of the sixteenth and seventeenth centuries. Prior to that was the medieval period. The medieval picture of reality was radically different from the one held by modern people in the West. Although medieval society was Christian, the type of Christianity was in many ways foreign to that of today. In fact, the difference between modern Christianity and that of the medieval period is significant precisely because the shared social imaginary is different.

The medieval mind conceived of the world as a cosmos rather than a universe. The cosmos was a hierarchy that was meaningfully structured and reflected the mind of God and, even more than that, the presence of God was held to be the underlying power that animated the forces of nature. This has been observed by numerous scholars and writers on the Middle Ages. To take one example, Rupert Sheldrake comments:

> Medieval Christian theology was animistic and God's being underlay the being of nature. God was in nature and nature was in God. Nature was alive, not inanimate and mechanical. The God of Medieval Christianity, which gave us the great cathedrals of Europe, was the God of a living world.[3]

This was not a pantheistic belief in the divinity of nature but reflected what in technical theological terms is often called 'participation'. That is, all things that exist are, in some sense, a participation in the being and energy of God: they come from God and they rely upon God for their continued power to exist at every moment.[4] The medieval mind understood God as both transcending and being immanent to his creation. God is an infinite being and so cannot be contained by the world that he has made, but he nevertheless dwells within every part of it at every moment and sustains it.

The modern period has undergone a significant shift which now sees God (if he exists at all) not as sustaining creation and being present within it at every moment and in every molecule but as a kind of craftsman who created the universe and now stands at a distance from it. The early modern philosopher William Paley invented a story that spoke of God as a watchmaker, which is very much the image that the modern world has adopted: if there is a God, he created the universe much like a watchmaker creates a watch. He set up its parts and made it tick but now it operates independently of him.

The classical view of 'participation' can be illustrated by comparing God and creation to a singer singing a song. The song is dependent at every moment upon the life, breath and sustaining power of the singer. The moment the singer stops singing the song, the song is over. The song is 'living' therefore because it is animated by the life of the singer. This is a good way of understanding the relationship of God to the cosmos in the imagination of the medieval period: the cosmos was like a song sung by God that was dependent at every moment and in every place for its existence.

But in modern times we no longer dwell imaginatively in a living cosmos that is animated by the power of God. Rather, we inhabit a dead universe that has a limited amount of power to sustain itself, and which will inevitably run out as the force of entropy takes its toll. Again, imagining the world this way has become the shared habit of atheists and Christians alike.

Because medieval society saw the cosmos as a reflection of the power and wisdom of God, they saw *meaning* within it. The creatures that God had made were reflective of his creativity and could even teach human beings spiritual lessons through their physical appearance or activities. Nature was not limited to physical organisms but was also regarded as a spiritual battleground of the forces of darkness and light: angels and archangels, demons and devils. Objects such as relics and consecrated bread and wine at the Eucharist, holy places such as the site of the crucifixion, were believed to be charged with spiritual power. Because the cosmos was alive with the presence of God, it 'spoke' in many ways to humanity. It was the voice of God and so communicated God's messages, his intentions, his wisdom and his power.

There is thus an enormous chasm between the conceptional world of the Middle Ages and that of the present time. Where is meaning and intention to be found today? Not out there in the world but only in the human mind. Human minds have intentions, share information and give meaning to things. But the process does not work the other way around: things in the world do not convey messages, information or meaning to the human mind. We think of ourselves as entirely separate from the rest of the universe: out there is cold, inanimate matter, and it is only in the inward space of the human mind that conscious and intentional thoughts occur. These thoughts are then visited upon the inert world and shape it in a particular way but the world itself contains no meaning whatsoever until we give it such.

We used to inhabit a meaningful cosmos, created by God and animated by his power, in which he spoke to us all the time through the things that he had made. Now, we are included in a universe that runs by itself and has no inherent meaning. The modern view of God is not the eternal singer of the song of the cosmos but the watchmaker who started the world off and has left it running by its own power.

I noted earlier that Charles Taylor's *A Secular Age* starts off with this important question: 'why was it virtually impossible not to believe in God in, say, 1500 in our Western society, while in 2000 many of us find it not only easy but even inescapable?'[5] In essence, the answer is that our social imaginary has changed. In the medieval period there was no other way of seeing the world than as the creation of God and as imbued with spiritual forces. In the modern period, we have at least two additional options: either the universe was created by God and now runs under its own steam *or* the universe just runs under its own steam and there is no God. Somebody holding the 'watchmaker' view of God may more easily consider his existence as simply one interesting fact about the universe. The atheist does not consider his existence at all.

This, then is how the social imaginary has changed. The vital question now is: *why* did this shift in the social imaginary come about and were the reasons for its changing sound ones?

From Method to Metaphysics (1): The Reformation

The reason that our view has so radically shifted can be traced to two seismic events of great importance. The first is the Protestant Reformation of the sixteenth century, and the second is the mechanistic revolution of the seventeenth.

The Protestant Reformation had as its goal the purification of the Church from what the Reformers saw as the errors and superstitions of Roman Catholicism. The Reformation was a hugely successful and influential endeavour in so far as millions of people and scores of nations became Protestant. Because medieval society was a Christian society, what happened in the Church necessarily had a huge influence upon everything else. And so, the Reformation was extremely important not just for religious dogma but for all culture too.

As we have seen, the Reformation did not spring from nowhere but was brought about by theologians who had particular ideas that they had picked up from the old medieval world. Some of those ideas were traditional but some of them were radical and novel ways of thinking about God and creation. The Reformation had the effect of making some of these new ideas popular and influential not just in the Church but in society more generally. And these ideas would go on to have a great impact not only upon the sixteenth century but upon all the centuries that would follow.

One of these new ideas significantly changed the way that people thought about God.* The older view was that God was the power animating everything that existed and he himself was self-existent. 'Self-existence' means that God's existence is part of his essence. That is, God could not not exist and, therefore, existence is part of who he is. This relates to the biblical name given to God – YHWH – which could be translated as something like 'I am who I am'. This type of existence contrasts with that of human beings or any other part of creation. Creatures do not possess existence as part of their essence but they come into, and pass out of, existence. It would make no sense for me to call myself 'I am who I am' in the way that God does because that does not accurately describe my relationship to my existence. I could call myself more accurately something like 'I was not, and now I am, and one day I will not be'. But God cannot say such a thing of himself because existence is part of his inherent essence.

The newer idea of God that came in through the Reformation encouraged people to think of God as a bit more like the things that he had made. To use slightly more technical language, people began to start thinking of God as *a being* rather than as the source of all being and even as *Being itself*. Eventually, God began to be thought of as a very large and very powerful man of some sort, perhaps one who could be located in some deep region of space. This idea was the seed of, and eventually led to, a current of religious thought called deism – the belief that God created the universe and set it running but that he himself

---

* The new idea described below is known technically as the 'Univocity of Being'.

is entirely disconnected from it. The reason that deism developed from the new way of thinking about God is because such thinking put *existence* above both God and his creation. No longer were God and existence the same thing but existence became a higher principle in which God and his creation participated. In the old way of thinking, God *was* existence and he gave out of his own self-existence to create the things that are made. Thus, there was a kind of flow of existence, like a fountain, that came from God and trickled down to his creatures. But, in the new way of thinking, that hierarchy of existence was lost and God began to be thought of as existing on the same plane as his creation.

From deism it was not a large leap to get to modern atheism and secularism. For the deist conception of God is similar to William Paley's watchmaker: he is the one who set the universe running but can be conceived as independent from it. Nature is like a machine that runs itself. The deist says about this machine that God made it and started it off. The atheist goes one step further and simply says that there is no need to believe such a thing: we can observe that the universe is like a machine that runs itself – why, then, do we need to believe in a celestial being that began the whole thing in the first place?

The old conception of God and creation guards against this movement of thought because it sees the world as radically dependent upon God for its existence at every moment and in every one of its features. If one grasps the idea that God *is* existence and that the existence of the cosmos is a kind of *donation* of God's existence then it is impossible to imagine that the cosmos could exist independently of him. In the old view, he does not simply start the universe but sustains it, like the singer singing a song. This is why he cannot be dismissed as unnecessary to it.

The historical point is, therefore, that the newer idea of God was first conceived in the late medieval period and was popularised and made influential during the Reformation and beyond. The move towards a God who was not self-existent and who was more like a very powerful human being began. This movement of theological and intellectual thought would create the conditions in which deism and, later, atheism and modern secularism were conceivable.

From Method to Metaphysics (2): The Mechanistic Revolution

The next important factor came with a revolution of the seventeenth century. What really happened at that time was not a 'scientific' revolution but a *mechanistic* one. This was the truly significant change: the shift in seeing the world not as a cosmos animated by the power of God but as a machine animated by the lifeless forces of nature.

Since the time of antiquity, there had always been different views on the correct general approach to investigating and understanding the world. There are basically two ways to come at the problem: the first way is to start with a broad theory about the world that is worked out using abstract propositions and philosophical reasoning. That broad theory is then applied to experience and observation. The other way of approaching the problem is by beginning with experience and observation, and moving from *those* things to more general theories about how the world is. In early modernity, because of people like Francis Bacon, the emphasis shifted comprehensively away from the approach that starts with abstract reasoning and towards the approach that starts with observation and experience. Bacon's inductive method was exactly that: a movement from the observation of repeated instances to more generalised theories. The success of this inductive method led to the overturning of previous abstract paradigms, particularly those associated with Aristotle, which had been greatly influential. It also led to huge success in gaining more knowledge about nature and in developing new technology. The inductive method became so powerful and influential that people began to assume not only that the method was useful but that induction pointed towards the way the universe really was: essentially, like a machine that runs through cause and effect.

At least two things followed from this. First, the shift in the social imaginary: from seeing the world as God's creation to seeing the world as a machine that functions according to the power of nature and therefore as apt to be exploited for the benefit of humanity and to its own detriment. The other aspect of this transformation was the rejection of the idea of a 'telos', or final causation, in nature. Final causation essentially means that a thing has a purpose or a goal towards which it is directed. In the pre-modern period, it was assumed that everything was moved not only by efficient causation (that which happens to a thing in time to effect it) but by final causation (that purpose *towards which* a thing is directed). The inductive method does not take account of final causation but only efficient causation. And this bracketing out of final causation eventually became the way people began to see the world: without purpose, without a goal, without a final meaning towards which things are called.

What happened, therefore, was that the method of induction shifted from being conceived of as a way of investigating the world to an all-embracing picture of reality. The supernatural realm and final causation were said not just to be unnecessary for scientific investigation but unnecessary full stop. The notion that there was a desire or a will within nature was dismissed by thinkers such as Thomas Hobbes as superstitious.* René Descartes declared that consciousness was only to be found in human brains, in the mind of God, and with the angels. This

---

* See Thomas Hobbes, *Leviathan* (Oxford: Oxford University Press, 2008), p. 11. Originally published in 1651, on this Hobbes comments: 'From hence it is, that the schools say, heavy bodies fall downwards, out of an appetite to rest, and to conserve their nature in that place which is most proper for them; ascribing appetite, and knowledge of what is good for their conservation, (which is more than man has) to things inanimate, absurdly.'

emptied nature of spiritual content. Previously, the world had been thought of as the theatre of God's glory, whereas 'nature' was apt to be, as Francis Bacon is reputed to have said, tortured and exploited so that it would yield up its secrets for the benefit of humankind. This change is captured particularly poignantly in the words of Roland Hart (the canine 'owner' and spirit-guide of David Bentley Hart) in the latter's wonderful book *Roland in Moonlight*:

> It's . . . tragic in the modern age, when mechanism isn't merely a scientific method, but a metaphysical and cultural and economic view of the natural world. Everything is thought to be a machine waiting to be consumed by other machines. Nothing is sacred in itself, no mystery is honoured . . . no tenderness shown. The age of the world-picture, of technology, of nature as the reservoir of purely material resources to be exploited and despoiled and then corrupted with toxins and microplastics and every imaginable chemical and synthetic pollution . . . The age of an economics devoted to absolute death . . . the total rarefaction of all life into lifeless numbers in a bank account. And all the delicate and lovely and mysterious spirits that indwell the things of nature all quite defenseless against the monstrosity of . . . humanity.[6]

It is called a mechanistic revolution therefore because it revolutionised the way that human beings saw the world. What was once a living, spiritually animated organism was now a dead machine that was apt to be 'tortured', exploited, and used for the purposes of human consumption and development. And this is the picture of nature that we have all inherited in the West.

The reason that we have been so successfully conditioned is due to the great success and seeming power of the modern scientific method. Philosopher Richard N. Williams puts it like this: 'Success at manipulating the world, as technology provides, strengthens our sense that science is showing us what really is the case in the world we inhabit."* But notice the assumption here that links the successful *method* of scientific development with a *metaphysical* or *religious* view of reality. The first is a way of investigating nature and developing technology. The second is a complete picture of everything. And inductive observation of the natural world does not eventually add up to a metaphysical picture of reality. It can tell us a huge amount about nature, and it can help us to develop technologies that are useful to humanity, but it does not have anything to say about the essence of nature in its totality, nor about what might lie beyond nature. A similar point is made by M. Scott Peck in his masterwork, *The Road Less Travelled*:

> In its laudable insistence upon experience, accurate observation and verifiability, science has placed great emphasis upon measurement. To measure something is to experience it in a certain dimension, a dimension in which we can make observations of great accuracy which are repeatable by others. The use of measurement has enabled science to make enormous strides in the understanding of the material universe. But by virtue of its success, measurement has become a kind of scientific idol. The result is an attitude on the part of many scientists of not only skepticism but outright rejection of what cannot be measured.

---

* Richard N. Williams and Daniel N. Robinson (eds), *Scientism: The New Orthodoxy* (London: Bloomsbury, 2016), p. 2. The American author Andrew Sullivan makes a different though related point about the power of science and technology in the age of the internet and the iPhone: 'Modernity slowly weakened spirituality, by design and accident, in favor of commerce; it downplayed silence and mere being in favor of noise and constant action. The reason we live in a culture increasingly without faith is not because science has somehow proved the unprovable, but because the white noise of secularism has removed the very stillness in which it might endure or be reborn' (Andrew Sullivan, 'I used to be a Human Being', *New York Times Magazine*, 19.09.2016, [https://nymag.com/intelligencer/2016/09/andrew-sullivan-my-distraction-sickness-and-yours.html]).

It is as if they were to say, 'What we cannot measure, we cannot know; there is no point in worrying about what we cannot know; therefore, what cannot be measured is unimportant and unworthy of our observation.' Because of this attitude many scientists exclude from their serious consideration all matters that are – or seem to be – intangible. Including, of course, the matter of God.[7]

What is true for the many scientists is actually true for all of us. In the Western world, the sense that the universe is a lifeless machine and nothing more has taken hold not just for unbelievers but for believers also. There is a sense that we all – Christian or otherwise – have a problem with belief in the supernatural, that it strikes us at a deep level as somewhat far-fetched. And this is because of the centuries-long wind of doubt and disenchantment that still blows through the avenues of our age. To quote Roland once again: 'And so, in an age of unbelief, everyone is an unbeliever to some degree. Belief now requires a decision, and a tacit application of will that never for a moment relents.'[8]

Roland's observation is profound: in pre-modern times, belief did not require a decision. It was simply clear that God existed, and that the world came from him and abided within him and because of him. But now that sense of the obviousness has faded with the coming of the mechanistic paradigm. *Now*, we must make a concerted effort of the will to believe.

Perhaps, the reader might observe, this is not a bad thing. Perhaps the mechanistic revolution really has elucidated the true nature of reality. Perhaps it was so easy – relatively speaking – to throw off the shackles of religious belief, to replace millennia of superstitious mumbo-jumbo with progress gleaned from a scientific methodology, for the very reason that science is finally uncovering what was in fact really there. And perhaps the reason it is so hard to hold a religious view in this day is because it will always be a desperate attempt to retain that which has been truly and rightfully done away with, consigned to the dustbin of the history of bad ideas and misplaced notions.

But we have seen that the so-called 'scientific' view is based upon a self-congratulatory historical narrative that seeks to blacken the name of Christianity and to arrogate to itself the achievements of medieval Christendom while claiming that it was Christendom that opposed their development. Once we recognise the falsity of this narrative, we can identify what really happened, which is that a very powerful method for learning about the world turned into a comprehensive metaphysic that sought to explain absolutely everything about the nature of reality. No doubt this simplifies what was a highly complicated historical process, but this does not change the fact that the shift from method to metaphysics is an arbitrary one and that there is nothing about the success of the inductive method per se that demands atheism or a naturalistic worldview. To explain why this shift is unjustifiable we will have to examine the limitations of science.

The Limitations of Science:
Science Cannot Explain Everything

My argument here is very simple and unoriginal: science is a *methodology*, and to suggest that it can be a *metaphysics* is to make a fundamental category error. But this error has been made repeatedly, and on such a wide scale, that it has actually come to characterise Western thought to an extraordinary degree.

If we take science to be something like the definition I have already offered (hypothesis, experiment, data, repeatability, and so on), then it should be obvious how grandiose and inflated the claims of the discipline have often become. Of course, great swathes of more modest and unblinkered scientists would never dream of making such claims for their discipline. But many prominent atheistic public scientists and non-scientists do, and it has been remarked upon before how unsophisticated highly trained scientists can be when speaking beyond the boundaries of their own subject. Richard Dawkins, for example, in *The God Delusion* speaks of the desire of the scientific establishment to find a 'Theory of Everything'.* Peter Atkins has said in public that science is 'omnipotent'.† Lawrence Krauss has written a whole book attempting to explain the question of how something can come from nothing by redefining the word 'nothing' so that it means 'something'.⁹ In each of these three cases (and in many more) a hubristic assumption has been made that science's ability to discover empirical realities about the natural world can somehow translate into a comprehensive understanding of literally everything.

But this can never be the case partly because scientific findings are always provisional, subject to change, and subject to reframing by some more dominant or overarching paradigm. To suggest that this enterprise can deliver up a final and concrete understanding of reality is to misunderstand the nature of science itself. It is also to suggest that the domain of science is, literally, everything when, in fact, the proper domain of science is far more limited.

What these atheistic thinkers overlook is that, at some point, empirical investigation comes up against theoretical limits. This is not to disparage science, but it is to say that it has a proper domain of enquiry, and to try and stretch it beyond this domain results in intellectual obloquy. Apart from anything else, the very premise that science can explain everything is self-refuting because such a premise cannot be verified scientifically: there is no scientific investigation, no empirical evidence, that can demonstrate its truth. One can continue to discover facts about the natural world and apply them to dazzling feats of technological or medicinal advance, but that would tell us precisely nothing about the existence or non-existence of features of reality *outside* this

---

* Dawkins speaks about this possibility without irony in *The God Delusion*. Cf. Richard Dawkins, *The God Delusion* (London: Black Swan, 2016), p. 173.

† See, for example, Atkins' debate with Oxford mathematician, John Lennox. Cf. Premier Unbelievable?, 'John Lennox vs. Peter Atkins – Can Science Explain Everything? LIVE DEBATE', accessed 14.03.2024, [https://www.youtube.com/watch?v=EER1-9nflJY].

domain of enquiry. This is a simple logical observation. To hold to the omnipotence of science is, therefore, not a scientific belief but a *philosophical* one, held without rational justification and in blind faith.

In addition, scientists and others must recognise that, at some point, the investigation of nature cannot proceed any further. This would be true even if scientists were able to understand the temporal beginning of the universe in the most minute detail. It would be true if they were able to elucidate comprehensively the reality of the laws of nature – perhaps by discovering some overarching law that determined all the other laws. It would be true if they were able to discover literally every empirical fact about every natural phenomenon that has ever existed. There would still remain questions of immense significance. In the case of the temporal beginning of the universe, the question would concern how, in the absence of further temporal and empirical events to explain it, whatever it was that existed at the beginning existed at all. Similarly, the existence of an overarching law of nature simply could not be explained by further investigation in the same direction. Science would meet its limit at this point, and this would not change with the development of more sophisticated tools or with any other technological advances. Even if all empirical facts about the universe were known by scientists, this would still raise the question of the existence of those empirical facts in their totality.

Further, the kind of question that arises when we come to the quantum vacuum that mysteriously existed prior to the universe, or to the overarching law of nature, or to the existence of a total universe of explicable and congruent physical occurrences, is of a completely different type. We arrive there in the realm of metaphysics and religion. To attempt to answer that question – most fundamentally, of why there is something rather than nothing – through the positing of further empirical facts is like trying to solve an arithmetic equation by dissecting a frog. There is the distinct sense that the person trying to do it doesn't understand the question that is being asked: which is, again, not a question of the development of matter, nor of its arrangement, nor of how biological organisms came to be in their present form, nor of any of the other most fascinating and important matters that the scientific enterprise can address. The question is more fundamental and belongs in an entirely different realm.

The Difference Between Beings and Being Itself

Here we must slow down and consider the metaphysical question that has been implied. There are various other domains that science simply cannot address in a comprehensive fashion, but we begin here because this one concerns the nature of existence itself. Once we accept that, at the very basic level, science has nothing to say about existence itself, the spell will be broken, and we will begin to see more clearly the proper domain of science and where it is guilty of trespassing into forbidden territory.

In the philosophy of religion, there is a perennial question: why is there something rather than nothing? This is not a question about how things came to be in their present form but about why anything exists at all. That question – of why the entire order of reality exists – cannot be answered by even a comprehensive account of the chain of physical events in time or by a comprehensive description of the way the world is at this precise moment in all of its chemical, biological and physical complexity. Even *if* such an account were possible, it would be a complete irrelevance to the question of why something exists rather than nothing. All it would be is a fantastic and brilliant and stunning description of the things that already are.

If we go back to Lawrence Krauss's book *A Universe from Nothing: Why There Is Something Rather than Nothing*, we can see something of this misunderstanding in action. The title itself gives the game away. It is an attempt to answer the age-old perennial question of metaphysics by demonstrating how 'nothing' came to cause the universe. But, even before any evidence is brought forth, no matter how incredible and unique it might prove, the project must be declared a total failure. And the reason is so simple: 'nothing' does not belong to the realm of something and cannot be admitted into such a discussion. Lawrence Krauss attempts here to redefine the word 'nothing' so that it no longer means 'nothing' but means 'something'. The moment we begin talking about nothing causing the universe, even if that 'nothing' is a quantum vacuum or fluctuation or whatever it might be, no matter how infinitesimally small in nature, it is not nothing. Nothing cannot cause anything. Nothing is simply a total absence of all things, such that to imagine it is only possible on a theoretical level; after all, what is 'nothing' like if we attempt to picture it in our minds? All that can be said of it is to repeat that it has no qualities, no causal power, and cannot be described beyond this. Therefore, for Lawrence Krauss to say that nothing caused the universe is a brave but ultimately doomed gesture.

This problem is often framed as one of beginnings: how did the universe begin? This is the question that Krauss is attempting to address. We can call it the 'temporal' approach to Being. 'Temporal' here simply refers to 'time'. So the question is: what caused the very first event in the history of the universe?

There really can be only two answers to this question. But these can be attempted only after we have understood two important words: 'contingency' and 'necessity'. If something is *contingent*, then it relies upon something else in some way. My existence is contingent upon my being produced by my parents for example. Another way of saying this is that, if a thing is contingent, it is possible that it could not have existed. So, I could not have existed had my parents decided not to have me. If a thing is *necessary* then it does not depend upon something else for its existence *and* therefore it could not not exist.

So the answer to the question just posed – essentially, what caused the universe? – can only be one of two possibilities. The first possibility is that the universe is necessary in itself and that it was not, in that sense, caused by anything. And the second possibility is that the universe is contingent and is dependent upon something necessary.* On the first possibility, it seems quite clear that the universe that we live in does not exist necessarily. One of the reasons we recognise this is that literally everything we have any experience of within the universe is contingent: every life-form, every star, every planet, every event. We are even told that space and time themselves came into existence as a result of something else. It is therefore correct to conclude that a universe made of entirely contingent things does not add up to something necessary.

The temporal argument from contingency applies to causal events in time. We observe contingent events happening, one after the other. If we trace the arrow of time backwards throughout history, all the way to the beginning, it must be the case that a necessary cause brought about the first contingent event. Contingent events cannot be caused by nothing, and cannot exist in an infinite chain, and therefore they must be dependent upon a necessary cause (meaning something that does not rely upon something else for its existence).

But the case can be stated more strongly. Indeed, Thomas Aquinas thought the argument from temporal contingency rather weak and cautioned Christians against using it lest they give the infidel a cause for scoffing. There is a different way of thinking about contingency. To use a spatial metaphor, we can imagine contingency on the 'horizontal' plane of time, but we can also imagine it on the 'vertical' plane of Being. If a thing is contingent, it simply means that it receives its power to exist from something

---

* It is, of course, possible that the temporal universe we inhabit is contingent upon something else which is also contingent upon something else. But this simply pushes the question back a stage further, so that it becomes: what caused the contingent cause of our contingent universe? The only other way out of this problem is to say there is an infinite chain of contingent causes, stretching back into eternity like an infinite Russian doll, that eventually produced our contingent universe. This answer is incoherent because it nowhere supplies a necessary cause.

else. A child is born of its parents. A meal is created by a cook. A blade of grass grows from a seed. And so on. Try and imagine that the entire order of Being is made up only of contingent things. This is an impossibility. Why? Because contingent things receive their power to exist from something else. And everything cannot receive its power to exist from something else because there must be something that provides the power to exist in the first place, something that is not contingent but necessary. These observations point to the reality of a necessary cause that has within itself both the property of self-existence and the capability to bestow the power to exist upon other things. Notice that this is *not* an argument that attempts to trace the arrow of cause and effect backwards to the beginning of the universe, but one that forces us to recognise the contingency of the entire realm of existing phenomena as we encounter them at any precise moment.

David Bentley Hart attempts to help us grasp a similar reality by considering our own existence.* You do not exist necessarily, but you depend upon all sorts of factors to sustain you in existence. Some are temporal (the things that happened in time to cause your existence such as your being born, being fed, and so on) and some concern what makes up the reality of who you are at a particular moment. You are composed of parts, which are composed of smaller parts, which are composed of smaller parts still, down to the subatomic level, which is itself mysteriously embraced by a dimly understood quantum field of some sort. The wider world is similar, also composed of parts and physical systems which are dependent upon other, more basic units of reality, and upon abstract logical, mathematical and natural laws. Taken together, all these contingent conditions that make up the existence of an individual, or of the wider world, do not at some point constitute a necessary cause of existence. Something

---

* The following explanation and terminology is taken from David Bentley Hart, *The Experience of God: Being, Consciousness, Bliss* (New Haven: Yale University Press, 2013), pp. 105–6

necessary, something beyond nature, must underly all of it. Hart puts it like this:

> In short, all finite things are always, in the present, being sustained in existence by conditions that they cannot have supplied for themselves, and that together compose a universe that, as a *physical* reality, lacks the obviously supernatural power necessary to exist on its own. Nowhere in any of that is a source of existence as such. It is this entire order of ubiquitous conditionality – this entire ensemble of dependent realities – that the classic arguments say cannot be reducible either to an infinite regress of contingent causes or to a contingent first cause.[10]

I mentioned Thomas Aquinas earlier who articulated the argument from contingency in the third of the Five Ways of the *Summa Theologiae*, written in the middle of the thirteenth century.* But these observations have been around at least since the time of Aristotle in the fourth century BC. Aquinas held that the universe had a beginning. But he held this as a matter of faith because he believed in the Christian revelation. Aristotle, on the other hand, believed that the universe existed eternally. Although Aristotle believed in an eternal universe, however, he still believed in the existence of God because he understood that contingent causes, even within an eternal universe, would need to be explained on the 'vertical' axis of causation. That is, in addition to the contingent things that exist, there must be a necessary power that gives its self-sufficient existence to those things which are merely contingent.

Notice the point: the 'horizontal' argument from temporal contingency was not held by Aristotle because he believed that the universe had always existed; nevertheless, the 'vertical' argument

---

* Incidentally, this is one of the serious errors in Richard Dawkins' *The God Delusion*. Dawkins simply misunderstands Aquinas as talking *only* about contingency in temporal matters and fails completely to grasp the 'vertical' aspect of his argument.

from contingency *was* held by him. That is, Aristotle believed that the universe was eternal in time and that it was also eternally sustained in Being by God on a 'vertical' level. So, even if science discovers one day that the universe did not have a beginning, even if science discovers that the universe has always existed in some kind of steady-state or oscillating pattern, it would not affect the argument from metaphysical contingency one bit. If the universe were eternal, the contingent events within it would not need a first cause in time, but the fact that there were contingent things that were sustained in existence by other contingent things would imply, at the deepest level, a necessary cause that holds all contingent things in existence.

Note here that the word 'God' has not been used to describe the necessary cause under discussion. This is because the point is about the proper domain of science. Science operates in the realm of contingency and not in the realm of necessity. None of the features of science already mentioned – hypothesis, experiment, data, public verifiability – has any bearing upon the realm of necessity. For necessity does not operate within the realm of contingent causation. Science may be able to tell us a lot about the realm of the latter. One day the blackboard may be completely filled, all equations known, all causes and effects, all biological organisms explained, all laws elucidated, and so on and so forth. *But* this would tell us nothing whatsoever about how there came to be a contingent order at all.

Ultimately this is about the difference between *beings* and *Being itself*. Science concerns *beings*: phenomena that already exist within the contingent realm, parts of nature, individual instances of species like grasshoppers, for example, or objects like meteorites. *Being itself* concerns the fact that there is existence at all – not the things that exist, but the *property* of existence. The phenomena that 'are' share in this property, but they do not possess it within themselves. (Recall the earlier description of contingent things which pass into, and out of, existence.) It may be that the real force of the question of *Being itself* cannot be felt easily by modern people. So fixated have we become by the realm of contingent things, by parts, machines and processes, that we have lost the capacity to ask it. Children appear more attuned to the joyful mystery of existence: that there should be anything at all – and particularly *this* or *that* thing – is not some worn-out triviality but a vibrant and immediate feature of their daily experience. It is splendorous and miraculous precisely because it is all so ludicrously extravagant and unnecessary. And yet, amazingly, it still *is*.

The Limits of Evolution

The question of evolution is fundamentally one of how less complicated organisms turn into more complicated organisms. Given what has just been said, it should be clear that evolution is not relevant to the question of Being. This is not to disparage the subject, but it *is* to say that evolution can only describe things which already exist.

It is important to point this out because the question of Being seems to be something that well-known evolutionary atheists such as Richard Dawkins seem incapable of grasping. Dawkins says that he is in love with the idea of more complicated things developing from very simple things. It is this type of thinking, he believes, that will eventually furnish us (or at least could theoretically furnish us) with a complete picture of reality. But the truth is that what it will never furnish us with – and *can* never furnish us with – is an answer to the question of why anything exists in the first place. Again, even if we could explain literally everything about the natural world, the question of Being would still remain. Evolution has nothing whatsoever to say about it.

Given that evolution has a proper domain within the study of nature, why has it taken on a quasi-religious status in the minds of many? It must concern the antagonistic narrative described in the first chapter: science in general has been pitted against Christianity to offer a rival account of reality, as an alternative religion. Evolution is seen as a central actor in that conflict, perhaps the most important. To the minds of many, it has done away with the need to believe that organisms are specially created and designed by God. It has contradicted the Christian Scriptures and not only contradicted but refuted.

Indeed, if the view is taken that the Bible and evolution contradict one another then the two viewpoints must act as enemies. One must be chosen and the other rejected. The anti-religious evolutionist will be glad to take up this challenge and insist that it is the Bible that is wrong and not evolution. And this, he will claim, is evidence not only of the falsity of the first chapters of Genesis but of the authority of the Bible in general and its supposed divine inspiration. If these terms are accepted (the Bible or evolution) and evolution is correct then, logically, the Bible is not. And it might seem that a Christian viewpoint insisting on these terms would be refuted fatally.

For the sake of argument, let's imagine that we find ourselves in that position: evolution is true and Genesis interpreted in a certain literal fashion is false.* The Christian could at that point return to his assumptions about the proper interpretation of Genesis and re-examine them. He could embark upon an investigation of evolutionary theory to find out if the tenets of it that contradict Genesis really are true. But, say he did all these things and concluded that there really were a contradiction and that the early account of Genesis was clearly false and proven to be so by the empirical fact of evolution. What would this *actually* mean? Yes, it would mean that the Scriptures are contradicted and, when looked at in a certain way, contain factual errors. There would be many people who would argue that other major doctrines of the Christian faith, such as that of original sin and redemption through Christ, cannot be true either. I am not suggesting

---

* Those familiar with the history of biblical interpretation will be aware that the word 'literal' can be understood in various ways and is problematically used in this context but the meaning is, hopefully, clear enough.

here that these issues are insignificant. To the contrary, I consider them to be extremely significant. But, what this discussion would not in any way affect is the question of the existence of God, the question of Being itself, and that of why something exists rather than nothing. We would still be left in a mysterious universe that receives the power to exist from an external cause.

To put this slightly differently, the viewpoint espoused by evolutionary atheists such as Richard Dawkins does not necessarily lead in the direction of atheism at all. At the most, it leads in the direction of the contradiction of a particular type of Jewish and Christian hermeneutic which sees the first chapters of Genesis as a literal account of the creation of the world.* But to abandon such a reading of the first chapters of Genesis does not demand atheism. It may demand a different type of reading of Genesis. It may demand a more creative approach to synthesising Genesis and evolutionary theory. It may imply that the Jewish and Christian Scriptures do indeed contain factual errors. But it does not imply that God does not exist. And it does not answer in any way the question of Being.

Some independently minded thinkers from religious and non-religious folds have suggested that the fact of evolution would imply a life-force within the universe that tends towards development, complexity and meaning. In his famous self-help masterpiece *The Road Less Travelled*, M. Scott Peck calls this force 'grace' and contrasts it with the force of 'entropy'. Entropy describes the way that all physical systems in the universe degrade and become chaotic over time. This law seems to hold everywhere with the one significant exception of life itself, which appears to be governed by a power that seeks not

---

* It should be noted that the interpretation of Genesis has varied throughout Christian history. There were prominent interpreters of Scriptures for many centuries prior to Darwin who saw the first chapters as an allegorical or mythical account of the creation and sat more lightly to what we would today consider a literal interpretation. The most important of these interpreters was St Augustine himself.

only the development of life but also its good.[11] Making a similar observation, the agnostic scientist and popular author Paul Davies states that the universe has a certain 'directionality' to it which moves towards consciousness and comprehension. He says that this cannot be an accident but points towards a purpose or meaning in nature which, when viewed in this way, gives a 'religious feeling' to it.[12] These examples demonstrate to us that the truth of evolution would indeed imply final causation in nature: that is, that nature not only develops as a result of temporal causation leading up to the present moment, but is actually directed towards certain ends or goals in the future. As we have already observed, the rejection of final causation was one of the developments of early modern philosophy, stemming from a mechanistic conception of the universe.

None of this absolutely proves anything, but it does show that, even if evolution turned out to be true in every one of its details, and even if it turned out somehow to be able to explain everything about the universe, then this is in fact more likely to point in a religious direction than a materialist one. This is because it lends credence to the idea that the natural world was created by a being possessed of particular intentions that appear to include the formation of biological life, complexity, diversity of species, beauty in nature, consciousness, will, emotion, and many other realities besides.

It is worth noting that there is considerable ambiguity as to Darwin's own view of the implications of his theory for theology. In the second edition of *On the Origin of Species*, for example, he writes that he 'infer[s] from analogy that probably all the organic beings which have ever lived on this earth have descended from some one primordial form, into which life was first breathed by the Creator'.[13] Additionally, he always denied explicitly that he was attempting to explain the origin of *life* but that he was concerned with the process of biological development. The short title *On the Origin of Species* conceals this subtlety, but the full and original title of Darwin's work makes it plain: *On the Origin of Species by means of Natural Selection, or the Preservation of Favoured Races in the Struggle for Life.**

What we are really coming up against here is a psychological phenomenon. Evolution is thought to be such a powerful tool for understanding biological life that some who encounter it become convinced that every other mystery of existence is solvable using the same heuristic. Again, this is really to mistake a theory that concerns the development of biological life for a doorway that leads to the elucidation of all of reality. There are, of course, many evolutionary biologists who would make no such outlandish claims for its explanatory power. But those scientists tend not to write bestselling polemical tracts against religion and, therefore, have to content themselves with more humdrum and everyday contributions to their discipline.

Science and Ethics

We have been speaking about the proper domain of scientific enquiry and have examined its relation to metaphysics. Not that this is the only area about which science has little to say. We now turn to the significant domain of human experience that we call ethics or morality, where science again has no ultimate authority.

This claim needs to be carefully explained because there is a possibility of misunderstanding. Take the comments made in 2015 by Liberal Democrat Tim Farron, then leader of the party. Farron had been quoted as saying in 2007 to a Salvation Army publication that 'abortion is wrong'. When confronted with this statement by the *Guardian*, Farron made the following rejoinder: 'I am pro-choice. I believe that abortion should be safe and legal and that the limit should be set by science.'[14]

It is not entirely clear what Farron meant by the limit being set by science, but what such a statement cannot mean, if it is to

---

* This point is made clear by Dame Gillian Beer in her introduction to Darwin's work. Cf. ibid., p. xvii make sense, is that science can somehow tell us when it is ethical or not to have an abortion. As we have already said, science concerns itself with discovering things about the natural world using hypothesis and experiment. If there are ethical values, then they are clearly not part of the natural world in the same way that a chemical or a biological organism is. Ethical values are abstract entities. Whatever they may be, they cannot be looked at under a microscope or secreted into a test-tube. The most highly trained scientist in human history, by virtue of his scientific training alone, has no more right to pronounce ethical judgements than the most scientifically illiterate person who has ever lived.

What can science give us in the ethical realm? Science can tell us empirical facts that have a bearing on ethical questions. In the case of abortion, science can tell us, for example, that there is no biological or genetic cut-off point at which a fertilised embryo, having started out as one thing becomes some fundamentally different organism that we might call a human being. But what we do with that information is an ethical question and not a scientific one.

To take another example, science can tell us how to create fertilised embryos in a laboratory and what these might be used for. But it cannot tell us if it is ethical to do such things or not. The questions of whether it is right to create embryos for stem-cell research or for IVF treatment are of an ethical nature, and the scientific methodology that makes it possible to carry these things out tells us nothing about whether it is right or wrong to do so.

There was considerable confusion about this during the Covid-19 crisis, during which our political leadership took refuge behind the slogan 'Follow the science'. This slogan, used seemingly on an hourly basis at points, implied that 'the science' could deliver up to us a pristine and unquestionable set of ethical answers concerning how we should deal with the situation. Again, 'science' can attempt to tell us certain things: how deadly a virus might be, how many people might catch it, what we can do to try to mitigate its spread, and things of this type, but it cannot tell us whether or not actions taken in consequence of these observations would be right or wrong.*

---

* Many have observed that even the so-called scientific pronouncements that were characteristic of the Covid era were more pseudo-scientific than the real thing. Computer modelling, for example, does not meet the criteria for genuine scientific endeavour but is simply a form of mathematical calculation, the outcome of which is dependent upon the variables inputted. Moreover, when, during the Covid era, certain predictions were made in the event that x, y and z were not done, if x, y and z *were* done then the original prediction could not be verified, which would mean that no test of the original predictions was ever undertaken. When predictions were made, on the other hand, and x, y and z were *not* done, the results which contradicted the initial predictions were routinely ignored. A good example of this concerns the original Imperial College London mathematical model that famously predicted 510,000 deaths in the UK and 2.2 million deaths in the US were no lockdown measures implemented. This model shaped the government responses of both nations. In the UK, it appears to have been a significant factor in fundamentally altering government policy from the initial 'herd immunity' strategy that had been announced to a total lockdown of the nation. This model was tested in real time through its adaptation by a team at Uppsala University to the case of Sweden which was not at the time implementing a lockdown policy similar to the rest of Europe. This adapted model, based on the original pioneered by Neil Ferguson, produced the 'conservative estimate' that, were the current strategy continued and lockdown measures not implemented, in May 2020 the peak intensive care load would exceed pre-pandemic capacity fortyfold and there would be deaths in the range of 96,000 and continuing to almost 100,000 by June. The current strategy *was* continued and by 29 April Sweden's death toll from Covid-19 was officially numbered at 2,462 (Phillip W. Magness, 'Imperial College Model Applied to Sweden Yields Preposterous Results', American Institute for Economic Research, 30.04.2020 [https://www.aier.org/article/imperial-college-model-applied-to-sweden-yields-preposterous-results/]). As of September 2020, Anders Tegnell, the chief epidemiologist for Sweden, could announce that Sweden had seen fewer than 6,000 deaths from the virus, and half of these had been in care homes (Fraser Nelson, 'Why Boris Johnson needs to speak to Anders Tegnell', *Spectator*, 18.09.2020, [https://www.spectator.co.uk/article/why-boris-johnson-needs-to-speak-to-anders-tegnell/]). By the most sensible metric (that of excess

During the Covid period, not only was it assumed that scientists such as Neil Ferguson and Chris Whitty were competent to make ethical pronouncements that enormously affected the lives of tens of millions of people, but it was also implied that the same scientists were qualified to make economic and cultural judgements about which predicted outcomes outweighed damage to various sectors of society. Again, all this was justified with the glib, oft-repeated slogan, 'Follow the science'.

But science can only tell us about the affairs of the natural world. It cannot tell us what we should do about them. The hardcore materialist who sees science as potentially able to explain everything worth knowing must be committed to the viewpoint that there simply *are* no such things as ethical values in any objective sense. Ethical values are simply things that material

---

deaths) Sweden was shown to have one of the best outcomes in the world with 3 per cent higher excess deaths than normal for the period beginning March 2020 and ending in late 2023, and was far more successful than other countries that had severe lockdowns such as New Zealand (8 per cent), Australia (9 per cent) and the UK (10 per cent) (Michael Simmons, 'Sweden, Covid and "excess deaths": a look at the data', *Spectator*, 10.03.2023 [https://www.spectator.co.uk/article/sweden-covid-and-excess-deaths-a-look-at-the-data/]). Not only did Sweden not incur the predicted 100,000 deaths from Covid but it significantly outperformed every other country in the world that implemented the lockdown measures that Sweden was told to adopt. This was a real-life test case of the Ferguson/Imperial College London model and it demonstrated in real time that the model was a catastrophic failure. The importance of this fact is hard to overstate given the disastrous effects of the implementation of lockdowns across the world. The failure of this model and the success of Sweden's response comprehensively demonstrates that lockdowns were unnecessary and implies that they did more harm than good. And yet hardly any official mention of this has been made. The official line in the UK, from the relevant politicians such as Boris Johnson and Matt Hancock, remains that all these damaging and draconian curtailments of human freedom and dignity were both necessary and successful. This is a complete falsity and the case of Sweden demonstrates both that fact and the utter failure of the Imperial College London model.

organisms decide to believe in and act upon because they prefer to organise their lives and societies in this way. This viewpoint is profoundly incoherent, but it is nevertheless the clear implication of a materialist worldview. Simply put: there are no ethics, there is only matter.

The problem here should be quite alarming to those who are willing to carry the logic through to the bitter end: if ethics are only what we prefer, then we might just as well prefer genocide to the common good, or a caste system to equality before the law. If there are no real ethical values, there is nothing except for convention and preference acting as bulwarks between us and far less-pleasant scenarios.

To return to the central point, whatever one's view on the reality or not of ethical values, the question cannot be ruled upon by science. That much is certain.

The Imaginative Poverty of Scientism

So far we have seen that the proper domain of science is the natural world and not metaphysics or ethics. Two fundamental questions therefore are completely outside the realm of scientific enquiry: why anything at all exists and how human beings should live.

The question of ethics is linked to the broader questions of justice and the reality of good and evil. These are issues that animate our very existence as social and spiritual beings, pervasive at every point in our conscious existence from childhood onwards, and yet they are outside the bounds of scientific enquiry. If we are to understand them, we cannot do an empirical test to find out the answers.

Alongside these questions, we should also put that of beauty, which relates more broadly to human expressions of art and culture. We will be looking at the experience of beauty in more detail in Chapter Six but it should be noted here that it is not something that can be understood in purely scientific terms without a radical impoverishment. Consider, for example, one's experience of an extraordinary piece of art or a sense of wonder at beholding a medieval cathedral. Most people would be highly reluctant to say that such experiences can be explained *merely* as some kind of material transaction consisting of neurons firing and chemicals in the brain in a response to visual stimulation, and that the works of art in themselves are *nothing but* the materials they are made out of: canvas and paint or wood, stone and glass.* Our inclination is to say that there is more going on, that this experience has more significance to it and, without overlooking the things that are really important about it, cannot simply be reduced to its material components.

We would – most of us anyway – want to say the same thing about love: romantic love, love for our children, families and friends. We would want to say that the love we feel and which animates and directs our entire existence cannot be explained totally by recourse to a physical description of chemicals in the body and neurons in the brain.

We would also want to say that the important decisions we make in life, which are almost always to do with the things already mentioned – ethics, justice, goodness, beauty, love – are not themselves physically determined, pre-programmed inevitabilities, and that our apparent free-will is not simply an illusion produced by our brains.

But, if we truly commit ourselves to the belief that science can explain everything about the world, then it must follow that all human experiences – including apparent encounters with good, evil, beauty, love and meaningful choice – are entirely reducible to physical description. If matter is the only thing that exists and science is the only tool we have for understanding what exists, then everything that exists is ultimately reducible to a specifically scientific explanation. There are therefore no objective

---

* The important point here is not to deny that the human body responds to the physical stimulus of the artwork, but that a physical description cannot give a comprehensive account of the human encounter with art or beauty, and that to imply such a thing is to miss the central point of these experiences.

ethical values but only those which are made up by human beings; beauty, love and all other transcendent intuitions are merely the result of chemical processes within the body. Human beings really make no choices at all because we are simply organic robots pre-programmed to do all that we ever do.

These matters are not rightly thought untrue because they strike us as unpleasant but because they are so obviously absurd. We know that morality is real, and we experience the unpleasant effects of trying to live in opposition to it. We know that beauty and love are more than the results of chemical processes in the body. And we know that the decisions we make are not an epiphenomenal* by-product of genetic determinism but are arrived at freely and deliberately, albeit under pressure from the various circumstances that we face in life. Every individual and every human culture that has ever existed has taken at face value these basic facts about existence. The only exceptions have occurred when cosseted intellectuals have theorised abstractly about the nature of things, come to absurd and bizarre conclusions, and then implemented their conclusions upon the societies in which they lived. The results have been inevitably disastrous because they constitute an attempt to inhabit and construct a false reality.

In modernity, many have undertaken to explain comprehensively these phenomena under the rubric of scientific materialism. This mindset is better called 'scientism' because it is really constituted by an ultimately religious set of beliefs. For example, a whole spurious subject area has sprung up by the name of evolutionary psychology which attempts to explain the highest

---

* The word 'epiphenomena/epiphenomenal' describes something which is a side-product of something else. In the philosophy of mind, an epiphenomenalist is somebody who believes that a mental state such as a thought or a decision is the by-product of a physical process that occurs within the brain. This view implies that the freedom to think and acts of will are simply illusory and that all mental states are entirely pre-determined by physical factors. The view says that our brains trick us into thinking that we have chosen or intended certain things, but this is not actually the case.

experiences of human existence in terms of evolutionary advantage: the reason why, for example, we human beings might find an open savannah awe-inspiring could be because our distant ancestors who preferred to look at open savannahs were better at spotting potential predators and so more regularly passed on their genes to the next generation. Or the reason why we enjoy a trip to the seaside or find the presence of a still lake relaxing is really because proximity to water offered some ancient hominid easier access to drinking water and so he was able to survive better and transfer his genetic material.

Even if one were to state these theories in more specific and technical terms, it is surely the sane and normal reaction to suppose that these great lodestars of human existence – beauty, love, freedom, and so on – cannot possibly be reducible to such a crude scheme of gradual development over time through selective adaptation and genetic mutation. And, to restate the point made earlier, if that were the case then surely to live consistently with such beliefs would terminate ultimately in meaninglessness, nihilism and despair.

At bottom, then, we must be honest and say that scientism will inevitably reduce those who consistently hold to it to a meaningless and empty, emotionally and spiritually impoverished existence. And this is because it cuts so sharply and terribly against the grain of reality.

The Consequences of Treating Science as a Religion: Dogmatism and Corruption

If we grant the point that science has developed into an illegitimately religious worldview, it should not surprise us to find that science itself has developed features common to religion. It has done so in the form of a narrow dogmatism that rules out certain possibilities prior to examination. But, owing to our conditioning in the materialist mindset, the dogmatic features of the modern scientific worldview are largely hidden from us.

The materialist worldview is founded upon various assumptions that are not themselves based on scientific evidence or any kind of rational basis. They are enforced by the academic and scientific community with a comparable zeal to that of any religious inquisition. Those who question these views or seek to investigate alternatives are, at best, simply ignored and denied prestigious positions or research funding or, at worse, treated as heretics and pariahs.

One such heretic is the Cambridge botanist and philosopher Rupert Sheldrake. Although a don at the University of Cambridge and eminent in his field, Sheldrake is often portrayed as a fruitcake and a traitor to the cause because he advocates for a less dogmatic approach to science. Sheldrake clearly articulates the unsubstantiated assumptions that the modern materialist mindset is based upon and critiques them as narrow and constrictive. For Sheldrake, science is limiting its own scope by holding to these assumptions and, if science were to be more flexible, it could perhaps make a great leap forward as the mysterious aspects of the universe were explored with a new openness. His books *The Science Delusion, Dogs That Know When Their Owners Are Coming Home* and others give examples of certain phenomena that many people are aware exist but which are simply ruled out as illusory on the basis of the materialist worldview. One of those phenomena is the common experience that dog and cat owners have of observing their pets waiting for them at the door when they return home from a trip out. Sheldrake has carried out thousands of observational studies indicating that, as the title of his book suggests, dogs and cats appear to have some kind of extra-sensory perceptive ability that simply cannot be explained by recourse to standard materialist explanations. Importantly, Sheldrake claims to be able to prove this using the scientific method. Modern science *assumes* certain things that form the basis of the accepted scientific worldview. Sheldrake helpfully lays out some of these assumptions:

- Everything is essentially mechanical. Dogs, for example, are complex mechanisms, rather than living organisms with goals of their own. Even people are machines, 'lumbering robots',[15] in Richard Dawkins's vivid phrase, with brains that are like genetically programmed computers.
- All matter is unconscious. It has no inner life or subjectivity or point of view. Even human consciousness is an illusion produced by the material activities of brains.
- The total amount of matter and energy is always the same (with the exception of the moment of the Big Bang, when all the matter and energy of the universe suddenly appeared out of nothing).
- The laws of nature are fixed.
- Nature is purposeless, and evolution has no goal or direction.
- All biological inheritance is material, carried in genes, DNA and other material structures.
- Minds are inside heads and are nothing but the activities of brains. When you look at a tree, the image of the tree you are seeing is not 'out there', where it seems to be, but inside your brain.
- Memories are stored as material traces in brains and are wiped out at death.
- Unexplained phenomena like telepathy are illusory.
- Mechanistic medicine is the only kind that really works.[16]

This scientific creed, as Sheldrake calls it, can be critiqued in the same way as many atheists would like to critique the Christian creeds. Are these ideas really as obviously true as we've been led to believe? The idea that organisms are nothing but pre-programmed robots, for example? That there is no significant difference between a human brain and a highly developed computer? That, since everything is material, human consciousness is merely a by-product of the material brain and can even be said to be *illusory* because it is not itself material? That all matter and energy simply popped into existence out of nothing at the moment of the Big Bang? That there are no purposes in nature, including the human and animal world? That evolution, assuming that its tenets are correct, has no purpose or goal but just *happens* to proceed in the direction of ever-greater complexity and fecundity? That your mind is *nothing but* your brain and its activity? That telepathic experience and other strange phenomena such as déjà vu are simply illusory? That there is nothing after death but the straightforward eradication of the human life?

When laid out in this fashion, it is surely clear that the materialist worldview is extremely fanciful and that it does terrible damage to the human experience. It is perfectly obvious, for example, that consciousness is *not* illusory. Even to utter such a thing is to be aware of a contradiction, as the awareness of uttering the statement indicates that one is conscious of doing so. The notion that the universe popped into existence out of nothing, for absolutely no reason, is philosophically incoherent and can only be held because of sheer blind faith in materialist dogma. The idea that biological life has no purpose or goal contradicts not only common sense (for what could be more obvious than the fact that humans and animals are *directed* towards certain ends?) but also scientific observations such as the discovery that DNA is a language made up of four letters which make words of three letters in length.

Taken seriously and lived out consistently, the materialist worldview would lead to the instant suicide of any human being who truly accepted it. And it would constitute the immediate, or at least inevitable, death of any civilisation that put its beliefs into practice consistently. Even in civilisations that are largely based upon the materialistic worldview, it is still the case that it is not lived out consistently because inherent human instinct understands intuitively that the premises of the materialistic worldview – no free will, no morality, no God, no transcendent realm, and so on – are false and unliveable.

M. Scott Peck says of the relationship between science and religion, 'The religious have not wanted their religion shaken by science, just as the scientific have not wanted their science to be shaken by religion.'[17] What he means is that religion and science are, at least on the surface, different expressions of the same instinct to find out the truth about the world. It is commonly reported that religious people are anti-science, distrustful and hostile to the findings of the discipline. Admittedly, there may be a modicum of truth to this but, as I have already argued, I believe that this phenomenon is hugely exaggerated. And yet there is also a degree of truth on the other side – that science is often hostile towards, and dismissive of, any evidence that might contradict its metaphysical assumptions about the nature of reality. Peck commends scientists, religious folk and truth-seekers who are beginning to examine phenomena such as spontaneous remission in cancer patients and seemingly successful examples of psychic healing.[18] And he argues that a partnership between modern science and the Christian religion is indeed possible.

An example of this alliance in action is found in the field of demonic possession. The existence of demons is, of course, ruled out *de facto* by the materialist worldview. And even Christians and those who would not consider themselves materialist might at this point find themselves shaking their heads with incredulity as though such things simply cannot be the case. But what empirical investigations have we done to prove that such a thing as demonic possession is merely a fantasy?

Richard Gallagher is a respected and credible psychiatrist with a huge amount of experience in the area of demonic possession. He makes the point that the majority of cultures throughout history have reported incidents of similar sorts concerning what might be called 'demons'. We are in a tiny minority, relatively speaking, in dismissing them, and yet we cleave to our dogma with mostly very little thought or further study. Gallagher himself started out as a sceptic of such phenomena but became convinced as he encountered in the course of his work people who were clearly manifesting symptoms of demonic possession that could not be explained by recourse to physical disorders in the body. Those people, at times, displayed remarkable supernatural (or paranormal) abilities such as the possession of psychic power which gave access to knowledge that could not have been obtained by normal means and the ability to speak fluently in other languages which they had never studied as adults or learnt as children. He also claims to have witnessed people levitating when manifesting demonic spirits.

Under the authority of the Roman Catholic Church, Gallagher formed partnerships with priests who specialised in this area. These priests consulted him specifically for his scientific and medical expertise. Gallagher helped these priests to determine whether there were physical bases for the apparent manifestations through the use of standard medical tests for such things as chemical imbalances in the body. This study helped the priests to understand when they were dealing with physical disorders and when they were not. In addition, Gallagher was able to use his psychiatric training to speak with the individuals in question to help them engage with the process.[19] This constitutes a good example of the way science and Christianity could work together productively if science and scientists were willing to lay down certain dogmatic presuppositions that sadly characterise the modern-day establishment. It also demonstrates a willingness on the part of Christians *not* to jump to the conclusion that every seemingly supernatural manifestation is indeed such a thing. Another good example of this type of collaboration is the Vatican-appointed Miracle Commission that is comprised of theologians and scientists who collectively investigate claims that certain virtuous persons have performed miracles after their deaths. This might sound far-fetched to many (including Christians) but it is nevertheless another example in which both scientists and Christians demonstrate a willingness to lay down dogmatic presuppositions in order to investigate potentially supernatural phenomena with an open mind.[20]

We might characterise those dogmatic presuppositions as primarily 'metaphysical' or 'religious' in nature. But, just as the medieval prelates are today accused of duplicitously holding to certain supposedly theological principles for nefarious ends, so we might wonder if the same is true for those who now invoke the supposedly irreproachable name of 'science'. In other words, dogmatism in science can serve multiple ends in the political, financial and social arenas, and many might reasonably surmise that we can observe this reality in action in multiple ways presently. This makes sense if we accept that a properly grounded ethical framework is in effect absent to the modern materialist scientific paradigm.* Science without ethics is essentially *amoral*. This does not mean that scientists and science will inevitably tend towards corruption and wickedness, but it *is* to say that science in itself cannot provide an ethical framework to govern human action and the ordering of society. We should be very cautious, therefore, when we hear public scientists claiming the right to pronounce authoritatively on political and ethical issues, as though their being scientists gives them the competence necessary to do such a thing. Perhaps the most telling example of this arrogation was a statement made by US Public Health official Anthony Fauci, who claimed in one interview that to question him (by which he meant to question the political decisions he supported in view of his supposed expertise in the relevant scientific areas) was to question science itself. Specifically, Fauci said, 'Attacks on me, quite frankly, are attacks on science.' As far as Fauci was concerned, he *was* the science, the science was authoritative, and therefore *he* was authoritative.[21]

In hindsight, many would agree that the global response to Covid-19 was somewhat *less* than rational in the main. Others would go further and consider it to be a moment when a perfect storm of mass hysteria, political expediency, and greed for financial gain and power coalesced and brought with them

---

* This is not to say that people who hold to the materialist paradigm are inherently immoral or that they cannot perform moral actions. But it is to say that there is not a properly coherent ethical framework for such actions according to a strict materialist paradigm.

unprecedentedly catastrophic outcomes. At the very least, we can observe instances of the way 'science' was used for ends other than the dispassionate and rational pursuit of truth. We have already mentioned the repetition of the phrase 'Follow the science' to justify political decisions to shut down nations, to force certain businesses to stop trading, to legislate for the compulsory wearing of masks, and so on. It hardly seems unreasonable to surmise that many of these decisions were taken at least partly because of politicians' own desire to protect themselves from public outrage should their responses to the problem be deemed insufficient. And it is not unreasonable to speculate that many of the advisors and politicians in Britain did not actually believe that the virus was as deadly as they were warning people it was. There were multiple instances of people in these positions saying one thing and yet doing another. One of the key architects of the Covid-19 lockdown globally was Professor Neil Ferguson, whose computer model predicted that hundreds of thousands of people would die in the UK without so-called non-pharmaceutical interventions. One of those NPIs was a nationwide lockdown that would (in theory) prevent infections and deaths because it would limit contacts between human beings. After the lockdown was put in place to enormous social, economic, spiritual, physical, cultural and otherwise holistic cost, it was revealed that Neil Ferguson was in fact breaking his own lockdown rules by having an affair with a millionaire climate activist called Antonia Staats.[22] This sort of behaviour was replicated multiple times by elite figures associated with the Covid-19 response, including, of course, the UK health secretary Matt Hancock who was conducting an affair in his own office during one of the lockdowns and the then Prime Minister Boris Johnson who was holding parties at 10 Downing Street during the same period. The infamous case of government advisor Dominic Cummings, who, with his wife and child, drove to Barnard Castle during a lockdown that he had supported personally, in a trip that he said had nothing to do with recreation and everything to do with testing his eyesight, could also be mentioned.[23] What did the elites know that the ordinary people didn't? Why were these political figureheads invoking the name of 'science' while at the same time ignoring the laws that they were drawing up in its name? Could it be that 'science' was just a convenient way of justifying a response that benefited them to the agonising detriment of everybody else?

The evidence of the enrichment of the scientific, political, technological and media elite is also abundant. It has been said that the Covid crisis brought about the largest wealth transfer from the middle classes to the elites in the history of humanity.[24] Pharmaceutical companies' wealth increased exponentially[25] and the wealth of other interested parties such as social media giants was also dramatically augmented.[26] The corporate media have been enriched by government subsidies[27] and doctors and pharmacists have received significant emoluments through the mass vaccination programme.[28]

The point of mentioning these things is to help us to recognise that the ideal of science alone as a dispassionate and rational way to understand the world in a comprehensive fashion has not necessarily resulted in the outcomes that we might have expected. In the case of Covid-19, the enormous emphasis on 'following the science' led not, in the main, to clear-eyed rationality but to a largely *irrational* response that was driven more by political cynicism and corporate greed than it was a genuine desire for the welfare of society.

In the modern age, science has been invoked as a replacement religion for Christianity. In this role, it is a failure simply because the domains of science and religion are different. There may be overlap at certain points but, fundamentally, science concerns itself with phenomena that exist in the natural world, and it cannot be pushed to give a comprehensive account of all reality. It cannot give us an answer as to why the universe exists. It cannot help us to understand ethics or the good life. And ultimately the most important things in our lives – the things that we really live for such as beauty, goodness and truth – are not reducible to the language of science.

We have told ourselves a story about the way science emerged in contrast to Christianity and liberated us from it. The truth is that science emerged from *within* Christianity and came to set itself up as a covert, rival religion, a religion that claims too much for itself and, like other religions often do, has become in many ways closed-minded, politicised and corrupted.

We will now begin to consider what is being lost as we turn away collectively from the cultural, moral and spiritual inheritance of Christianity. We have observed in this chapter that science cannot give us a satisfactory account of beauty and transcendence. Now we will go on to explore that claim at greater length.

III

Aesthetics: Why Secularism Cannot Ground Transcendence

And all is seared with trade; bleared, smeared with toil;
And wears man's smudge and shares man's smell: the soil
Is bare now, nor can foot feel, being shod.
                    Gerard Manley Hopkins, 'God's Grandeur'

We now turn our attention to the collective problems caused by
the decline of Christianity, particularly in terms of ethics and
the broader issue of the trajectory of Western civilisation. In
this section, however, we return to a claim made in the previous chapter, that a materialist view of the world cannot help
us to understand or embrace aesthetic experience. In addition,
the materialist view cuts us off from the possibility of achiev-
ing transcendence. The word 'transcendence' can mean many
things, of course, but here it refers simply to the ability of the
mind or the soul to conceive of, and perhaps commune with,
something higher, or beyond, the bare material reality of sense
perception. Additionally, the word 'aesthetics' can be used in
different ways, but here I mean simply our subjective experience
of the world: how the world presents itself to us as either pretty
or ugly, good or bad, painful or pleasurable. Aesthetics does not
concern logical deduction from premises, but is about the way
reality discloses itself to us through our sensory and emotional
life.

Aesthetic experience is often linked with the very highest
moments in life. We often associate it with arts such as music,
literature or architecture. But this can be extended to experiences
of beauty in nature that bring us a sense of peace or connection

135

with the world. We might also talk about heightened emotional experiences such as 'falling in love' or the affection one feels for one's children or parents. Aesthetic experiences are, ultimately, what human beings live for. They are the things that make our lives bearable because they take us out of the humdrum, ordinary grind of daily existence and reveal to us the meaning of that toil. Without aesthetic experience, the human soul diminishes, weakens and eventually loses the will to carry on. Ultimately aesthetic experiences are all tied together because they refresh the soul through an encounter with beauty in one of its various forms. Beauty, in other words, is essential to us.

On the surface, this set of observations is fairly uncontroversial. We know that we cannot exist without beauty, without moments of release and transcendence. We know, ultimately, that life is not about a simple maximisation of hedonistic pleasure, but that pleasure, beauty and significant moments are a sign of some greater purpose, some greater state or depth to which we can aspire and at certain points inhabit. There are, of course, strict materialists who would deny this, but it is nevertheless the case that most people are drawn towards some version of this idea.

But we have a serious problem, which is that the metaphysical framework that undergirds modern thought has no way of understanding beauty without critically and fundamentally undermining it. According to the materialist paradigm, the arts are not a portal to truth, beauty and goodness because such things are subjective and limited to human opinion. Therefore the arts can only ever be an expression of individual subjectivity, the torpor and chaos of the human soul, like Tracey Emin's unmade bed which speaks only of her loneliness and alcoholism. Either that or the arts can be diminished to the status of a vapid distraction that endures for half an hour or more before we must re-enter the miserable world of everyday experience. Romantic and familial love and friendship are merely the results of chemicals firing in our brains, the broader biological context for which is produced by the evolutionary process. Similarly, nature only 'speaks' to us because we are programmed by our genetics to be drawn or repelled to certain aspects of it. Any uplift that we sense through this or any other kind of encounter with beauty is ultimately reducible to material processes over which we have only the illusion of agency or control.

Because we have no real account of beauty, we inevitably relegate it to a secondary consideration. And if we don't do that then we intentionally undermine it by creating art and living conditions that purposefully contradict aesthetic conventions such that we end up producing ugly things that ultimately create ugly people and ugly societies.

Once again, this phenomenon found its most perfect expression to date in the Western world's response to the Covid-19 virus. In the UK, sectors of society were literally subdivided into 'essential' and 'non-essential'. In that context, what was meant by 'essential' seemed to be those goods and services that were deemed necessary by the government to ensure the material continuation of society and human life within it. But no formal definition was ever given. Whatever the words 'essential' and 'non-essential' actually meant, it was absolutely clear that considerations of aesthetic beauty and spiritual life did not meet the cut. The arts suffered catastrophically and gathered worship was prohibited.* Social interactions

---

* What actually happened during 2020 when the churches were closed down and what was the Church of England's role? There has been considerable speculation that the Church of England hierarchy could have allowed its buildings to remain open to some degree and even for certain acts such as private prayer to continue. It is certainly true that clergy were instructed to discontinue the opening of church buildings, but it may also be true that this instruction actually *influenced* the UK Government in its decision to remove a legal exemption to lockdown in the case of private prayer in churches. The timeline goes something like this: on 17 March 2020, the Archbishops of Canterbury and York banned public worship but allowed churches to remain open for private prayer. In a joint letter they wrote, 'Please do of course keep the church buildings open for private prayer wherever possible as we know so many do all the time' (+Justin Cantuar and +Sentamu Eboracensis, 'To All Church of England Clergy', Church of

England, 17.03.2020, [https://www.churchofengland.org/sites/default/files
/2020-03/17-03-20-joint-letter-from-the-archbishops-of-canterbury-and-
york-re-coronavirus.pdf]). Five days later, the bishops in London ordered
their churches to close completely, even for private prayer, although priests
living adjacent to their churches were allowed to enter them to pray and
celebrate Holy Communion (+Sarah Bishop of London, +Christopher
Bishop of Southwark, +James Bishop of Rochester, +Stephen Bishop
of Chelmsford, 'A statement from the Bishops of London, Southwark,
Chelmsford and Rochester', Church of England, 22.03.2020, [https://
www.churchofengland.org/news-and-media/news-and-statements/church
-continues-be-alive-and-active-our-buildings-must-close]). A day after
this, on 23 March, Prime Minister Boris Johnson announced a general
lockdown across the UK but an exemption was made for churches to stay
open for 'solitary prayer'. As the following article makes clear, the Roman
Catholic Diocese of Westminster was swift to order its churches to remain
closed even for private prayer, even though an exemption had been made
(Dorothy Cummings McLean, 'UK govt order "places of worship" shut
down, Catholic bishops comply', Lifesite News 24.03.2020, [https://www.
lifesitenews.com/news/uk-govt-orders-places-of-worship-shut-down-cath-
olic-bishops-comply/]). A day later, the Archbishops of Canterbury and
York followed suit, stating in a joint letter, 'Our church buildings must now
be closed not only for public worship, but for private prayer as well.' They
went one step further than this, however, and added, 'this includes the priest
or lay person offering prayer in church on their own' (+Justin Cantuar and
+Sentamu Eboracensis, 'From the Archbishops and Bishops of the Church
of England, to be shared with all clergy', Church of England, 24.03.2020,
[https://www.churchofengland.org/sites/default/files/2020-03/20200324-
letter-from-archbishops-and-bishops_o.pdf]). Even though a legal exemption had been made that allowed both clergy and laity to enter churches
to pray, the archbishops banned both groups from doing so. There was
no legal reason to do this. It was a decision that they took independently
from legal considerations. Finally, when the legal regulations were published
on 26 March, no exemption for private prayer was mentioned, even though
it had been on 23 March when the lockdown was first announced. It
was permitted, however, for clergy to broadcast acts of worship from
their churches, but this had been unilaterally ruled out by the archbishops (Matt Hancock, 'The Health Protection (Coronavirus, Restrictions)
(England) Regulations 2020)', Public Health England, 26.03.2020, [https:
//www.legislation.gov.uk/uksi/2020/350/pdfs/uksi_20200350_en.pdf]).

were not only prohibited but were the very *target* of the restrictions. The whole concept of 'social distancing' constituted an Orwellian contradiction in terms that nevertheless spoke of the need to remain isolated from one's friends and family upon pain of infection or arrest. The point being that the only real 'good' that was sought by this hysterical response to an ambiguous pathogen was the avoidance of immediate infection, illness and death from Covid-19. Literally no other considerations were admitted: anything, even the absolute spiritual, moral, aesthetic and social destruction of human society, was better than facing the threat posed by this virus. Surviving Covid-19 – even if that meant the destruction of everything that is worth living for – was the only value that was promoted. Thus humanity experienced a kind of death to itself as it capitulated to a highly speculative and questionable utilitarian calculus of material survival. And this was not just a mistake that could have been handled differently. This was, in fact, a *disclosure* of the denuded and impoverished state of the soul of Western civilisation, a revelation of the nothingness that is really there beneath our affluence and technological sophistication, fig leaves protecting us from our total spiritual nakedness.

Yet the essential point is that there is simply an enormous chasm between our experience of the world and what we have been conditioned to believe about it. We live in a confused dichotomy in which we act as though aesthetic experiences are deeply meaningful and significant while *believing* that they are nothing but the offshoot of the evolutionary process and entirely reducible

---

Whatever happened behind the scenes, it is absolutely clear that, in the Church of England, the churches were rendered far more inactive than they needed to be from a legal perspective. We do not know if the legal exemption for private prayer could have been secured in the final legislation of 26 March, but, given this timeline of events, there is every reason to believe that it could have been, and that parish churches up and down the country could have remained open all the time during the lockdowns. The fact that they weren't was a symbolically tragic token of the decline of our Church and nation.

to the terms of material causation: nothing but chemicals, nothing but synapses, nothing but physical processes, and so on. Thus, when something like Covid comes along, it makes sense to jettison them because they can hardly be thought of as real.

Vertical versus Horizontal Life

We have discussed how the medieval person saw the world as animated by the presence of God. It is very hard to appreciate this clearly because such a worldview is entirely alien to our modern one. We therefore have to use our imaginations.

There were various features to the medieval outlook. First, the pre-modern person did not experience (as we do) the world around as entirely separate from himself. Rather, the human individual was (to use Charles Taylor's phrase) 'porous' to the world outside. There was no absolute barrier between the individual and the world. He was vulnerable to nature in a way that modern people are not. And he was also vulnerable to the supernatural. He could be ministered to by angels or harassed and possessed by evil spirits. This contrasts with our outlook in which the individual is 'buffered' (Taylor's terminology again), meaning separate – and therefore protected – from the world 'out there'. The reasons for this shift are complex but they are, broadly speaking, to do with the fact that modern people have come to see meaning not in all reality but only in human minds. Thus, in modernity we *project* meaning, and therefore action, onto the world around us, and therefore feel ourselves to be separate from it. In the medieval period, meaning could also be directed towards the human being from the realms of nature and supernature. The important point, though, is that we *feel* ourselves to be separate from nature and the supernatural whereas our medieval forebears did not. They were open to these realms but also vulnerable to them.

Second, the world and the things in it were not understood primarily in terms of mechanical and material causation but of the spiritual reality that they embodied. For example, a snake was symbolic of moral evil and deception, light was symbolic of spiritual and intellectual illumination, and so on. Thus, the world did not appear to pre-modern individuals as dead matter animated by efficient causation but as a symphonic tapestry of symbolic spiritual resonances.

Third, the arts such as music and architecture were not 'disembedded' from spiritual meaning as they are in modernity. Rather they were acts of religious devotion and potential conduits of the divine. Thus, the immense cost in terms of time and material of building a Gothic cathedral was justified upon the basis that this was, in very literal terms, the construction of a dwelling place for the divine presence.

Fourth, the sacraments of the Church and its liturgy were not seen as ambiguously channelling the divine presence. Rather they were explicit evocations and manifestations of the divine. The sacrament of the Mass was the high point of this process as the place where heaven and Earth met in the consecration of the bread and the wine which, though retaining the material composition of those elements, nevertheless *became* the body and blood of Jesus. There were also various other forms of sacramental resonance, such as the holiness of pilgrimage sites and the spiritually charged nature of objects like saints' bones and relics.

All this points to the medieval world as one in which heaven and Earth were intertwined. This was not a world in which human beings were simply matter confined to the Earth and destined to become one with it again, but one in which man was both human *and* divine, inhabiting a region somewhere between the apes and the angels, a blend of spirit and dust, originating in God and hopeful of finding his end in him once again. In this sense, human culture could play a role not only in expressing this reality but also in channelling it through the arts, through liturgy, and through the political ordering of society.

This is what we might call 'vertical life', which is an experience of being in the world that orientates human beings 'upwards' towards the transcendent realm. In the medieval period, this sense may have been overwhelming and perhaps even terrifying at points, as it surely was in the case of Martin Luther who, prior to his rediscovery of the gospel and subsequent reforming practices, was consumed with fear at the notion that God would judge him for his sins, however minor, and send him to hell for eternity. What we can most certainly say about pre-modern people is that the problems that confronted them as a result of their worldview were radically different from ours.

If medieval man experienced life as primarily 'vertical' then modern man primarily experiences it as 'horizontal'. This means that modern Western people are orientated towards immanent concerns as opposed to transcendent ones. We can describe this further in terms of the types of goals the average person pursues in life. In modernity, these goals might be, say, the desire to receive a good education, so that one might get a good job which is enjoyable and which earns one a decent amount of money in order to live in a reasonably comfortable manner, or the desire to be married and to have children. Or it might be more hedonistic and concern having multiple pleasurable experiences through sexual relationships, social life, alcohol or recreational drugs.

The political and educational spheres are largely set up to facilitate the achievement of these goals which are really seen to be the highest ends in life. Religious concerns are either folded into these immanent, horizontal goals or treated as weird outliers which really have no relevance to the modern world and the people who live within it.*

In many ways, it is easy to see the advantages of this way of looking at things: on the surface, it eases the pressure somewhat such

---

* A good illustration of this would be then Prime Minister Rishi Sunak's speech in March 2024 in which he said, 'It is not the colour of your skin, the god you believe in, or where you were born that will determine your success but just your own hard work.' Thus, religious concerns of every sort are, according to Sunak, subordinate to the 'hard work' that can bring an individual social status and security. *Telegraph*, 'In full: Sunak says British democracy is being targeted by extremists', accessed 25.03.2024, [https://www.youtube.com/watch?v=4naItWf7kZI].

that one is never in the position that Martin Luther found himself: terrified of God, scrupulously examining his sinful conduct in the hope that he might achieve a sufficient level of repentance and piety so that he can avoid everlasting damnation. One is therefore free to achieve the ends that one decides are right for oneself. And these may be extremely wholesome ends like some of those just mentioned. One is freed from the obligations that used to be held over people by religion: no church attendance necessary, nor prayers, tithes or rigid moral restrictions. There are various other points that could be made about the benefits of eschewing religion and specifically Christianity. There is the sense that we have (along with society) grown out of those beliefs and now occupy a more sophisticated and perhaps even brave position within the world. We are no longer primitive and superstitious but sophisticated and free from the existential terror brought about by 'religion'.

But there are enormous downsides too. The overarching problem with reorientating life so that it is lived only on the 'horizontal' level is the loss of transcendent meaning and experience. This is a phenomenon that Charles Taylor describes as existential 'flatness', as though an opaque canopy which blocks out most of the sunlight has been erected above our heads. We desire to break upwards and out of this situation, but we don't have the ability to do so. We experience life – at least to some degree – as stiflingly immanent, and we feel ourselves somehow unnaturally rooted to the ground, crushed or cramped in our souls.

This might take the form of a sense that life is simply meaningless. We might, like the preacher in the Old Testament book of Ecclesiastes, have a moment of realisation within the ordinary course of human existence that, although certain things might be enjoyable and give some fleeting pleasure, life as a whole seems to lack an overall sense of purpose and direction. In the most extreme moments of such awakenings, it might seem that the purposes for which we had been living previously are drained of their power sufficiently to ground a human life and that there is nothing worth living for at all.

On the other hand, flatness can be felt in the everyday: the pleasures of hedonistic pursuits wane and more intense experiences are sought to replace them. This is often the case in the novels of the great contemporary French writer Michel Houellebecq, whose protagonists are not infrequently sex-obsessed middle-aged Parisian men who experience existential crises because they can no longer find joy in sexual encounters with their partners, with prostitutes or with complete strangers. Houellebecq accepts all this frankly but he holds out no hope that a transcendent outlet might be found to contrast with this miserable reality.

But flatness might just be the sense that the repeated cycle of going to work in a bland office and doing a reasonably meaningless job day after day, year after year, diminishes the soul and leaves one wondering what one's life could or should have been. This type of scenario was famously depicted in the BBC comedy series *The Office* and embodied in the character of Tim Canterbury, who, seemingly alone among the characters, harboured the desire to do something other with his life than selling printer paper. He is frequently rebuked by colleagues such as Gareth who simply can't understand why he is so dissatisfied. At one stage, Tim has a conversation with an overweight colleague called Keith during a lunchbreak. Keith asks Tim what he watched on television last night, to which Tim replies that he didn't watch anything. Keith then tells Tim that he watched a repeat of an episode of the British medical drama *Peak Practice*. 'Boring, isn't it?' Keith says. 'Staying home and watching *Peak Practice* with your wife?' Tim agrees, to which Keith replies, 'Not for me. I like it.'

Aesthetic ugliness and indifference to beauty contribute to the sense of flatness. Charles Taylor speaks of 'the cardboard quality of bright supermarkets, or neat row housing in a clean suburb; the ugliness of slag heaps, or an aging industrial townscape'.[1] In Britain, most historic cities have been seriously blighted by the imposition of depressing modern buildings that would not look out of place in Soviet Russia, made from concrete and glass with flat surfaces and hard corners and edges. These buildings stand in absolute discontinuity to traditions of architecture even from relatively recently that sought both congruence with pre-existing settings and aesthetic beauty. The introduction of loud one-way systems and, in some places, Los Angeles-style freeways has further contributed to the aesthetic decline of these cities. The encroaching sense of malaise and existential ennui is therefore literally embodied in the surroundings of modern people, and it is no wonder that, as the environments around us die, so our souls are gradually confined and starved of life.

Aesthetics and Horizontal Life

The broad historical process that I am suggesting could be summarised in this way: Western civilisation has cut itself off from the source of transcendence, namely God. First, we demoted him to the status of a very large and powerful human being and then we forgot about him altogether. There were certain advantages to this (or so we thought) but one of the significant drawbacks was that we lost the ability to conceive of human life as having any kind of transcendent end. As a result, our capacity for manifesting and understanding beauty and the aesthetic diminished drastically. This was because our souls, as it were, no longer orientated themselves upwards to God but only sideways towards the rest of the world and inwards towards ourselves. There may be other more specific factors involved but this is the overwhelming reason that the visual arts, including architecture, have declined into ugliness and narcissistic forms of self-expression. As a result, many people in the West tend to experience life as lacking a vital transcendent dimension and have a sense of being crushed or, perhaps, lost, as though simply meandering about without any purpose, wondering what all of this could possibly mean.

And yet, even in the secular world, flatness is not all there is. On the other end of the spectrum there is 'fullness'. If flatness is the feeling of being lost, fullness is the feeling of being in the right place. It is a sense that we are orientated properly towards our fellow human beings, to the environment in which we live, and to the spiritual realm. It is, to put it more simply, a condition of all-embracing peace. Fullness is not something that any of us live with permanently, but we have glimpses of it. Traditionally, these glimpses have been sought and found in Christian practices. Even though they are transitory, they help us to anchor ourselves morally and spiritually, such that we develop a sense of where we are going and where we eventually want to be.

Between flatness and fullness there is a middle space which can be inhabited by religious believers or by secular people but in different ways. The common factor is that the middle space gives us a sense that life is reasonably meaningful, bearable and, broadly speaking, not too bad. It may even be the case that life is quite good sometimes and has the potential to get better.

For the secular person, the sense of meaning that characterises the middle space is often obtained through general human goods such as a stable and happy marriage or relationship, family life, a fulfilling vocation or an attempt to make a general contribution to the well-being of humanity. For the believer, however, the significance is found not so much in these things in themselves but in their relationship to God and eternity. The believer may find, for example, that having a family is deeply fulfilling, but often this will be accompanied by the sense that it also has a deep spiritual significance, even if that significance is not felt often in the humdrum of everyday routine.

Yet the main difference between the believer and the secular person is that the believer maintains that he is, at least in a partial way, connected to the source of fullness, namely God himself. This is often found in explicit religious experience, which, as it were, 'fills up' the believer, putting him in contact with the divine and lifting him out of the mundane experience of life. Once the believer returns to ordinary life, he is reorientated towards God and can live in the middle condition in a peaceful way knowing that his life is, generally speaking, moving in the right direction. But it is essential to the believer that he maintain this point of contact, at least occasionally, because if he does not then the sense of connection with the divine will gradually fade away.

Making Sense of Fullness

There are various ways to approach this apparent desire for fullness. The first course is simply to dismiss or ignore it. On that view, one would say that there is no transcendent realm from which we can receive spiritual uplift, nor are there aesthetic or religious experiences that can help us to orientate ourselves morally or spiritually in this world. All that there is is the material realm and various desires caused by chemicals in the body, synapses in the brain, and so on. Further, to insist upon a transcendent realm that speaks 'from beyond' to this world is to denigrate and to demote the *actual* lives we have. Life in the middle state is all there is² and to imagine that there is something else is inevitably going to spoil whatever goodness we might find in it.

This was part of Nietzsche's famous critique of Christianity and Platonism, claims of another world and life beyond this one which so neutered and emasculated men who otherwise might have been able to rise above their weaknesses and become truly great and powerful. For Nietzsche, Christianity was a substitution of the real for the imaginary. As he wrote in *The Antichrist*: 'Neither Christianity neither morality nor religion has any point of contact with actuality.' He detailed the imaginary effects, beings, natural history and psychology posited by Christianity and said that this 'fictitious world', conjured up by the corruption of priestcraft, which includes the notions of heaven and everlasting life, necessarily opposes itself to the natural world and to what human beings really are:

Once the concept of 'nature' had been opposed to the concept of 'God,' the word 'natural' necessarily took on the meaning of 'abominable' – the whole of that fictitious world has its source in the hatred of the natural (the real!), and is no more than the profound uneasiness in the presence of reality . . . *This explains everything.*[3]

And so, for Nietzsche, 'The "kingdom of heaven" is a state of the heart – not something to come "beyond the world" or "after death".'[4] The point being that we have to make the best of the world that we live in now or else the only thing that we really have will pass us by as we strain out for an illusion. Nietzsche had a particular idea of what that meant: rejecting charity and pity, and developing oneself into an Übermensch – that is, a superman who subjects the weak to himself in order to augment his own feeling of power.

Many accepting Nietzsche's critique of Christianity might have less extreme solutions. For example, those who reject God and the afterlife might say that it is *through* this rejection (and therefore the affirmation of ordinary life) that we can truly see the good in things. These things might be less spectacular than heaven but they are nevertheless all that we have and, seen in the right way, are the closest we are ever going to get: shared experiences of friendship in childhood and adolescence, having a meaningful job, falling in love, seeing one's children born and grow up in one's presence, walking in the woods on a sunny day on the cusp of autumn, and so on. If we spend our lives fixated on a realm beyond this one, then we are in danger of missing the inherent goodness in life, and this would indeed be the greatest loss of all.

There is certainly power in this critique. It might be the greatest defence that the secular person can make against the Christian worldview. But it is hard, upon this view, to prevent oneself from slipping into a form of nihilism. Try as we might to resist, it really does seem as though people are inclined to look for some deeper meaning in life, especially within what I have been calling aesthetic experience – points of contact with extreme physical or visual beauty; encounters with beauty in nature and the arts; significant moments around birth and death. This is why Charles Taylor concludes that the desire for fullness seems to speak in favour of the believer who understands it as a sense of elusive transcendence. The reason that we desire fullness and that we see it in various fleeting but nevertheless crucial moments in life is because there *is* something beyond this world that is really communicating something of itself to us. There *are* places and moments at which the borderline between these two worlds becomes thinner or perhaps even seem to disappear altogether. And simply to deny all this and to disparage it as 'illusory' or 'fictitious', as Nietzsche did, is to do violence to this shared human experience.

This point can be clearly made with reference to the arts. There is, again, an enormous chasm between what we experience through the arts and what secular people are ultimately committed to believing about them. My favourite example is that of a great Gothic cathedral such as Chartres or Notre Dame, but you could take any work of the Gothic period as an instance. The Gothic period was a moment of extraordinary flowering of artistic genius. Through two simple technical innovations – namely, the movement from rounded to pointed arches and the development of flying buttresses – the new style was born. But the technical innovation was, in that sense, only the conduit for the spiritual vision that dwelt within the hearts of the great geniuses who would put it to use. Gothic cathedrals became towering microcosms of the entirety of God's creation, illuminated by unearthly light, adorned with images, painted and carved, of the great chain of Being, from foliage and brute beasts to angels and demons and upwards, ever upwards, to the realm of heaven and to God himself. This is most beautifully epitomised in, for example, the Octagon at Ely Cathedral, which gives one the sense of being almost literally drawn up into the heavenly realm as one's soul is lifted through the beauty and colour of the rising pillars, sprung ceiling and vibrant stained glass. And at the top of it all – right at the centre and at the highest point – is the face of God.

The materialist worldview commits us to saying that every encounter with beauty or artistic effort towards its creation terminates in a reductive evolutionary or material explanation. That is, any sense of transcendence or beauty that might enliven or refresh the soul can only ever really be understood as a physical transaction that can be reduced to an ultimately biological explanation. This is the clear implication of materialism, but it simply cannot be correct.

Another way of putting this is that there are in essence two options. It could be that the materialist account really is correct and that the sense of meaning, power, transcendence, beauty or uplift that we might find in the arts at their highest is merely a kind of illusion caused by bodily processes. The other option is that we reject strict materialism and adopt an understanding that we are more than soulless organic robots, so the highest arts do not produce merely the *illusion* of transcendence but actually have the capacity to put us in touch with a higher realm than that of the material sphere. To put this in technical language, we either reduce our phenomenology of beauty* or we expand our ontology.† The former requires diminishing (arguably drastically) our account of the arts and aesthetic experience. The latter requires admitting that there is more that exists than the material realm. But it is only through doing the latter that we can really give an account of the arts and aesthetic experience that seems to do justice to them. We might also argue that materialism inevitably diminishes art by denying the possibility of transcendence and that this invariably leads to artistic output which is ugly and self-indulgent.

---

* To remind the reader, 'phenomenology' here means experience without reference to abstract theory.
† 'Ontology' here simply refers to that which exists and the topic of existence.

Subtler Languages (1):
The Arts, Sports and Alternative Spiritualities

At this point we may have arrived at an agreement that bare materialism is simply insufficient to give an account of the most important and significant experiences of our lives. But this hardly commits us to the Christian worldview or indeed to any traditional religious outlook. We may have a vague belief that there is something more and we may choose to act on that in a number of different ways.

'Subtler languages' is a phrase that describes the way many people cope with the need for transcendence in a secular age.[5] Traditional religious belief appears to have been discredited but people still need to break up and through the sense of immanence and flatness I have been describing. In the absence of religion, they need something else that gives them a sense of spiritual uplift.

Unquestionably the arts and various forms of entertainment are subtler languages. At the lowest level of culture, television is a fairly routine way of simply 'checking out' and relaxing for a while before we have to return to the stresses and difficulties of ordinary life. This can hardly be seen as a positive venture towards some kind of transcendent uplift but is really an expression of desire to achieve temporary escape from difficult existential or practical anxieties. Great literature, music and the higher arts present more obviously edifying avenues. Classic literature, for example, can be widely engaged with by secular people even if they do not share the religious presuppositions of the authors. Reading Dostoyevsky or Dante can furnish the secular person with insight into the human condition and the drama of existence. This often goes beyond mere intellectual stimulation and puts the reader in touch with a sense of a deeper reality in the world.

Music is the art form which provides the greatest capacity for spiritual uplift. This is partly because music is the least material of the art forms. It comes from material instruments but ultimately sound is something that takes flight upon the air and, as such, is the closest thing to spirit that we encounter in the ordinary course of our lives. Music also demands that the listener dwell within it in an almost meditative state. If it is broken unnaturally into segments then it loses its overall coherence and power. Like literature, music has undergone what Charles Taylor calls a 'disembedding' process. Literature and music used to be embedded in the world of Christianity. They presupposed the existence of God and the truth of Christianity. They were thus created and performed within that belief system. But, as the Christian worldview has declined, the arts have been 'disembedded' from that context and placed within the context of secular materialism. The result of this is that Christian art still exists but it is now performed and/or understood within a different frame of reference.

To give an illustration, Mozart's *Requiem* was composed in somewhat mysterious circumstances but, like all requiem Mass settings of the time, it was made for specifically religious reasons: namely, to be used in the liturgical context of an actual funeral Mass for somebody who had died. Nowadays it would rarely be used for this purpose. In the modern world, we hear Mozart's *Requiem* in a disembedded context. For example, we might have it on at home as background noise. Or we might go to a performance of it in a concert hall or even in a church. But we would see it specifically as a performance and it would not be meant as an intercession for the eternal repose of a deceased soul. We could only relate to it on *that* level in a theoretical way. The primary purpose of going to the concert would be to listen to the beauty of the music, to be moved emotionally by it.

The point is that *this* experience is open to the unbeliever and believer alike. As we sit in the church or in the concert hall listening to a performance of some formerly religious work such as a requiem Mass, the question of whether or not God exists, whether or not the soul endures beyond death, of the existence of heaven and hell, are not in any way the point. Those questions can be entirely ignored. The art has been disembedded from its Christian context. A subtler language has been invented: Christian music without ontology.*

This can be said of the visual arts too in, say, a tour round a particularly spectacular Gothic cathedral or a visit to a Venetian art gallery. Such things can provide a deep sense of meaning or spiritual uplift. But – and this is the crucial point – the people who engage in them are not forced to confront the question of the reality underlying either the works themselves or their experiences of them. This is the attraction of a subtler language: uplift with ontology, transcendence without religion. It provides the secular person with a spiritual life without committing to traditional religious belief. It is, in the words of Louis Dupré, a form of 'atheistic transcendence' and can 'easily develop into a substitute for religion'.[6]

This religion substitute idea is sometimes plainly articulated in mass culture. For example, it is routine for avid football fans to describe loyalty to their clubs in religious terms. The significance is at least twofold: on the one hand you have the ecstasy of gathering together with tens of thousands of fellow supporters to cheer and sing in a mutual sense of shared purpose. Premier League football fans know (particularly if their team is often successful) how intensely euphoric these gatherings can be. But there is also a community aspect which is particularly seen in places like Newcastle where there is only one club and the shared sense of devotion to it binds the community together in a tangible way. This is vividly captured in an Amazon-made documentary series about the upturn in fortunes of Newcastle United FC as they are bought by a rich Saudi-backed consortium and given a new lease

---

* This, of course, presents a problem for the contemporary Church as musicians sometimes have little sense that they are offering worship to God but instead possess the idea that church services can give them an (often paid) opportunity to perform classical music to a captive audience. Challenging these assumptions can be described as an attempt to re-embed that which has been disembedded.

of life. In the trailer for the series, a number of fans can be heard saying things such as:

This is a one-club city, so it is the absolute beating-heart of being a Geordie; St James' Park is our church. It is Newcastle in its entirety. For me it's that sense of belonging. It's that sense of community. It is the great equaliser in the city. It doesn't matter if you have money, if you don't have money, if you're black, white, brown, from the west end, from the east end, from the south, the north, we all sort of just fall towards it when match day comes.

After which some children who appear to be about seven years old all agree that they can't live without Newcastle United, that they love the club with all their hearts, all their passions, 'everything'.[7] It is not difficult to see the echoes of traditional Christian devotion here.

The classic expression of subtler languages is the phrase 'spiritual but not religious'. This phrase in many ways epitomises the technical definition of a subtler language because it makes a distinction between the outward and visible forms of traditional religious belief (religious) and the interior and apparently more meaningful journey of the soul towards the divine (spiritual), unsullied by the murky and distorting impositions of corrupt institutions.

The 'spiritual but not religious' concept is, once again, best understood historically as a radicalisation of the Protestant critique of the Catholic Church at the time of the Reformation: the Church corrupts the inner life of the soul and hinders one's access to God and so *must* be rejected if the individual is going to find true, interior connection to the divine. The concept can be traced to the Romantic literary movement of the nineteenth century which placed great emphasis upon the experience of transcendence, particularly in nature, and finds its home now in various forms of new age belief or in more general claims to be 'a spiritual person' but to be unsure of the institution of the Church or, perhaps more commonly, of 'organised religion'. And yet the fact that people who use this self-description still desire a spiritual life, even though they are disillusioned with the Church, perhaps speaks of the deficiencies of secularism and the malaise of the soul it produces.

The 'spiritual but not religious' idea is closely linked to a not-so-subtle subtler language and that is the language of the occult and satanism. The rise of interest in new age beliefs, neopaganism and more explicit forms of occultism is described by Richard Gallagher in his work on demonic possession, *Demonic Foes*. He notes, for example, that various surveys have found that 25 per cent of Americans believe in astrology, that 41 per cent believe aliens have visited the Earth and that three-quarters believe in at least one paranormal notion such as Bigfoot, haunting spirits or telekinesis.[8] He writes, 'Almost every city around the world has storefronts advertising fortune-tellers and psychics,' and he mentions the opportunities that the internet and social media have provided for the mass-marketing of these services. But, alongside these seemingly less macabre beliefs in the paranormal, the growth of interest in the occult and diabolism is also on the rise:

A recent *New York Times* article highlighted a self-identified witch who organized a well-attended 2019 conference for students of witchcraft hosted at New York University. After recording a lesson of her popular podcast about the ancient craft, she showed off her home altar – overlaid with a statue of the goddess Diana, candles, crystals, pendants, and a book of spells – in her Park Slope townhouse.[9]

Additionally, in May 2023, the BBC reported on a conference organised by the Satanic Temple: 'More than 830 people snapped up tickets for its late April convention, dubbed SatanCon,' wrote American correspondent Rebecca Seales in enthusiastic tones. She went on to describe various intentionally blasphemous rituals such as 'unbaptisms' in which participants are garbed in floor-length hooded cloaks and black face masks reminiscent of those worn during the Covid period. Their hands are then bound with a rope which is cast off to represent their liberation from the moralising constraints of Christianity. A Bible is then desecrated by having its pages ripped out. These actions are intended to symbolise the overturning of that person's Christian baptism. The article also describes attempts by satanists to have diabolic images erected in public areas and to start satanic after-school clubs. Most disturbingly of all, the satanists not only advocate for 'abortion access' but they have an online clinic that provides abortion pills by mail and an abortion ritual which they encourage people to recite as they carry out the abortions at home. The interesting point to note is the manner in which the BBC reported this, with no acknowledgement that any of it might be offensive to Christians or harmful more generally. It is simply the straightforward promotion of satanic religion.[10]

The sort of satanism described by the BBC is actually a very tame version of forms that are prevalent in Western culture. The author of the article is keen to stress that the satanists described 'don't actually believe in a literal Lucifer or Hell' but 'say Satan is a metaphor for questioning authority, and grounding your beliefs in science'. It is unclear whether this is honest on the part of the Satanic Temple and the BBC or a thin-end-of-the-wedge attempt to interest readers in seemingly more 'benign' forms of satanism before introducing them to more hardcore versions of diabolical worship.*

---

* This exact formula was earlier that year utilised in the *Daily Telegraph* in an article entitled 'Young sacrifice belief in God on altar of Satanism' which attempts even more explicitly to distance satanism from 'macabre occult rituals, virgin sacrifices, chalices of blood and belief in the actual Devil' and to associate it with various forms of progressive political activism (*Telegraph*, 'Young sacrifice belief in God on altar of Satanism', accessed 27.03.2024 [https://www.telegraph.co.uk/news/2023/01/14/young-people-turning-satanism-instead-stuffy-christianity/]). It is quite mysterious why anyone would feel the need to turn to a metaphorical expression

Richard Gallagher is (as already noted) one of the most experienced psychiatric practitioners dealing with demonic possession in the West today and he notes multiple examples of individuals whom he has encountered personally who became either oppressed or possessed by demons after engaging in satanic ritualism. A typical story involves an individual who, either in the context of a satanic cult or individually, pledges himself to Satan in exchange for something such as success or animal magnetism. The most explicit example Gallagher gives is of a possessed woman whom he calls Julia who had joined a satanic cult fronted by a charismatic leader called Daniel who was 'devoted to Satan and prayed to him all the time'.[11] Daniel is an example of somebody who prayed to Satan and received privileges from him in return. Julia called herself Queen Lilith and the cult worshipped not only satan but Asmodeus, 'the demon of lust'.[12] The satanic cult engaged in promiscuous sex and ritual orgies. These ritual orgies were often linked to so-called black masses which (like the softer 'unbaptisms' described by the BBC) are an intentional parody and inversion of the equivalent Christian rite, in this case Holy Communion.

And yet, far more disturbing than any of this, is Gallagher's description of an exchange in which Julia told him that Daniel, the cult's main leader, grew tired of her when she found out she

---

of satanism in order to engage in progressive politics. Indeed the whole concept of being a satanist but not believing in a literal devil is reminiscent of the tragic attempt on the part of liberal clergy in the Church of England to promote a form of Christianity that does not believe in a literal God. It also represents religious belief at its darkest and most self-deluded and recalls C.S. Lewis's fictional demon Screwtape's desire to create human beings who are 'materialist magicians'. Through Screwtape, Lewis imagines a breed of men who, in the future, will engage in occult practices while denying the reality of the spiritual realm, thus opening themselves to the service of the demonic while lacking any true understanding of their actions. Cf. C.S. Lewis, *The Screwtape Letters* (New York: Bantam Books, 1995), p. 19.

couldn't get pregnant any more. When Gallagher asked Julia what she meant, she responded as follows:

> I was the cult's main breeder . . . I could get pregnant easily, which gave me a special status in the group. We had someone who could perform abortions, a physician's assistant, I think, a repulsive guy. We used fetuses for ceremonies. Daniel encouraged it and said he and Satan would honor and reward me greatly for this 'service' and be eternally grateful for my role . . . Julia said Daniel told her that people had been doing this kind of 'service' to Satan for centuries. The group considered themselves pagans, he argued, and he claimed that a lot of pagan cultures were essentially demon worshippers, but the Aztecs did far worse in sacrificing *living* humans – mostly women and children.[13]

Clearly, this cult is operating with a different ontological paradigm to that of the Satanic Temple described by the BBC, believing very much in the literal reality of the existence of Satan and not using this language as a symbol for progressivist activism.

The hardcore version of satanism operates as a subtler language but in a not-so-subtle form. On the one hand, Christianity is explicitly rejected but not for the reasons given by average secular people. Satanic literalists reject Christianity not because God and the spiritual world do not exist but because they do and because the satanists have decided to worship the Dark Lord instead. This is how they find their sense of transcendent uplift and escape from the everyday mundanity of the secular realm: in diabolical adoration.

Subtler Languages (2): Jordan Peterson and Self-Improvement

Self-improvement has the capacity to give to the individual a sense of undeniable, almost god-like, power. This is why self-improvement must be understood as another type of subtler language. It is like a secularised form of the Christian notion of sanctification, which concerns growth in holiness over the course of a human life.

Perhaps the most important contemporary voice in the sphere of self-improvement is that of the Canadian psychologist and intellectual Jordan Peterson. Peterson rose to global prominence after he released a series of YouTube videos denouncing a piece of draconian hate-speech legislation concerning transgender pronouns tabled by the Canadian government. Well known for his lecture series on the book of Genesis and for his two psychological manuals of self-help, *12 Rules for Life* and *Beyond Order: 12 More Rules for Life*, he also has a popular podcast and has made countless media appearances.

Peterson is an anomaly because he clearly sits at odds with the dominant political paradigms that characterise Western culture. He is highly critical of postmodernism and of leftist strands of thought that tend towards communism and other forms of political collectivism. He also believes that in times past Christianity functioned as a bulwark against the relativism and nihilism that is so pervasive in the modern day. And yet, despite these apparently fringe views, he is still an intensely popular figure and must be counted as one of the most prominent intellectuals on the planet.

There are many factors that have made Peterson the cult-like figure he is, not least his dynamic rhetorical style, his ability to hold a crowd in the palm of his hand, his unusual emotional openness, his honesty and directness, his eccentric but smart dress sense, and many other things besides. But at the heart of the complexity, there is a very simple and powerful message: 'life is suffering and the way to overcome suffering is to take personal responsibility, to work hard on yourself primarily, and to try and improve things. The alternative is chaos, indolence, self-loathing, and self-destruction. It might seem that the first option is not great, but it's a hell of a lot better than the alternative. So what option do you have?' The function of religion, in Peterson's thought, is '*moral* . . . rather than descriptive. Thus, [traditional religions] did not concern themselves with what the world was, as a scientist might have it, but with how a human being should act.' Peterson's view is that 'our ancestors played the world as a stage – a drama – instead of a place of objects'.[14] Thus, for Peterson, religious imagery – including Christian imagery – is always symbolic and represents something of the everyday experience of people who conjured up these stories and, by extension, with all humanity. For example, in a chapter entitled 'Compare Yourself to Who You Were Yesterday, Not to Who Someone Else Is Today', he writes the following:

> Attend to the day, but aim at the highest good.
>
> Now, your trajectory is heavenward. That makes you hopeful. Even a man on a sinking ship can be happy when he clambers aboard a lifeboat! And who knows where he might go, in the future. To journey happily may well be better than to arrive successfully . . .
>
> Ask, and ye shall receive. Knock, and the door will open. If you ask, as if you want, and knock, as if you want to enter, you may be offered the chance to improve your life, a little; a lot; completely – and with that improvement, some progress will be made in Being itself.[15]

On the one hand, this passage clearly takes Christian motifs, such as that of heaven and prayer, and turns them into symbols for self-improvement: thus, 'heaven' is not the dwelling of the literal God and the destination of the soul after death, but the place that we are bound towards if we are aiming at 'the highest good' (which is not specifically defined but to do with, broadly speaking, becoming a more virtuous person). The prayer taught by Jesus on the Sermon on the Mount is not about literal intercessions for divine intervention, but about mental focus: asking, knocking as if you want to enter. Yet the other feature here, which is characteristic of much of Peterson's output, is that he uses ambiguous, quasi-religious language that always allows for the possibility of some form of spirituality. Thus here, 'You may be offered the chance': the passive voice leaves open the question of who is doing the offering. And, of course, his talk of progress 'made in Being itself' could be interpreted in a purely materialistic way or as a reference to the highest possible spiritual Being and its manifestation in the world. Peterson doesn't say which. This ambiguity is, once again, very similar to that of the other subtler languages that I have written about: it gives a sense of spirituality without committing to any traditional religious paradigm or doctrinal beliefs.

There is something unmistakably powerful in Peterson's message and indeed in the whole notion of self-help more generally. Being told that there are specific ends that are valuable and about which people can actually do something gives them a sense of agency and direction in a world that very often offers them little of either. Again, Peterson is very specific about this. How do you find out what goals to pursue? Look at what has been meaningful and valuable to other people:

> You need a family, you need friends . . . career, educational goals, plans for time outside of work, attention to your mental and physical health et cetera. That's what life is about, and if you don't have any of those things, well, then all you've got left is just misery and suffering, so that's a bad deal for you.[16]

Statements like this tell us that Peterson's philosophy, at least in *that* form, is really another philosophy of immanentism, albeit a very powerful one. Life is about temporal ends – family, friends, career, health, and son on – and religious symbolism is always related to human experience. Heaven, in other words, is really about Earth and making Earth as heaven-like as possible. Christ is an archetypal image of the perfect man and not the literal presence of God in this world. What Peterson's philosophy of life does not seem to give us, therefore, is a transcendent outlet. We find significance in the things of this world *only*. And the question of whether there is some kind of overarching significance that bestows meaning upon all these lesser, albeit very important, things is not of central concern. There *are* meaningful aspects in life, in other words, but where this meaning comes from is not determined, at least not by Jordan Peterson.

This raises the question of what you can do when the things that ordinarily bestow meaning in life begin to lack purchase. What do you do, for example, when you don't have any goals, and when the pursuit of family, friends, job, pleasure, and son on comes to seem worthless? In one of his public lectures, Peterson was asked this question. In answer, he began by talking about the Old Testament Law as prohibition against sin and comparing it with the New Testament ethic of the pursuit of the good. So how do you know what the good is?

> The first thing you do . . . is you have to look around you, within your sphere of influence, your direct sphere of influence, and fix the things that announce themselves as in need of repair, and those are often small things . . . They can be . . . your room. Put it in order . . . What's important is that you learn how to distinguish between chaos and order and to be able to act in a manner that produces order . . . And so practising that is a real useful form of meditation and it's also . . . a divine act . . . You can do something as simple as just sit on your bed and think, 'Okay, there's probably five things I can do today so that tomorrow morning is slightly better than this morning was' . . . But if you ask yourself, like you're asking something, which I think is a form of prayer, if you ask yourself instead of telling yourself, 'What is it that I can do to set things more right today that I would actually do?' It's usually some small thing because you're not that disciplined . . . Then you can go do it. You put the world together a little more when you do that and that spreads out but you also . . . construct yourself into something that's better able to call order forth from chaos and that makes you just incrementally stronger and then the next day you can maybe take on a

slightly larger task and you get the benefit of compound interest if you do that. It's a tremendously powerful technique. And I think if you do that, at some point, instead of just having to just fix things up that are not good you'll start to get a glimmer of the positive things that you could do: the positive things that you could do that would actually constitute a vision.[17]

Here we see once again Peterson's tendency to take a religious motif and translate it into the terms of everyday activity. The Old Testament is about prohibition, about not doing bad things. Therefore, we should stop doing bad things in our lives. Those things might be quite mundane, like living in an untidy room. It is from *that* point that we can start to think more creatively about what it might be like not just to *not* live in a chaotic environment but actually to start improving the world. This is, in Peterson's view, the meaning of the change from the Old Testament's negative mood to the more positive tone of the New Testament. So, we tidy our rooms, and, as we do so, we start to realise the almost spiritual quality of order. Recognising the goodness of order, we think about how we can bring greater amounts of it to the world around us. We start to take more responsibility upon ourselves and a vision begins to emerge. Again, bringing literal order to a room is likened to 'a divine act', understanding the difference between chaos and order is 'meditation', asking yourself how you can be better is 'a form of prayer'.

Peterson's advice amounts to a type of horizontal transcendence. He seems to be able to give people a sense of deep significance through a simple yet powerful set of observations about the nature of human existence using religious symbolism drawn from mythological or sacred texts. But the relevant point is that he never asks his listeners to commit themselves to some form of traditional religion, to vertical transcendence.

What can one make of Peterson's answer to the question of what to do when one has no goals? On the one hand, it may be taken as quite a shallow response: bringing about order in the midst of a chaotic world will give your life direction and it will give you a sense of meaning and accomplishment. You will start to respect yourself more and you can go from there. In that sense, it's simply a restatement of his basic philosophy of action.

But Peterson's answer can also be interpreted as an invitation to explore the nature not only of order within the world but of ultimate reality. There is huge anecdotal evidence that many people – particularly young men – have found in Peterson a so-called 'gateway drug' to traditional, orthodox forms of Christianity. It seems that these young men have indeed tasted something truly divine in the act of imposing order and are therefore seeking a deeper communion with the source of this harmony. Not content merely to tidy their rooms, to gain muscle and learn new skills, to marry and raise children, these men are finding in this call to personal responsibility an accompanying sense that there *is* indeed a deeper meaning to growth and order that can only be understood spiritually and that finds its home in our relationship to God.

The Tragedy of the Secular

The concept of subtler languages can explain so much about Western secularism that many more words could be written and many more examples given. Perhaps it has gone out of fashion to some extent in the new millennium, but we could mention here the enormous interest that developed in the twentieth century in UFOs and the paranormal. It has been suggested by theologians and academic theorists that these fixations are best described as a kind of contemporary, post-Christian sensibility.* Another subtler language is the replacement of religion by politics, about which more is said later. My argument here is that all this really speaks

---

* For a theological critique of this phenomenon see Fr Seraphim Rose, *Orthodoxy and the Religion of the Future* (Platina: Saint Herman of Alaska, 2004). For a more academic and contemporary approach, see D.W. Pasulka, *American Cosmic: UFOs, Religion, Technology* (New York: Oxford University Press, 2019).

of the deep need that we retain – even in a secular world – to find something beyond, to find something transcendent.

If we assume that some sort of bare materialism is the ultimate reality that undergirds all existence then any sense we have of transcendence or beauty or spiritual uplift is simply an evanescent glimmer of light upon the surface of an infinite darkness, out of which we emerged and wandered for a while before returning into the nothingness from which we came. Jordan Peterson's philosophy of chaos and order, when not understood in explicitly Christian terms, cannot save us from the nihilism against which he has spent his whole life railing, because the implication of his logic is that nihilism and chaos are at the heart of reality. We can bring greater levels of order into our environments but ultimately the horizon of death threatens and promises us the dismantling of all we have built out of the materials of our lives. This observation may be the reason why so many people who have followed Peterson have concluded that there must be some sense of *ultimate* order that undergirds everything else and that can best be understood in terms of orthodox Christianity. The various forms of individualistic self-expression so commonly offered to these people are not only redolent of a petulant, self-centred and adolescent attitude but also seem to cut against the grain of reality; they do not work because they are not grounded in reality. Bringing order out of chaos *does* work, however, and it *does* speak of the truth because reality is ultimately grounded not upon chaos and caprice but upon order and eternal harmony.

Another way of putting this is to borrow the language of C.S. Lewis who, in his autobiography *Surprised by Joy*, spoke of the sense of profound contradiction that he discovered in his thinking while he was an atheist. There was more than one strand to this, but perhaps the most significant was his discovery that his philosophy of knowledge sat very much at odds with his way of inhabiting the world: 'We had been, in the technical sense of the term, "realists"; that is, we accepted as rock-bottom reality the universe revealed by the senses.' That is, Lewis believed that the material world was the ultimate and only reality. In his view, there-fore, abstract thought, moral judgements and aesthetic experiences were all a by-product of the material world and were not in them-selves objective or independently existing. They arose somehow from material reality but could not be real or ultimate in the same sense as the former. Neither could it be the case that they spoke of objective standards that existed independently of the material realm. Morality and aesthetics, upon this view, must be subjective and therefore dependent upon the individual's preference.

Lewis came to understand that this philosophy of knowledge did not sit well with almost everything he truly believed about what was most important to him. He was, after all, a scholar and a teacher of English literature and he certainly did not think that one book was as good as another and that there was no objectively existing stand-ard of literary quality. 'We maintained that abstract thought . . . gave indisputable truth, that our moral judgement was "valid", and our aesthetic experience not merely pleasing but "valuable".'[18]

Lewis came to see, in other words, that he would have to give up one side of this equation if he were going to have a consistent worldview: either material reality is all there is and judgements about literary quality, aesthetic beauty and moral judgement are merely subjective preferences, *or* there are true standards of goodness, truth and beauty by which aesthetic and moral judge-ments can be made. But if the latter is the case, then it necessarily follows that there is a deeper reality to this world than the ma-terial realm, that something else undergirds it, that there are not only physical laws but also spiritual, moral and aesthetic ones. Lewis's atheism could not survive such an observation.

The Dreaming Spires of Oxford

One of the implications of the rejection of Christianity is the loss of its transcendent aesthetic. It is difficult to imagine that the descent into ugliness and irrationality will not only continue but worsen if we persist in the same way.

To my mind, there is no better example of this than when we look at our ancient university city of Oxford. The architecture of such a city literally embodies in different places the Christian and post-Christian worldviews. And it is not difficult to see which of the two produces aesthetic and transcendent beauty and which produces ugliness and monstrosity. It is obvious to everybody that the college buildings so explicitly grounded in Christian thought and belief are not only marvels of great architectural beauty but they somehow speak of the objective reality of truth, goodness and beauty within the context of a collegial, intellectual environment. In the case of a building like the Old Bodleian Library, we observe the remnants of an entirely different educational system. Defunct doorways that used to lead to the lesser subjects of music, mathematics, rhetoric and astronomy literally lead onwards to the central door of the greatest subject, that of divinity, *Regina Scientia* or 'Queen of the Sciences'. The whole building is patterned physically upon a metaphysical schema that sees all human knowledge as nested within the highest and greatest knowledge which is that of God himself. This is reflected in the university's motto, taken from Psalm 27:1: *Dominus illuminatio mea* ('The Lord, my light'). Christ Church, Corpus Christi, Magdalen, Jesus, St John's, St Peter's, St Anne's – these college names and many more speak of the worldview that undergirded and informed and created this vision for a medieval collection of colleges, the members of which together sought knowledge of truth, both human and divine. And because this collective endeavour was thought to be grounded in an eternal and objective reality, it was one that continued from one generation to the next. The American political philosopher Patrick Deneen speaks eloquently of this:

> The primacy and beauty of many of the most prominent college buildings such as the campus library and the chapel reflect this original purpose of a collegium: the transmission of hard-won knowledge from one generation to the next, a practice of utmost

seriousness meant to inspire awe and admiration. While today's campuses often still retain the remnants of the architecture of the collegium, more often than not even these older buildings today house undertakings inspired by a wholly opposite animating philosophy, and are almost always today overshadowed by the grotesque buildings that, we are told, reflect progress and the abandonment of the backwardness of the past.[19]

Deneen notes the ironic practice of leading prospective students through the older parts of the campus where the beautiful and inspiring buildings are located and intentionally avoiding the very architectural monstrosities that speak of the contemporary philosophy of the institutions: namely, individual self-expression and technocratic expertism. These soul-crushing erections of glass and concrete, twisted into unnatural shapes, are intentionally designed to undermine and subvert conventional rules of harmony and order. If there is any governing philosophy to them, it is in the display of how modern man has conjured up the ability to create buildings that in their design explicitly reject considerations of natural laws such as gravity and the duty to make them cohere elegantly with their surroundings. Unlike the Old Bodleian, the Radcliffe Camera, the Church of St Mary the Virgin, and the many hundreds of chapels, libraries and other buildings that make up the medieval buildings of Oxford, these modern forms speak only of the transitory moment in which they were created. Nobody can pretend that they have been built to last for very long. The Christian imagination, on the other hand, causes buildings to spring up that are intended to stand for thousands of years, that are intended to be there until the literal end of history at the return of Christ.

There could be no greater and more obvious picture of the superiority of the Christian worldview to that of the modern post-Christian world. Loss of the truth bleeds not only into the relativisation of the good but also into the rejection of the beautiful and the embrace of ugliness. Humankind no longer rises above itself and creates enduring works that speak of God's transcendence but instead indulges in the banality and emptiness of self-expression. There is an inevitable link between what we believe about the ultimate nature of reality and the kind of world we produce for ourselves to live in. Who can deny that the world is now so much uglier than it used to be and is only accelerating in this direction? Once again, the only thing that can bring us back is to re-embrace the Christian worldview that produced the only part of our world that we really want to hold on to. And this is true not only for the aesthetic but also for the moral dimension, as I will now go on to demonstrate.

IV

Ethics (1): The Myth of Moral Progress and the Christian Revolution

To begin with, [man] is nothing.

Jean-Paul Sartre, *Existentialism is a Humanism*

The Myth of Moral Progress

'The arc of the moral universe is long, but it bends towards justice.' This phrase has most recently been associated with former US President Barack Obama who was fond of repeating it in various settings. Shorn of its original context, the phrase appears to support what might be called a progressive, liberal view of history. Similar themes to those already discussed reappear when we consider what this phrase means: that humanity was held in a prison of fear and superstition for many centuries or even millennia, but that we have now moved beyond the sources of these beliefs (religion and, specifically, Christianity) and are straining towards a world that is increasingly free and just, as we battle against the old prejudices and hatreds and inevitably defeat them one by one. Once again, we can trace these ideas in their modern form to Enlightenment philosophers who emphasised rationality over the inherited traditions of the past and claimed that reason alone could lead us towards a better civilisation. It goes without saying that the implication of this progressive view is that the past is inferior to the present, that things are getting better as a result of the joint efforts of mankind, and that those who do not accept such an understanding are 'on the wrong side of history'.

Obama's invocation of 'the arc of the moral universe' lends these ideas a sort of mystical power, as though it is a certainty that humanity will one day fulfil its destiny by creating a flaw-less utopia here upon Earth, that the wickedness of prejudice, discrimination and intolerance will inevitably be defeated, and that the barriers that separate us will finally be broken down for ever. And yet the phrase has a history which cannot be separated from a Christian vision of the world that mitigates strongly against progressive utopianism. Again, it is not that progressive utopianism is an idea that arrives out of the ether and is opposed at every point to Christianity, but rather that it is a distorted form of Christianity. It is a man-centred version of Christianity in which humanity, and not God, is the saviour. It is a man-centred version of justice that sees sin not as a power that lives within the human heart but as a social phenomenon that is characteristic of certain oppressive groups. It is a man-centred version of salvation that has faith in heaven, but it is a heaven that is brought to Earth through rationality and the effort of human beings.

Yet the phrase was originally coined in 1853 by a clergy-man, Theodore Parker, and is most commonly associated with Martin Luther King, Jr and the American civil rights movement. It was quoted in his speech of 31 March 1968 at the National Cathedral, Washington DC, and is inseparable from the Christian context:

> We're going to win our freedom because both the sacred heritage of our nation and the eternal will of almighty God are embodied in our echoing demands . . . We shall overcome because the arc of the moral universe is long, but it bends towards justice. We shall overcome because Carlyle is right – 'No lie can live forever.' We shall overcome because William Cullen Bryan is right – 'Truth, crushed to Earth, will rise again.' We shall overcome because James Russell Lowell is right . . .
>
> Truth forever on the scaffold.
> Wrong forever on the throne.

And behind the dim unknown stands God,
Within the shadow keeping watch above his own.[*]

King's rhetoric – here as always – is steeped in a Christian vision of the world: the reason that lies and injustice will not overcome ultimately is because God will bring *his* purposes about, regardless of how unlikely this might seem at any time.

King was not ambiguous in his thinking on these matters. In a sermon on a similar theme, he articulated a sophisticated theological view of historical progress that cautioned against both 'superficial optimism' and 'crippling pessimism'. In this he was very clear about the limiting reality of sin and the inability of humanity to bring about the kingdom of God by itself in this age:

> The Kingdom of God as a universal reality is *not yet*. Because sin exists on every level of man's existence, the death of one tyranny is followed by the emergence of another tyranny. But just as we must avoid a superficial optimism, we must also avoid a crippling pessimism. Even though all progress is precarious, within limits real social progress may be made. Although man's moral pilgrimage may never reach a destination point on Earth, his never-ceasing strivings may bring him ever closer to the city of righteousness. And though the Kingdom of God may remain *not yet* as a universal reality in history, in the present it may exist in such isolated forms as in judgment, in personal devotion, and in some group life.
>
> Above all, we must be reminded anew that God is at work in his universe . . . he is striving in our striving . . . he is working through history for the salvation of his children. As we struggle

---

* It is not clear to me that this speech has been published, but a recording of it can be heard on YouTube. Cf. Reelblack One, 'Dr Martin Luther King, Jr – Remaining Awake Through a Great Revolution (1959)', accessed 03.04.2024, [https://www.youtube.com/watch?v=TiMKcH8o_Yo].

to defeat the forces of evil, the God of the universe struggles with us.*

This quotation is a textbook example of the orthodox Christian view that God's kingdom, as a result of the reality of human sin, can only appear in this age in a limited form. Christians believe that they can embody the kingdom personally through putting away sin and demonstrating God's love to the world. They believe that the kingdom is manifested in a more complete form in the society of the Church and in its worship. And they believe that the kingdom can come in limited ways in and through the structures of human society. *But* the kingdom will come in its fullness only with the return of Jesus Christ. This will be an event that cuts across human history and it will take the world by surprise.† This is often pithily summed up in the short phrase: 'Now, but not yet'. The kingdom of God can come to Earth *now* in part but *not yet* in full.

The point of all this is that King's vision was far removed from a liberal political view that has no place for God in the progress of humanity, that ignores the reality of sin and that says we will

---

* Taken from a sermon called 'The Death of Evil upon the Seashore', in Martin Luther King, Jr, *The Power of Love* (London: Penguin Books, 2017), pp. 87–8.

† Theologically literate readers will notice that I am articulating what is technically called a 'pre-millennial' view of the return of Christ. The 'post-millennial' view (put simply) says that, prior to the second coming of Jesus Christ, the Church will be increasingly successful in its evangelistic efforts and that the majority of the world will become Christian. The Church will then be the dominant power upon Earth and will establish its rule for a thousand years. This millennial rule will be followed by the King himself, Jesus Christ, coming back to Earth to sit upon his throne whereupon he will rule for ever. Although there are features of this view that are undoubtedly compelling, it seems to me that it is not supported either by Scripture or by the traditional thought of the Christian Church. There has, admittedly, been a lot of disagreement about this throughout the history of Christianity.

inevitably bring about a heaven here on Earth. For King, the civil rights movement was a moment in which the justice of God broke out in a new but limited form. And, as he says in the sermon above, the tyranny of racial segregation would inevitably be followed by some other tyranny yet to be named *just as* racial segregation followed on from the tyrannies of colonialism and slavery.*

In place of the liberal progressive view of history, I would like to suggest something quite different, namely that our whole understanding of morality is really based upon Christianity, and that it doesn't even make sense to talk about an 'arc of the moral universe' outside this context because, were we actually to confront the 'morality' of a pre-Christian or truly non-Christian civilisation, we would find it barbaric and cruel beyond imagination.

The Ethical Confusion of Our Time

At the beginning of his classic work *After Virtue*, Alasdair MacIntyre asks us to imagine a world in which the natural sciences such as chemistry, biology and physics suffer a terrible catastrophe. The knowledge of these disciplines, as well as their overarching frameworks, is lost to humanity almost completely. After this catastrophe, some enlightened people seek to revive the sciences even though they have largely forgotten what they are. Yet all they have is fragments of knowledge from the past:

---

* In my view, King's understanding of colonialism was imbalanced and tended to see all colonialism as necessarily evil and liberation from colonial structures as an unalloyed good. He failed to see the good intentions in some colonisers and did not predict the political, economic and social difficulties that would result from independence for many nations: 'The oppressed masses in Asia and Africa have won their freedom from the Egypt of colonialism and now move toward the promised land of economic and cultural stability' (ibid., p. 84). The problem with this view is that independence has hardly resulted in economic and cultural stability for a multitude of formerly colonised countries.

... a knowledge of experiments detached from any knowledge of the theoretical context which gave them significance; parts of theories unrelated either to the other bits and pieces of the theory which they possessed or to the experiment; instruments whose use has been forgotten; half-chapters from books, single pages from articles, not always fully legible because torn and charred. Nonetheless all these fragments are reembodied in a set of practices which go under the revived names of physics, chemistry and biology.[1]

These partially reconstructed subjects are discussed in schools, academia and popular culture, but the discourses about them are deceptive. People believe that they are talking about the same subjects that were lost prior to the catastrophe but, because the overarching contexts of these disciplines have been forgotten and all that remains is fragments, they are in fact not speaking about the same subjects at all. They might argue about the merits of different theories such as relativity, evolution or phlogiston theory, but they would have nothing to refer these conversations back to – no framework that would allow them to evaluate their knowledge – and so the conversations would have an arbitrary dimension, as though each person were simply choosing the theory that happened to be his favourite or that he preferred for whatever reason.

The point of this story is that the language of morality is in the same state of disorder as the language of the natural sciences in the fictional world described by MacIntyre.

What we possess ... are the fragments of a conceptual scheme, parts which now lack those contexts from which their significance derived. We possess indeed simulacra of morality, we continue to use many of its key expressions. But we have – very largely, if not entirely – lost our comprehension, both theoretical and practical, [of] morality.[2]

If this is true, then at least a couple of things follow from it. First, it will not be obvious to us that we do live in such a situation. This is because, like those who recovered what they thought were the natural sciences, we use the language of ethics, but we are unaware that we have lost a sense of the overall context. Like them, the only way we might realise this is through an understanding of broader historical perspective.

And the second thing that follows is that there will necessarily be great inconsistency in our shared moral discourse. There will be points at which various moral frameworks appear to coincide with each other but there will also be points of contradiction between them. Even more amazingly, there will be points of contradiction *within* individual moral frameworks themselves. An example of this might be a progressive viewpoint that on the one hand espouses radical feminism and support for gay rights, while on the other it supports Islam and the political aims of terrorist groups such as Hamas. This viewpoint can be held only because there is no consistent, overarching moral framework to refer it back to. Both viewpoints are *felt* to be correct, and it does not occur to the one who holds them that there are significant ideological contradictions between them.

MacIntyre's parable has huge explanatory power. We do indeed live in a morally confused time. The issue is not simply that we lack the philosophical tools to resolve our ethical quandaries but that we are dispossessed of the conceptual framework for making *any* judgements about morality whatsoever. We might *feel* that certain things are right or wrong, but we have no way of justifying these feelings apart from simply insisting upon them in an increasingly indignant tone of voice. In this context, what is felt by the majority to be a just political cause is dependent not upon some rational scheme of moral evaluation but upon government spin and media emphasis. Secular humanists sometimes make the totally unconvincing claim that such morality as we do possess is innate and self-evident. And yet such claims can be dismissed immediately by a historical and contemporary survey of cultures that have completely different ethical outlooks from our own. If it is insisted upon that our moral understanding is both correct and innate, we must accept both that we are claiming superiority to other cultures and the implication that we have the moral authority to tell the rest of the world what is right and wrong. These implications, however, cannot be squared with the emphasis that Western nations place upon the evils of colonialism, racism and the importance of diversity and equality.

We are in a terrible mess and there is no consistency in public moral discourse, in the media, in political life or in educational establishments. This is because there is no shared overarching moral framework to which we can refer that will help us evaluate ethical judgements. Each person is simply doing and saying what appears to be right in their own eyes. And this does not lead to consistency but to utter confusion.

The overarching moral framework that we have lost came to us through Christianity. The Christian worldview was influenced by Greek and Jewish civilisation and developed into its most sophisticated philosophical form in the High Middle Ages when the synthesis of these great civilisations came together in the work of Thomas Aquinas. That framework has been lost following the catastrophe of the decline of Christianity and the advent of secularism. Now we retain ethical fragments from the Christian past, but we have lost the ability to put them together consistently. It is like a large puzzle that has been poured out on the floor with the frame taken away and the original picture removed. We may be able to make some sense of it here and there, but we will never be able to put it back together again.

In other words, the ethical ideas of Christianity have been retained in part but belief in the actual religion of Christianity has declined. This has created great confusion which modern secular people find hard to acknowledge because they lack the conceptual tools to understand the situation in which they find themselves.

The Implication

If this is true then it signifies something important about the future. If it really *is* the case that our sense of morality – incoherent and unsubstantiated as it is – comes to us from Christianity, and if it is the case that Christianity really *is* in decline in the West, then it follows axiomatically that some kind of post-Christian moral consensus will emerge. And it follows that that post-Christian moral consensus will be substantially different from the Christian moral consensus that preceded it.

The argument of this chapter is that, in many ways, we can already see the post-Christian moral landscape taking form in the Western world and that this provides us with a warning as to what may be coming next. Perhaps the most significant and profound aspect of Christian morality that is fading from view is the conception of humanity and our place within God's creation. We have forgotten the historical fact that Christianity gave us our understanding of the sacredness of every human being regardless of social class, ethnicity, biological sex, age, health status, or any other potentially disqualifying factor. We have forgotten the fact, in other words, that Christianity gave us an entirely new vision of what a human being is. We have absorbed the Christian view of humanity so deeply that we are not aware of its historical contingency and of how it differs from that of other cultures and religions. It *is* not and *has* not been obvious that every human being should be treated with fairness and justice, on the basis that each one has a certain sense of dignity and sacredness about him. The only reason we have an intuition that we should be treated thus is because of Christianity. Now that Christianity is declining, we are seeing a new vision of humanity emerging. And that vision of humanity will prove to be a terrifying departure with catastrophic consequences. Indeed, as I have said a number of times, we can already see that, for all our talk of equality and diversity, the lives of many are being forfeit to the ideology of post-Christian secularism.

The Christian Revolution

As has been indicated, the simplest way to illustrate the uniqueness of the Christian outlook is to examine the world into which Christianity was born and to see the stark difference between the two. If we do this, we can recognise quite clearly that the world *we* inhabit – and to a great extent still value – was formed by Christianity. Nor is this a particularly controversial statement. It may contradict the Enlightenment fiction of the Christian 'Dark Ages', but it is nevertheless a straightforward historical argument that has been recounted by many writers, both popular and academic. Among them are, for example, distinguished political philosopher Larry Siedentop, who links the Christian invention of the individual with modern-day liberalism.[3] There is the irascible and brilliant polymath David Bentley Hart whose *Atheist Delusions* goes to great lengths to demonstrate the absurdity of the then-fashionable New Atheist claim that Christianity and more broadly 'monotheism' is a source of gross immorality, when in fact the New Atheists actually derived their moral ideas *from* Christianity. And then there are more popular authors such as the historian Tom Holland, whose 2020 work *Dominion: The Making of the Western Mind* argues that Western modernity, including seemingly unrelated phenomena such as the permissive society and the advent of political correctness and wokery, is largely the product of Christian thought.[4] In that book, Holland argues that the shifting conception of crucifixion illustrates the central difference between the pagan outlook of Rome and the novel vision of Christianity. The cross in the Roman world was a sign of torture and an instrument of power wielded against the weak and the outcast, whereas, in Christianity, it became a symbol of self-sacrifice and the triumph of the meek over the proud. Perhaps even more pertinently, contemporary feminist writers such as Louise Perry have begun to recognise Christianity's role in shaping a sexual ethic that ultimately benefited and protected women who were otherwise subjugated and abused. This is a phenomenon that Perry wrote about to some extent in her 2022 work *The Case Against the Sexual Revolution.*[5] Therefore, nothing in the following argument is intended to be particularly original. The reason that it bears repeating is because it is a crucial part of the argument of this book that modern notions of morality rely upon their origin in Christianity.

Polytheism and Atheism

The first observation that must be made is that ethics is always downstream from theology. To put it more specifically: what we believe about the nature of reality at its deepest and most foundational level will determine how we orientate our lives and ultimately the kinds of ethical decisions we make.

It has occasionally been said by certain atheists that monotheism is the cause of most of the world's ills. To the contrary, it is in fact only monotheism that can ground any kind of absolute standard of morality at all. The concept of there being only *one* God is, of course, one of the principal inheritances of the Judeo-Christian tradition. The widespread dissemination of this belief in the form of Christianity created the basis upon which the Western social, cultural and legal order was built. We have already seen that the concepts of reason and rationality rely upon the notion of a stable cosmic and physical order that was put into place and is upheld by a single, omnipotent God. The same is true of ethics.

Judaism and Christianity came to birth in polytheistic cultures in which there were no absolute standards of right and wrong. What was considered right or wrong was based upon the preferences of a particular tribe's god. It is important to note that the gods of polytheistic religions are emphatically *not* the same kind of beings as the Absolute Being of Judaism and Christianity. Rather, the gods of the Ancient Near East into which Judaism was born and the gods of the Greco-Roman world into which Christianity came are more properly thought of as demiurges. They exist in heavenly or spiritual spheres, *but* they do not possess the attributes of the Most High God: namely, self-existence, omnipotence, omnipresence, omniscience, and so on. We have already seen that the attribute of the true God that sets him apart from everything else in all of creation is that he possesses the power of existence within himself and 'donates', as it were, the power to exist to all of his creation. If the gods of the Ancient Near East or the Greco-Roman world did exist they would only have done so by virtue of the fact that they had been created by the Most High God who possesses existence within himself. This is a key distinction because it makes clear the point that the gods of polytheism do not pretend to possess the same kind of universal jurisdiction as the God of the Bible. Rather the gods of polytheism are limited in their power and therefore squabble and fight with each other for dominance.

Significant ramifications follow. First, within the polytheistic framework, there are only regional and tribal standards of morality. There is no universal, transcendent ethic which applies to all people, at all times and in all places. Thus, if Ba'al or Molech demands child sacrifice, then child sacrifice must be made. There is no higher court of appeal that might condemn child sacrifice as inherently wicked.

The second point is that polytheism implies (either metaphorically or literally) that, at the foundation of reality, there is violence, chaos and war. Indeed, in many of the creation myths of polytheistic cultures, such as the Babylonian *Enuma Elish*, the world is literally born out of a primeval struggle between warring gods. In the polytheistic imagination, existence is not fundamentally love, light and peace but violence, war and death. Indeed, all of reality is born out of struggle, and struggle is simply the reality of the world.

Regardless of our personal religious convictions, Western people are nevertheless shaped by the notion that there is an ultimate standard of right and wrong, and that, at the heart of reality, there is not violence, chaos and war but peace, love and joy.

These convictions are indeed failing but they are nevertheless still present to a great degree. To take one trivial example of this, as a parish priest I take many funerals for people who do not go to church regularly and have little to no Christian faith. Yet it is my overwhelming experience at such times that folks who have lost loved ones speak of the departed as being in a better place, being with God, being 'called home', being at rest, and so on. And they speak of one day being reunited with them. This might seem innocuous, but it reflects a cultural imagination that has been shaped by monotheistic Judeo-Christian thought. Outside our framework, it makes no sense to think about human death in this way. Humans are, in that case, trivial by-products of cosmic or biological forces. The ultimate reality is not peace and light but death and chaos. It is only because we have been so radically shaped by Christianity that we have the imaginative apparatus to see it differently.

This is why the charge that 'monotheism' has been the source of such manifold evil is so deeply misguided: it is not even in the empirical denial that monotheistic religions have been the source of violent or unjust actions, but in the fact that the whole notion of a single, binding, transcendent morality is unthinkable outside a monotheistic framework, and that moral goodness is, in a sense, a reflection of something deeper and higher than human culture, that morality is ultimately grounded in the fact that reality, at its very heart, simply *is* the fullness of goodness, life, joy and love.

A similar critique to that levelled at polytheism can be applied to atheism also. This is because atheism, just like polytheism, denies the existence of the Most High God and the moral order over which he presides. The atheist denies the existence of the polytheistic gods too, but this ultimately makes no difference to the relativistic ethical scheme that logically proceeds from such beliefs. As the Jewish philosopher Yoram Hazony puts it:

> The atheist deciding what is true and right for himself becomes, in effect, one god among many others. This case is the same as

that of the Egyptian Pharaoh, who was also considered one god among many others. From a biblical point of view, every atheist is just another small-time Pharaoh – a man who denies the existence of the one normative moral order and sees the world as composed of countless local standards of what is true and right.

According to the biblical understanding, every atheist is a polytheist, and every polytheist is also an atheist. Atheism and polytheism are metaphysically indistinguishable, just as the moral relativism that follows from each of them is the same. The only alternative to the pagan metaphysics, and to the moral relativism that follows from it, is the recognition of the one God, creator of heaven and Earth, who rules his creation in accordance with a single moral standard.[6]

In a sense moral relativism is only the presenting issue of the atheistic viewpoint. For the atheist, just as much as for the polytheist, the universe is founded upon a play of competing forces – upon power, struggle and violence. The political philosopher and theologian John Milbank has argued that what he calls 'an ontology of violence' came to prevalence in the thought of early modern philosophers whose works largely shaped the Enlightenment political tradition.[7] Thomas Hobbes is a key name in this regard, for it was Hobbes who said that the state of nature (by which he meant the way the world was in itself, prior to being civilised by humans) is red in tooth and claw, characterised only by the war of all against all. According to Hobbes, human beings are motivated primarily by the desire for power, and they pursue this power in order to stave off death and subdue their enemies. For Hobbes this was the ultimate goal of politics: simply the delaying of death for as long as possible. All civilisation is, therefore, upon a Hobbesian viewpoint, a kind of temporary shelter against the sway of competing forces of violence. The extent to which society can protect us from violence and death is the extent to which it is successful. But there is no more noble or transcendent end for a political community than this limited aim.

If early modernity was influenced by an ontology of violence then so is modernity's successor, postmodernity. If we understand the Enlightenment project as attempting to found human society upon universal reason, then we can take the postmodern project to be a kind of intensification of this aspiration. Postmodernity, first, takes note of the failure of the modern, rational project, namely, that in the wake of two world wars and the manifest impotence of Enlightenment thought to provide a single standard of morality upon which all can agree, the postmodern thinker simply cannot conceive of a single standard of rationality or morality upon which human civilisation should be based. Rather, there are merely individual standards, standards based on the preferences of individuals. And the wants or preferences of the individual are ultimately the highest court of opinion. There is no transcendent standard to which we can appeal. In addition to this postmodern rejection of Enlightenment rationality is added a vigorous and passionate embrace of an ontology of violence – that is, postmodern philosophers such as Jacques Derrida and Gilles Deleuze explicitly argue for a metaphysics of indeterminacy, chaos and 'flux'. For these postmodernist thinkers, at the heart of reality is not a stable order to which we can refer in our quest for truth and goodness, but rather a play of competing forces. People like Derrida, Deleuze and Michel Foucault argued for such a metaphysics in order to free human society and language from what they said were the dominant and corrupt institutions of the patriarchy, colonialism and other influences of this sort. But, in fact, the metaphysics they espoused simply propagated the violence that they superficially denounced. And this is because, in the absence of a *single* standard of right and wrong, the only ultimate standard is power. And power is only established through conflict and violence. John Milbank calls these thinkers 'neo-Nietzscheans' and comments that they cannot 'wriggle out of the implication that, while nihilism may be "the Truth", it is at the same time the truth whose practical expression must be fascism'.[8]

And so, neither atheistic modernism nor atheistic postmodernism can offer us any grounds either for a single, transcendent source of morality *or* for the belief that reality is at bottom good and peaceful. Rather, existence is founded upon struggle, and the ethical implication is that power is the ultimate goal of humanity, and the individual will and its preferences are the highest court of appeal, even if those preferences turn out to be diabolical in nature.

Contrast this with the Christian vision that is the culmination of the highest pagan philosophy and Jewish religious thought. First, there is a Most High God who is not only the lawgiver upon Mount Sinai but also the source of truth, goodness, beauty and Being itself. The reason that an action is good or evil is not because of some arbitrary obedience towards, or transgression of, a moral rule but because of its conformity to the nature of God. God calls us to reflect in our lives that goodness that inheres within himself. This is where we must throw away all our anthropological conceptions of God: he is not like a man just writ large and more powerful. Nor is God just the source of moral pronouncements. Rather he is reality itself, and all that exists is contained within the benevolent embrace of his eternal being. True virtue is a participation in the nature of God, a conforming of the human life to his goodness. This may sound too explicitly theological for some, but, as has already been pointed out, all ethical talk ultimately boils down to theological convictions.

The Christian Scriptures are replete with the notion that God is within himself a harmonious correspondence of unity and difference, and that creation is called out of nothingness to reflect that divine harmony. This is hinted at in the Old Testament and is brought to full fruition in the New Testament revelation of the reality of God as a Trinitarian unity of love. In the creation of mankind in Genesis, for example, 'God said, "Let us make mankind in our image, in our likeness"' (Genesis 1:26), and many Christian commentators have seen this 'us' as the earliest reference to the Holy Trinity.* Mankind is created not as a simple unity but as a differentiated harmony of man and woman: 'So God created mankind in his own image, in the image of God he created them; male and female he created them' (Genesis 1:27). This same theme can be seen in the New Testament most clearly in the Gospel of John, which both references and develops the earliest part of the book of Genesis: 'In the beginning was the Word, and the Word was with God, and the Word was God' (John 1:1). The Word (or *Logos* in Greek) is, of course, Jesus Christ, who is said to be 'with' God but also to *be* God. 'He was with God in the beginning' (John 1:2), John writes a second time as though to repeat the point that Jesus is not simply identified exactly with God but that he is, in some sense, another expression of God. The Christian Church, in its reflection upon the New Testament, came to understand that God is best understood in Trinitarian terms. That is, God is made up of three 'persons' – Father, Son and Holy Spirit – but is within himself one 'substance' or 'essence'.

This might seem abstract, but the relevant point is that the doctrine of the Holy Trinity gives us a way of understanding reality that is profoundly joyful and filled with life and hope. Consider the words of Christ in the high priestly prayer in the Gospel of John: 'Father, I want those you have given me to be with me where I am, and to see my glory, the glory you have given me because you loved me before the creation of the world' (John 17:24). Before the world began, the Father, Son and Holy Spirit were unified in a harmonious relationship of infinite love, joy, peace and delight. It was out of that unified harmony that creation itself was born.

---

* As with many points of scriptural exegesis, this is the subject of some debate and disagreement. Cf. Michael S. Heiser, *The Unseen Realm: Recovering the Supernatural Worldview of the Bible* (Bellingham: Lexham Press, 2015), p. 39. Heiser believes the plurality is a reference to God's 'divine council' of *elohim* (that is, lesser gods). In general, I am very persuaded by Heiser's thought, but I think he is too restrictive in his interpretation of Genesis 1:26–7.

Creation has suffered a catastrophic fall into sin and darkness, but it nevertheless retains that original yearning to return to its home in the life and the light of God.

The Christian vision could not be further away from the pagan notion of the world as an entity born out of a violent contest between warring gods. And its *outworking* could not be more different either: for the Christian vision says not that death and violence and struggle and flux and emptiness and futility are the final end of things, but that, underneath all the pain and suffering and chaos that we experience in this world, there is an infinitely loving, harmonious and peaceful God who calls us to draw near to him and, to the extent that we are capable in the midst of our human weakness and limitations, to bring his dwelling place to bear upon the Earth.

Christian Humanism

If the doctrine of God is a central distinctive feature of Christianity then equally important is its conception of humanity. It is sometimes fashionable for modern people to believe that the pagan world was essentially similar in its intellectual and cultural attitudes to our own post-Christian age. But nothing could be further from the truth because it was Christianity that invented the understanding of the individual with which Western people are familiar. Our intuition, for example, that all human beings should be treated fairly and given appropriate levels of respect and care comes from Christianity. Very simple points can be made about the ancient world that highlight its contrast with the Christianity-influenced world that we live in today.

To begin with, the Greco-Roman culture into which Christianity was born was literally patriarchal. The word 'patriarchy' has been co-opted by modern-day progressives who use it to refer to a world that gives greater advantages to men than it does to women and in which men hold women under their subjugation. But there is a fundamental difference between any kind of so-called patriarchy that might exist today and that of the pagan world. This is because the patriarchy of the ancient world was not seen as an injustice that needed to be fixed but as a deeply embedded religious and cultural reality.

The Enlightenment historian Edward Gibbon is one of the most famous proponents of the idea that the ancient world was similar to that of Enlightenment modernity: secular and therefore free of religious bondage. Such a view is truly unthinkable when we examine the historical facts. Larry Siedentop, in his important work *Inventing the Individual*, makes the point in some detail. To begin with, the Greco-Roman world saw itself not as a collection of individuals, as we might see ourselves today, but as a collection of families. Within that collection of families, the father was the ruler, the king and the high priest. The cult of the family was inherited from the earlier Indo-European world and was centred around the household hearth which functioned as a shrine dedicated to the worship of dead male ancestors. Women, slaves and foreigners were seen as categorically inferior because they could not function as ruler, king and high priest, and because they would not be worshipped as gods when they died. Indeed, it was only the eldest son who could inherit the family hearth. The domestic sphere was fundamentally predicated on the notion of inequality. It could not conceivably have been otherwise. In this system, the father was essentially a god in waiting and he had the power of life and death over his wife and children.[9]

Adult male citizens were the centre of civic and social life. Women, children and slaves were seen not only as inferior by convention but as inherently lacking certain qualities which were deemed to be typical of the male citizen. Specifically, women and children were held to have a limited measure of reason (or, as it was in Greek, *Logos*). They were considered weaker in all respects and therefore inferior. There was no sense in which the weak should be pitied; they were not to be cared for or protected but were acted upon by the strong and were servants to them.

All this was a fact of life. It was based upon a fixed religious and metaphysical picture of the world. This point is worth stressing because it is sometimes said that, without Christianity, the ancient world would have more quickly developed into the secular world that we enjoy today. This viewpoint is historically absurd because the ancient world was both deeply religious and deeply conservative. There is no reason whatsoever to believe that it would have developed into something like the secular world that we live in today. This observation is made all the more likely by the addition that many philosophers and theologians have argued that secularism is an outgrowth of Christianity and intrinsically linked to its central anthropological premise: namely, that all human beings are possessed of intrinsic value and should be treated fairly. There was no such belief in the Greco-Roman world.

The father's power over life and death was *not* theoretical but literal. This can be seen in the attitude of the ancient family towards the practices of abortion and the exposure of infants. To begin with, abortion *was* the subject of debate in the ancient world. But it was not the sort of debate that is had in the modern day, which would concern the inherent value of the unborn child and the ostensible right of the mother to end its life. The debate in the ancient world concerned the *husband's* right to make decisions about the woman and about what happened to *his* child. It should be borne in mind that these decisions often led not only to the death of the child but also to the death of the woman because of the primitive methods of pre-modern abortion. J.M. Bakke notes the claim that fatalities in connection with abortions were one of the most common causes of death for women in the Greco-Roman world.[10] To emphasise the point, it was in the second century AD that legislation was laid down to criminalise abortion, but this was, again, exclusively to ensure the rights of the father not to be deprived of his offspring without his consent. These laws were nothing to do with the value of the unborn child or the rights of the mother.

The widespread denunciation of abortion as an immoral practice in itself was a result of the spread of Christianity. This attitude can be traced to one of the earliest Christian documents outside the New Testament, *The Didache*, which contains an explicit prohibition of the practice,[11] and all the evidence of the succeeding centuries is that Christianity viewed the practice of abortion as gravely sinful and as constitutive of the destruction of the image of God in the unborn child. Indeed, there is no other historical reason to account for the widespread denunciation and criminalisation of the practice.

Perhaps more shocking to our modern sensibilities is the Greco-Roman practice of exposure, which consisted of a newborn baby being abandoned outdoors by his or her family to be taken as prey by the elements or wild beasts. Bakke notes that 'the practice of exposing children was both well-known and socially accepted'.[12] Whether or not a child was exposed was the decision of the father: 'the father had the legal right to decide the life and death of the other members of the family, and it was he, at least in the final instance, who decided whether a child should be accepted into the family or exposed'.[13] There were several reasons why children might be exposed, among them poverty, illegitimacy, religious superstitions based on omens of doom, and the presence of physical deformities. Children with the latter affliction were often drowned along with the more generally weak and unhealthy.[14]

There was also, of course, a major bias towards the preservation of boys over girls. Some inscriptions from the Oracle at Delphi reveal, for example, that, out of 600 family records there preserved, only six families had more than one daughter – the reason being that boys were considered superior to, and more useful than, girls and that girls were therefore more routinely exposed.

It is true that sometimes children survived exposure because they were taken in as foundlings. But this normally happened, not through charity or pity, but so that they could be used as slaves and prostitutes. An archaeologist, Lawrence E. Stager, tells the story of what he and his colleagues found when they excavated a villa in Ashkelon: '[We made] a gruesome discovery in the sewer that ran under the bathhouse . . . The sewer had been clogged with refuse sometime in the sixth century AD. When we excavated and dry-sieved the desiccated sewage, we found [the] bones of . . . nearly 100 little babies apparently murdered and thrown into the sewer.'[15]

Once again, these practices were socially acceptable and legal at the time. There is a fundamental gap between the intuitions of those ancient people and ours today. We have been conditioned by two millennia of Christianity to be repulsed at such things as child murder. No such civilising influence had come upon the people of Greco-Roman antiquity.

The Greco-Roman world also had a completely different view from ours on the subject of paedophilia. In the Greek world, the practice of pederasty was normal between free urban citizens. It was routine for older, freeborn men to engage in homosexual sex with children from the age of twelve upwards. This was considered to fit within the social hierarchy as long as it was the older man who was the active partner and the child the passive. This active/passive dichotomy was also the way that heterosexual sex was viewed, with the man playing the dominant role in the exchange. The Romans were slightly more picky and critiqued pederasty involving freeborn children because they would one day grow up to assume the same status as the ones who dominated them. It was considered perfectly fine, however, to exploit slave children sexually, and child prostitution was, once again, common and socially accepted. We in the Western world have rightly developed disgust at paedophilic desire and the sexual exploitation of children. But there is no explanation as to how this has happened apart from Christianity.

Simply put, Christianity invented humanism. That is, Christianity invented the idea that human beings have a unique place in the order of the cosmos, a place that is not dependent upon certain character-istics such as sex, age, class and race. There are two strands to this from a theological perspective. The first is that Christianity took up the Jewish notion that all human beings are made in the image of

God. Thus, all human beings are superior in dignity and status to the other creatures that God has made. They occupy a mediating position between the angels in heaven and the beasts upon the Earth. Speaking of humanity, the writer of Psalm 8 says,

> You have made them a little lower than the angels
> and crowned them with glory and honour.
> You made them rulers over the works of your hands;
> you put everything under their feet:
> all flocks and herds,
> and the animals of the wild,
> the birds in the sky,
> and the fish in the sea,
> all that swim the paths of the seas.
>
> Psalm 8:5–8

But beyond that, the doctrine of the incarnation and the message of the Christian gospel were simply revolutionary by the standards of the ancient world. The incarnation is the Christian belief that, in Jesus Christ, God became man and yet he did not divest him of his divinity but joined it to his humanity. Thus, humanity became connected to divinity in the person of Jesus Christ. One of the earliest theologians of the Christian Church, Saint Athanasius of Alexandria, said of this, 'He indeed assumed humanity that (humanity) might become God.'[16]

Notice here a stark contrast with the Indo-European and Greco-Roman notion, implicit in the religion of ancestral worship, that only the first-born men were gods in waiting and that therefore they could rule over their family with complete power. The Christian view is that *all* human beings – and not only the first-born sons – are beckoned to divinisation, to be united to God through his Son Jesus Christ.

Further, in the Christian Church a vision of a new human family was being brought to birth. The members of that new family were to treat each other with self-giving love and respect. When there were disagreements, they were required to repent, to ask for and to offer forgiveness, and to demonstrate personal humility. All this was predicated upon the idea that the atoning death of Jesus Christ had laid down a pattern of self-giving love that his disciples were to imitate in their relationships with one another, and that unity in the Church was not based upon arbitrary social characteristics but upon faith in Jesus Christ. The apostle Paul is especially clear in this regard, going as far as to say, 'So in Christ Jesus you are all children of God through faith . . . There is neither Jew nor Gentile, neither slave nor free, nor is there male and female, for you are all one in Christ Jesus' (Galatians 3:26, 28). Paul did not mean that members of the Christian Church had divested themselves of their biological characteristics or their social status. Rather, he meant that they shared a common identity and were united in a new human family through faith in Jesus Christ.

Thus, through the gospel, racial tension and animosity could be transcended. Speaking of the millennia-old hatred that existed between the Jewish and Gentile world, Paul wrote to a Gentile church saying, 'For he himself is our peace, who has made the two groups one and has destroyed the barrier, the dividing wall of hostility, by setting aside in his flesh the law with its commands and regulations. His purpose was to create in himself one new humanity out of the two, thus making peace' (Ephesians 2:14–15). The specific theological mechanism that Paul spoke of might not be especially clear to the modern reader, but what *is* clear is that Paul believed it was through Christ that historic animosity between different races could be overcome, and that those who had lived at enmity with one another could be reconciled within the Christian Church.

In the same letter, Paul addressed wives and husbands:

Wives, submit yourselves to your own husbands as you do to the Lord . . . Husbands, love your wives, just as Christ loved the church and gave himself up for her . . . In this same way, husbands ought to love their wives as their own bodies. He who loves his wife loves himself. After all, no one ever hated their own body, but they feed and care for their body, just as Christ does the church – for we are members of his body.

Ephesians 5:22, 25–6, 28–30

It is common for modern people to regard passages such as this as patriarchal and oppressive but, in the context in which it was written, it was extremely radical and elevated immeasurably the status of wives relative to their husbands. Remember that, in the world in which this letter was written, the husband had the power of life and death over his wife and his children. In contrast, the apostle Paul says that husbands are to give themselves up for their wives in the same way that Christ died on the cross for the Church. A greater reversal of values is hard to imagine. It is true that Paul saw marriage and indeed the Church as consisting of a hierarchical order. For example, he wrote that 'the husband is the head of the wife as Christ is the head of the church' (Ephesians 5:23). But the role of 'head' here meant that the husband had a greater responsibility to act in a spirit of sacrificial love towards his wife. The wife, in her turn, is to offer to her husband submission and respect.*

---

* On the specific verb used for 'submission' (ὑποτάσσω –^hypotassō), David Bentley Hart comments, 'In the case of wives and husbands, the issue here does not seem to be merely one of domestic authority (which in the first century would have been regarded as a matter of positively banal obviousness), but also one of reciprocal service and protection. Hence, the verb has a very different connotation than does, say, ὑπακούω (^hypakouō), which is used in the next chapter of the obedience of children to parents or of slaves to masters. In the world of late antiquity a household was under the authority of the paterfamilias; but it is also the case that, in an unpoliced society, households were often small fortresses with bolted outer gates and inner doors, wives were often much younger than their husbands, and male labor was the foundation of most of the economy. So, here, a husband's reciprocal responsibility to his wife – who is under the shelter of his household – is to lay down his life for her, on the model of Christ's self-sacrificial headship.' David Bentley Hart (trans.), *The New Testament: A Translation* (New Haven: Yale University Press, 2017), pp. 386–7.

Whatever modern people think about the specific theology of marriage in the letter to the Ephesians and elsewhere in the New Testament, it should be observed that our contemporary notion of equality between the sexes originates in these Christian ideas. Any standard that we use to judge them is a standard that would not exist without Christianity.

Christianity also put forward a radical vision of the role of children within the family. In the two so-called 'household tables' of the letters of Ephesians and Colossians, the apostle Paul spelled out the ideal reciprocal relationship between children and their parents. Children are to obey and to honour their parents as per the fifth commandment, whereas fathers are told not to provoke their children to anger (Ephesians 6:4; Colossians 3:21) but to 'bring them up in the training and instruction of the Lord' (Ephesians 6:4). While the ancient world had seen the father as having no obligation whatsoever to his children, such that he was permitted even to kill them if he did not want them for any particular reason, Christianity asserted something quite different: just as the husband was to lay his life down for his wife, so was he to expend himself in raising his children as disciples of Jesus Christ. Paul's attitude is congruent with the approach of Christ himself, who not only gave his time and attention to children but held them up as examples to follow:

'Truly I tell you, unless you change and become like little children, you will never enter the kingdom of heaven. Therefore, whoever takes the lowly position of this child is the greatest in the kingdom of heaven. And whoever welcomes one such child in my name welcomes me.

'If anyone causes one of these little ones – those who believe in me – to stumble, it would be better for them to have a large millstone hung round their neck and to be drowned in the depths of the sea.'

Matthew 18:3–6

When children were brought to him so that he might lay his hands on them and pray, his disciples rebuked the people, but Jesus said, 'Let the little children come to me, and do not hinder them, for the kingdom of heaven belongs to such as these.' When he had placed his hands on them, he went on from there.

Matthew 19:13–15

Again, such an attitude towards children is far more recognisable to modern people than those of the Greco-Roman culture which considered them as essentially expendable and inferior because they lack a fully developed sense of the Logos, and regarded sexual relationships with boys as young as twelve as normal and healthy.

Finally, on the issue of slavery, if we look at the historical record, we find once again that the critique of this practice emanates exclusively from within the Christian tradition. It is important to bear in mind that when the New Testament was written slavery was a ubiquitous and commonly accepted practice across every world empire, including those of the Greeks and the Romans, and that this had, quite literally, always been the case for as long as human history has been recorded. To abolish slavery would have required a major conceptual change and to put such an abolition into practice would have meant the economic and social overturning of entire societies that relied upon it. And yet the New Testament contains within its pages the seeds of abolition. In the letter to Philemon, for example, Paul asks the wealthy and powerful Philemon to forgive a slave he owned for running away. He appealed to the true relationship of slave and master which was, in this case, transcended by the fact that the slave Onesimus and his master Philemon were 'beloved brothers' in the Lord (Philemon 16). Elsewhere, Paul condemned 'enslavers' outright, with the word in the original context referring specifically to those who take human beings captive to sell them into slavery (1 Timothy 1:10).

It took time but eventually the Christian critique of slavery would develop and result in the outright condemnation of the practice. The first recorded instance of a specific denunciation appears to be that of Gregory of Nyssa in AD 369. In a sermon on a text from the book of Ecclesiastes, Gregory wrote:

> You are condemning to slavery human beings whose nature is free and characterised by free will. You are making laws which rival the law of God, overturning the law appropriate for humankind. Human beings were created specifically to have dominion over the Earth; it was determined by their creator that they should exercise authority. Yet you place them under the yoke of slavery, as though you are opposing and fighting against the divine decree.[17]

It has already been noted that slavery would all but die out in the Christian world by the end of the first millennium, and would only be revived at the advent of early modernity when empires such as the French, Spanish and subsequently the British resumed the practice. This was an admittedly bleak and terrible deviation from the Christian past, but, again, it would be challenged in the eighteenth and nineteenth centuries by figures such as William Wilberforce and the evangelical Clapham Sect who based their critique upon a specifically Christian understanding of the dignity of humanity that was being effaced in the enslavement of others.[*]

But the point that bears repeating in all this is that if, in the modern age, women or children are treated badly, if there has been racial prejudice or continues to be any form of slavery, then it is only Christianity that has made possible any critique of these

---

[*] From an American perspective, Yoram Hazony writes that the reintroduction of slavery to Western nations brought about disastrous consequences and so those nations sought to retrace their steps and to restore the conditions that existed prior to that terrible decision: '[This] is what happened in 1863, when Abraham Lincoln proposed that the evil of slavery, that unspeakable digression from the course of English constitutional history, would be abolished' (Hazony, *Conservatism*, p. xx).

societal imperfections in the first place. Without Christianity they would very likely be normal aspects of everyday human existence. The reason such critiques exist at all is because of the radical new vision of humanity that was bequeathed to the world through Jesus Christ and the Christian religion.

V

Ethics (2): Confused Ideas and Disturbing Trends

Confused Ideas

I wrote above about Alasdair MacIntyre's *After Virtue* and the story of an imagined world that had rediscovered fragments of the sciences after a catastrophe in which the overall framework of science had been forgotten. People argued over various scientific theories and ideas, but they had no background knowledge against which to judge these discussions. MacIntyre introduced this story to help us to see what has happened with ethical discourse in the modern age. We still argue passionately about what is right and wrong, and we still live as though right and wrong are indeed valid categories and yet, because we have lost the background knowledge that gave those terms meaning, we cannot really know if our judgements are valid or not. When we disagree on a moral judgement in the political or personal realm, what authority can we invoke to adjudicate between competing positions? In the secular sphere, the answer, ultimately, is that there is no objective authority, no background discussion to which we can point and therefore situate our moral claims. Moral discourse, shorn of religious and metaphysical context, is nothing but subjective preference. And so, in the post-Christian age, all we are left with is feelings about what is right and wrong.

The historical perspective helps us to understand what has really happened. Human beings in the Western world have been shaped profoundly by the Christian worldview and have absorbed much of its ethical outlook. However, because we no longer inhabit the imaginative world of Christianity and have shunned its metaphysics, the Christian outlook has become distorted and confused. We now operate with a contradictory bricolage of ethical standards and presuppositions that are best thought of as a deviant form of Christian ethics, a kind of heretical departure from the faith that has, regardless of whether we know it or not, shaped us all.

Nihilism, Freedom and Individualism

There are a few well-known trends that we can observe. The first is simply nihilism, the belief in nothing at all except for the primacy of the individual will. David Bentley Hart goes as far as to say that 'To be entirely modern . . . is to believe in nothing'[1] and: 'Modernity's highest ideal . . . requires us to place our trust in an original absence underlying all of reality, a fertile void in which all things are possible, from which arises no impediment to our wills, and before which we may consequently choose to make of ourselves what we choose.'[2] If the modern world has any originality about it, it is simply that it has (out of the destruction of the Christian religion) invented the notion that material reality is all that exists, that human beings are nothing more than a part of that material reality, and that, underlying all human experience and biological life, is simply nothing at all. There is thus no metaphysical court of judgement, no teleological structure to the universe or to human life, no purpose for which we were put here. What should we do, given this uncanny and bizarre situation in which we find ourselves? The only answer can be that, in the absence of any binding claim upon our existence, we should simply do whatever we choose. Choice, in this sense, becomes the highest and only ideal. What is chosen is not really the point. Rather *that* it is chosen – and chosen freely – is the issue of importance. 'To begin with, he is nothing,'[3] as Jean-Paul Sartre said. All that man can do is to make of himself whatever he chooses.

In many ways, this type of nihilism joined to the primacy of the will is a perfect example of a post-Christian confusion. In the absence of God or an underlying spiritual reality, of course it follows that humanity is not created for any particular purpose and that there is no given and authoritative set of ethical standards by which we should live. The confusion comes from the notion that there is an inherent good in the exercise of the individual will and that the will ought to be an object of respect and even reverence to others. It is true that belief in no God and no supernatural world *frees* the individual, in a completely radical sense, to act in whatever way he or she chooses. But this observation has no ethical aspect to it. Upon such a view, there is nothing morally good or bad about the exercise of the will because there is no ultimate and objective standard of morality by which to judge anything. There is nothing to adjudicate between the freedom of the will of *all* and the freedom of the will of the mighty. Why should the strong limit their freedom to respect that of the weak? Upon such beliefs, what really is the liberty of human beings in any case and why should it be respected? Once again, the only reason that we possess the instinct to liberate the weak from the oppression of the strong is because of the religious worldview that has shaped the West. Modern nihilism of the sort described here is therefore a kind of incoherent mixture of materialistic atheism and Christianity.

Freedom is a central concern of Christianity. In fact, the whole concept of free will derives from Christianity and thus provides the basis for modern individualism. As the atheistic philosopher John Gray writes:

> . . . the belief that human beings are marked off from all other animals by having free will is a Christian inheritance. Darwin's theory would not have caused such a scandal had it been formulated in Hindi India, Taoist China or animist Africa. Equally, it is only in post-Christian cultures that philosophers labour so piously to reconcile scientific determinism with a belief in the unique capacity of humans to choose the way they live.[4]

And yet Christianity does not understand freedom in the modern sense as freedom from constraint. Rather, the Christian religion understands freedom as the ability to achieve the purpose for which human beings were created: namely, eternal union with God. Thus, the greatest impediment to true freedom is not a religious creed or a set of unchosen cultural obligations but sin, which is a deviation from God's path for the human soul and which brings the individual will into the bondage of destructive and addictive habits of behaviour. Each person is called to the exercise of his will such that it may be liberated from the harmful consequences of sin and so that he might become eternally free to enjoy union with God. Again, there is a radically egalitarian aspect to this because the Christian creed has always held that this eternal destiny is offered not only to the elite class of male citizens or to a priestly caste but to all human beings regardless of social status. Thus the individual choices of every human being are of central importance within the Christian outlook. Not that this is an arbitrary celebration of freedom from restraint as it is in modernity however; it is, rather, indicative of the belief that every human being has been made in the image of God and is called by him to choose virtue over sin, holiness over depravity. The Church of England's Book of Common Prayer captures this idea most perfectly in the Second Collect for Peace, when it describes God as one 'whose service is perfect freedom'.[5] In the modern outlook, such a formulation would be a simple contradiction in terms, for to serve any will other than one's own is the polar opposite of freedom. And yet, in the Christian view, it is precisely *in* serving God's will that we can be freed from the tyrannous and sinful habits that enslave us.

Identity Politics and Wokeness

In recent years, we have seen the emergence of a new form of moral and political ideology which is often called 'wokeness' and which is associated with the concept of identity politics and political correctness. In the immediate historical context, wokeness has probably arisen because of an inherent flaw within the liberal political project. Liberalism offers as its two central values liberty and equality. But equality is notoriously hard to deliver in a world in which liberty is given to individuals of varying gifts, abilities and advantages. Therefore, these two values – liberty and equality – become pitched against each other in a kind of zero-sum game: if there is too much liberty, there cannot be equality. But conversely, if equality is forced upon people, it necessarily entails a confiscation of liberty. The woke outlook derives from a frustration with the lack of equality that liberalism is able to offer. The woke solution to the lack of equality is less freedom and more political and legal intervention: the only way that society can be truly equal is if people and structures are forced to be such by the law.

Wokeness is, at least superficially, concerned with marginalised and oppressed people and it says that a just society promotes the well-being of the weak and the downtrodden. It doesn't need repeating that this is a concept derived from the Judeo-Christian tradition, beginning with the liberation of the Jews from the tyranny of Pharaoh and culminating in the death of Christ himself on behalf of all. However, there are various components of the woke outlook that distort this Christian inheritance such that wokeness is really a kind of anti-Christianity. These components are best understood as an updated form of the Marxist paradigm.

To begin with, wokeness focuses itself upon unjust structures within society and claims that the problems of society can be solved by the transformation of those structures. Due to the legacies of Western colonialism and slavery, these structures are held to be historically and inherently racist and discriminatory. They are held to promote an ostensibly normative pattern of humanity which is exclusively white, heterosexual, able-bodied and male. Wokeness, therefore, possesses a doctrine of sin which is quite different from that of Christianity. In the latter, sin is something that originates in the human heart. Sin is the responsibility of the individual person and is confronted through repentance in light of the atoning death of Christ on the cross. In the woke outlook, sin is something not within the individual but *out there* in the unjust structures of society. Sin is not dealt with through individual repentance but through political activism. Repentance *is* called for but only on the part of some – namely, people who are any combination of white, heterosexual, able-bodied and male* – and this is not because of specific individual sins that these people have committed but because they belong to an oppressive class and because they have inherited that class's subconscious predisposition towards racism, sexism, homophobia, and other types of discrimination.†

Wokeness is neo-Marxist because it divides humanity into two groups constituting the oppressors and the oppressed. In Marx's philosophy, the oppressors were the capitalist bourgeoisie whereas the oppressed were the downtrodden proletariat.‡

In the communist outlook, the proletariat could only be free of societal oppression through the overthrow of the bourgeoise elite.

---

* The idea that discriminatory behaviour is subconscious and not engaged in on purpose is a central part of critical race theorist Robin DiAngelo's book *White Fragility*. According to DiAngelo, any attempt on the part of white people to excuse themselves of being racist (such as comparing themselves favourably in contrast to neo-Nazis) is simply a strategy of evasion which they must abandon if they are going to confront adequately the real problem. Racism is, thus, not a choice on the part of white people, but it is an inherent aspect of their existence that must be accepted and repented of continually. Cf. Robin DiAngelo, *White Fragility: Why It's so Hard for White People to Talk about Racism* (London: Allen Lane, 2019).

† It is also the case that repentance is required of those who, while not part of the oppressive (straight, white, male, etc.) class themselves, have subconsciously become complicit in upholding these power structures. Thus, in the woke view, people who are black from a racial perspective can nevertheless be called 'white' if they participate in the upholding of societal structures that support white racism.

‡ The simplistic Manichean dualism of Marx's philosophy is apparent at the very beginning of *The Communist Manifesto*: 'Freeman and slave, patrician and plebian, lord and serf, master and journeyman, in a word, oppressor and oppressed, stood in constant opposition to one another . . . Society as a whole is more and more splitting up into two great hostile camps, into two great classes directly facing each other: Bourgeoisie and Proletariat', Karl Marx and Friedrich Engels, trans. Samuel Moore, *The Communist Manifesto* (London: Penguin Books, 1888), pp. 2,3.

The struggle was held to be between the social classes and was understood in economic terms. In the woke outlook, the emphasis has changed from class and economics to categories of people who are said to possess certain types of privilege: white privilege, male privilege, straight privilege, and so on. The oppressed are those who have been discriminated against historically by those who possess these privileges and who do not possess any of these privileges themselves: non-white people, women, gay people, and other marginalised groups. In contrast to the classical Marxist view, the woke outlook does not concern itself primarily with social and economic class. Rather, the woke view is preoccupied with a matrix of oppression based upon race, biological sex, sexual orientation, and other types of perceived disadvantage. It results in a situation in which people of economic and class privilege can nevertheless be said to be highly oppressed, whereas those of a very deprived economic and social background are held to be inherently discriminatory because of their skin colour, biological sex, sexual orientation, and other factors.

Wokeness, like Marxism before it, is, I would argue, a kind of bastardised version of Christianity. The concept of sin is transferred from the individual to the structures of society, and sin is overcome not by God in Christ but through social activism and ultimately revolution. Utopia is secured not through the return of Christ but through political progress. Unlike Christianity, there is no benevolent underpinning to the world and no real belief in the image of God in humanity. In the woke view, the marginalised are simply organised into different groups and pitted against one another in an effort on the part of each to prove that *they* are the most oppressed and therefore the most entitled. The vision of a God who sacrifices himself on behalf of sinners is therefore fundamentally transformed into a kind of fetish for victimhood.*

---

* This is precisely the mistake that was made by the journalist Matthew Parris in his disastrous foray into atonement theology in two articles released around Easter 2023. The second of these articles was a truly

Ultimately, wokeness is not reflective of a peaceful God who seeks to reconcile his wayward creatures to himself through the sacrifice of his Son but speaks more of the ontology of violence and the chaos of primeval flux: at the bottom of all reality is simply difference, struggle, the competing sway of the forces of life and death. The structures of society are merely an oppressive embodiment of this reality and thus those who have found themselves on the wrong side of this eternal dialectic must arise and take the power back in an act of pure aggression. Racial harmony can only be achieved through the reversal of the white–black power imbalance. Justice between the sexes can only be won through the raising of women to a status higher than that of men. Vindication for gay people and those of atypical sexual orientations can only result from the queering of society and the displacement of the heteronormative outlook. Human culture is understood not as an environment in which true harmony within difference can emerge but as the arena of struggle, displacement and aggressive liberation. Relationships between people are not opportunities for self-giving, friendship and mutual enjoyment, but zero-sum vectors of mutual oppression. This is all indicative of a deeper

---

extraordinary attempt to critique two millennia of theological reflection on the atonement (with which Parris revealed himself to be completely unacquainted) whereas in the first of these articles – released on Easter Sunday – he attempted to argue that Christ's 'victimhood' was the foundation of the Christian religion. Parris singularly failed to understand that Christ's being a victim was in no way the main point of the atonement, nor did his victimhood *in itself* make him virtuous or his actions redemptive. Rather, it was the fact that Christ *gave* his life as a gift for others, and that that life was of such great value, the atonement became the basis for humanity's salvation and therefore the Christian religion. It is in the woke outlook that being a victim is *in itself* deemed to make a person virtuous. Cf. Matthew Parris, 'I'll choose heroes before martyrs any day', *The Times*, 07.04.2023, [https://www.thetimes.co.uk/article/ill-choose-heroes-before-martyrs-any-day-dls6z2xqk] and 'The Problem with St Paul', *Spectator*, 22.04.2023, [https://www.spectator.co.uk/article/irelands-violent-men-of-peace-2/].

nihilism than even that of the liberated individual will. It is a nihilism that sees not nothing at the bottom of everything, but struggle, suffering, violence and pain.

Climate Activism

There is one further ethical sensibility that is significant in the late modern Western world and that is the climate activism epitomised by Greta Thunberg and protest groups such as Just Stop Oil and Extinction Rebellion. This outlook does share some commonality with wokeness because it also emphasises oppressed groups. In this case, the oppressed are those who are held to suffer disproportionately from the effects of climate change, such as those who live in developing countries affected by floods and the younger generations of the Earth in general, who believe that there will be no world left for them to inhabit and thus fall into a kind of anxious despair.*

The climate alarmism narrative is best understood as a reversal of the Judeo-Christian idea of humanity as a mediator between the beasts of the field and the angelic realm of heaven. In this view, men and women are the crowning achievement of God's creation and are given dominion over the Earth to steward it and to flourish upon it. The climate alarmism narrative counters the Christian view by saying that humankind is not the crown of

---

* The relationship between the two is embodied in the politics of Greta Thunberg. For example, at a rally in November 2023, after the outbreak of war between Israel and Gaza, she invited Palestinian women to speak in support of the Palestinian cause. A man jumped on the stage in protest and said that he had 'come for a climate demonstration, not a political view'. After he was removed to the sound of loud booing, Thunberg joined the crowd in a chant of 'no climate justice on occupied land' – whatever that is supposed to mean – and said, 'As a climate justice movement, we have to listen to the voices of those who are being oppressed and those who are fighting for freedom and for justice.' Maroosha Muzaffar, 'Man grabs Greta Thunberg's microphone at Amsterdam climate protest', *Independent*, 13.11.2023, [https://www.independent.co.uk/climate-change/news/greta-thunberg-amsterdam-climate-protest-palestine-b2446187.html].

God's creation but a cancer upon the Earth which endangers its very existence.* It attributes to the Earth a kind of sacral status that elevates it in importance above the concerns of human beings, and thus it can be seen as a new form of paganism that worships the natural order as divine and has no transcendent conception of a spiritual realm beyond it.† In this way, the vision of man given to the world by Christian humanism is done away with and, in its place, man is subordinated to nature and should be sacrificed for it. Figures such as David Attenborough and Stanley Johnson say that there are too many human beings living on the Earth and so the number of people must be reduced dramatically. But what ultimately is the point of the Earth if it is not to provide a

---

* The 'humanity is a cancer' idea can be found in many places and the logic of it dates back perhaps to Thomas Malthus, who said in an anonymous pamphlet of 1798 that, while the human population will continue to rise, food supplies will not. Humanity will therefore encounter a shortage of food, which will entail war, famine and sundry types of death. More recently, the broadcaster and biologist David Attenborough has called humanity 'a plague upon the Earth' and has said, 'Either we limit our population growth or the natural world will do it for us.' Louise Gray, 'David Attenborough – Humans are plague on Earth', *Telegraph*, 22.01.2013, [https://www.telegraph.co.uk/news/earth/earthnews/9815862/Humans-are-plague-on-Earth-Attenborough.html].

† In his book *Pagans and Christians in the City*, Steven D. Smith argues that the fundamental difference between Christianity and paganism is that the latter had no conception of a transcendent realm beyond this world. Paganism, therefore, deifies and worships aspects of the natural world. Christianity, on the other hand, contains a supernatural component. The picture is complex because Christianity says that the sacred *is* present in the natural realm in many ways *but* that there is also a transcendent dimension to which manifestations of the sacred within nature point. Put more simply, Christianity says there is something beyond the natural world and that the worship of humanity is properly directed there. Smith says that, as we move away from Christianity, we are replacing it with an updated, modern form of paganism. Cf. Steven D. Smith, *Pagans and Christians in the City: Culture Wars from the Tiber to the Potomac* (Grand Rapids: William B. Eerdmans Publishing Company, 2018), pp. 1–15.

home for humanity to flourish? And who is going to choose who is sacrificed and who isn't?

In *Straw Dogs*, John Gray quotes the scientist and environmentalist James Lovelock approvingly, calling mankind 'a plague of people', 'an exceptionally rapacious primate' and (rather lamely) 'Homo rapiens'.[6] Lovelock calls us 'the human plague' and forecasts a population collapse in the near future which will mean that 'by the year 2150 the biosphere should be safely back to its preplague population of Homo sapiens'.[7] It is odd to read such statements written by human beings advocating cheerfully for the destruction of their own species. But there is a logical consistency here. Gray's book is based on the premise that there really is no difference between humans and other animals. Indeed, Gray makes the point that if Darwin is all we have to go on, then there really are no species in a fixed sense. As he writes, 'Darwin's discovery was that species are only currents in the drift of genes.'[8] So, not only is there no difference between humans and animals, but there is no such thing as humanity at all. Gray's point is that any type of human exceptionalism – whether that is Christianity or secular humanism – is based on an empirical falsity, which is that human beings are somehow special or unique compared to the other animals. According to Gray, they are not. And, because humans use up the planet's resources and cause a myriad of species to go extinct, the best thing for the planet would be that humanity simply disappear or, at the least, be vastly reduced in number and environmental impact.

However, this call for voluntary depopulation can only really be thought of as a preference that exists in the minds of people like Gray and Lovelock. For if human beings are just like any other animal, then just like any other animal, there is no objective moral code that they *ought* to adhere to. Why, then, save the planet for the other animals? It seems, once again, that we are back to a perverse and distorted Christian notion of self-giving sacrifice.

The subordination of the Christian religion to paganism could not be better embodied than in the display of the giant illuminated globe, *Gaia*, in Anglican cathedrals such as Durham, Rochester and Exeter. It will of course be argued that *Gaia* is simply a celebration of the beauty of the Earth and does not need to be interpreted as a form of pagan idolatry. However, the name '*Gaia*' is literally the name of a pagan goddess who is the embodiment of the Earth and through whose sexual union with Uranus, representing the sky, bore other races of demi-gods. The rationale given by all three cathedrals appears to make no specific mention of the Christian God at all, nor of Jesus Christ, but speaks, for example, of the desire for *Gaia* to create an 'over-view effect', which is described as 'a feeling of awe for the planet, a profound understanding of the interconnection of all life, and a renewed sense of responsibility for taking care of the environment'.[9] Durham Cathedral offers various options for interactions with *Gaia*, including a sunset silent disco and morning yoga. In both images advertising these events, women are pictured between the camera and *Gaia* with their arms held aloft in its direction as though worshipping it. Another image shows a small boy with his hand outstretched towards *Gaia* as though he is in prayer.[10]

Many will be inclined to see in this symbolism an overturning of the Christian humanist tradition and will be convinced that there is more to this than simply a harmless artistic installation in an Anglican cathedral. Rather, *Gaia* represents a focal point for a community to gather around a post-Christian and pagan religious vision of the world renewed through collective human activism.

This survey of major ethical trends in modernity surely points to great confusion and contradiction. The individualistic nihilism described posits the individual will and its free exercise as the source of morality. And yet the whole concept of free will came from Christianity and requires it in order to make sense. Indeed, upon a materialist paradigm we have little reason to believe that it actually exists at all. The neo-Marxist woke paradigm is simply replete with distorted Christian notions of liberation for the oppressed and the destruction of the wicked, and yet it is hopelessly twisted into a violent competition for power disguised as a plea for sympathy for victims. And the climate alarmism narrative ultimately posits the destruction of humanity for its own good, not acknowledging the fact that these notions of self-sacrifice are Christian in origin and can have no basis in material reality, since material reality cannot produce ethical obligations.

In other words, these ethical trends are still reliant, however unknowingly, upon Christian ideas. In order to develop a truly post-Christian ethic, one would need to look to a philosopher such as Friedrich Nietzsche. Nietzsche understood that concepts such as pity for the weak and concern for the marginalised originate in Christianity. Rejecting this, he argued that power is the central good of existence and championed its exercise over and against the weak and the pitiful. He saw this as a far more consistent outworking of atheism and materialism than contemporary ethical formulations. According to Nietzsche, the exercise of the will is itself the only and final good. Any other ethical claims are merely the fantastical chimera of a lost and rejected Christian age.

Disturbing Trends

If what has been said so far is true and the ethical inheritance of the Western world derives from Christianity and is still, to some extent, dependent upon it, then it follows logically and inevitably that, as Christianity declines, this ethical inheritance will disappear. We are heading towards a post-Christian age in which the moral framework of Christianity simply will not apply. In this post-Christian framework, mankind will no longer be seen as specially created by God and exalted above the beasts. He will be no longer the bearer of the image of God and therefore owed compassion and justice. Rather he will be simply another animal. And his species will be viewed as a plague upon the Earth. He will not have the right to life. He will not have the right *not* to be removed from this Earth when he becomes an inconvenience or a detriment to it. He will not have the right to fair and equal treatment. He will not have the right to food or running water. In fact, he will not have the right to anything because rights will be understood to be fictional concepts conjured up by governments and international courts which can be changed at their behest. The post-Christian age will be therefore the post-human age. And it has already begun.

Abortion

In addressing this issue, it should first be said that this is a very painful and difficult subject. I will argue below that the wide-spread practice and acceptance of abortion is indicative of a culture that has lost touch with the Christian understanding of humanity as made in the image of God. But this is not to marginalise the very real hardship that women can face when they find themselves unexpectedly pregnant. The point here is that abortion is an industry that is a component of the system-atic exploitation of women, and is thus not liberating or healing for them or anyone else involved. I believe that abortion not only destroys children, but damages women immensely. Compassion for women *and* children is, therefore, at the heart of what follows.

One of the most striking summaries of the arrival of this post-Christian age is provided by the Roman Catholic Cardinal Robert Sarah. Sarah grew up in a primitive village in Guinea, West Africa, and became the youngest bishop in the Roman Church at the age of thirty-four, having been appointed by John Paul II. He was influenced by that Pope's critique of Western modernity which he called a 'culture of death'. Cardinal Robert Sarah added that the West is intent on imposing this culture onto more traditional and less economically developed ones. There is therefore a hypocrisy in the Western narrative which preaches tolerance and equality, and wrings its hands over its colonial past, and yet has no qualms whatsoever about impos-ing its own values upon traditional cultures such as the one from which Cardinal Sarah came.

This is evident in the case of the worldwide proliferation of abortion. Sarah notes that, in 2014, one pregnancy out of four globally was terminated, which means that just over forty million abortions happened in that year alone. He observes that, in France, they have about one abortion for every three births. He also speaks of the situation in Africa:

> I see the astronomical sums that are promised by the Bill and Melinda Gates Foundation, which aims to increase exponentially access to contraception for unmarried girls and women, thus opening the way for abortion . . . What are the hidden motivations of these large-scale campaigns that will end in tens of thousands of deaths? Could it be a well-designed plan to eliminate the poor in Africa and elsewhere? God and history will tell us one day.[11]

The abortion debate in the West is usually framed between the right to life for the child and the right to choose for the woman. This is ultimately a futile dialectic which misses the crucial point. This is because rights are ultimately arbitrary unless they are grounded in a transcendent and therefore religious worldview. If they are not thus grounded, they can be confiscated easily by the powerful or trumped by those with ostensibly greater rights. The real question in the debate concerns the sacredness of humanity: are humans made in the image of God, loved by God, and destined for an eternity with him? Or are we, as John Gray says, just like the other animals, if not worse, because we are, quite literally, a plague upon the planet? Those are the real questions that affect the outcome on abortion.

If humanity is marked with the image of God then this applies to all human beings including those yet to be born. Surely, to deface the image of God by killing an unborn child is therefore an extremely grave evil. And yet, notice that this logic is the same logic that safeguards human life in *all* cases: the only reason it can ever be truly wrong to murder is because, first, there really are such things as right and wrong and, second, to murder a human being is a transgression of the moral law. And *this* is because human beings are made in the image of God and are endowed with a peculiar sense of dignity and sacredness. When we reject the notions that right and wrong are given to us objectively by God and that human beings are made in his image, not only does abortion become a definite possibility but ultimately anything and everything does. And this includes things that, at this time, may seem quite far-fetched.

Once again, we are faced with a logical choice, which is that we rediscover the Christian vision of a humanity in which all people, including the unborn, are made in the image of God and therefore should be treated with care, dignity and respect, *or* we continue down the kind of path proposed by John Gray and David Attenborough, which will involve the depopulation of the planet by various means.

Globalised abortion coheres with this agenda. It constitutes an industrialised form of eugenics on an enormous scale. Those who associate the word 'eugenics' more with the Nazis than modern-day liberals might be shocked to hear this, but it is nevertheless true. For example, the campaign group Don't Screen Us Out note that, in the UK, 90 per cent of babies found by pre-natal scans to have Down syndrome are aborted.[12] They also campaign against the blatantly eugenicist law that extends the twenty-four-week time limit for abortion for children who have Down syndrome, cleft lip and club foot to the point of birth. This is a truly extraordinary law which means that a fully formed child of nine months or even older can be legally murdered even a few minutes before birth if he or she is unlucky enough to be found with a slightly rotated foot.

The National Health Service website notes that the method for abortions after fourteen weeks is called 'Dilatation and Evacuation'. The information on the website is scant, but we are told that 'D&E' 'involves inserting a special instrument called forceps through the cervix and into the womb to remove the pregnancy'.[13] At the age of fourteen weeks, most children are about the size of an orange and many are beginning to grow hair on their heads and eyebrows. Their hearts have already been beating for ten weeks. Inserting forceps into the womb 'to remove the pregnancy' involves the literal crushing of this orange-sized human life, the snapping of the spine, the breaking of the skull, the deadening of the beating heart. It is an act of truly monstrous violence, visited upon the most vulnerable in all human society. It is almost unbearable to imagine the force needed to destroy children in the same way who have reached the twenty-four-week mark and beyond it. And yet UK law provides for children to be destroyed immediately prior to birth if they have Down syndrome, club foot or a cleft lip.

Nor are the practices of 'partial-birth abortion' and so-called 'live-birth abortion' merely theoretical. To give an example of the kind of techniques used in these practices, in 1996 a motion tabled in the UK Parliament proposed the banning of partial-birth abortion and cited instruction given by the Royal College of Obstetricians that doctors should ensure babies are killed prior to birth, in extreme cases by injecting the babies' hearts with potassium chloride or by 'withdrawing the foetus through the birth canal until only the head remains inside when the bottom of the skull is pierced and the brains sucked out, thus collapsing the head'.[14] Fortunately, most Western people still find such practices to be utterly barbaric, but there is evidence that late-term abortion, partial-birth abortion and live-birth abortion are becoming increasingly acceptable. For example, statistics show that in Canada in 2020/21, 127 live-birth abortions were carried out. These children were born alive and then were abandoned to die outside the womb.[15] And, at the time of writing, there are various proposals being suggested, particularly by Labour MPs, for the legalisation of abortion up to birth.[16]

What such examples disclose is the arbitrariness of rules around the timing of abortion. It is quite obvious that, referencing the example from the UK Parliament, there is no moral difference between sucking a baby's brains out immediately prior to birth or doing it immediately afterwards. But, to avoid the charge of murder, the abortionist must make sure that it is done before. The same logic is true of abortion at any time in the period of pregnancy. Limits of twenty-four or twelve weeks are just as arbitrary. All these time limits do reflect the futile debate about the right of the mother versus the right of the baby. But the question is ultimately about what a baby *is* and, in a broader sense, what humanity is. If human beings are nothing but organic sacks of meat thrown up by the evolutionary process, then nothing at all is really morally wrong because there are no such things as morals. We can kill as many children as we like just as they did in ancient Rome. But if human beings are made in the image of God and are possessed with a sanctity unique among the creatures of the Earth, then to murder a human being at any point is a grave transgression of the moral law. This applies to all people, men and women, from the womb to the tomb* and is especially true when it comes to the killing of the weak, the vulnerable and the innocent. There is no category of person that fits this description better than the unborn baby residing in his or her mother's womb, relying helplessly upon her for protection and nourishment. To invade that vulnerable space with implements of death and to kill the child growing there is one of the gravest acts of moral evil possible. The fact that the Western world has convinced itself that this act is not only justifiable in certain circumstances but it somehow constitutes a moral good for women to have the right to do this to their own offspring is perhaps the single most important piece of evidence that the world we live in now has cast off its Christian inheritance and has entered the post-Christian world of pagan depravity.

---

* The vast majority of Christian ethicists would recognise a distinction between murder and killing, however, and would admit that there are at least some circumstances in which the taking of life does not constitute murder. Examples of these instances might include soldiers killed in a just war or capital punishment.

Euthanasia

The post-human culture of death is not only manifested in the abortion industry but is becoming increasingly prevalent in the practice of, and support for, euthanasia. The argument for euthanasia is always framed in terms of compassion for the person who is suffering and would prefer to be put out of their misery. There is, of course, a certain logic to the view that, if there is no further meaning to human life than the experience of pleasure and the avoidance of pain and if there is no world beyond this one and no God to whom we are accountable, a person's excruciating suffering is pointless and therefore should be ended as soon as possible by a merciful and swift death. This is yet another example of post-Christian nihilism. Indeed, the same logic could be applied to human life at any point: once I am no longer happy, once I am no longer enjoying myself, once I feel a certain amount of pain as opposed to pleasure, then why not simply end my existence? This is why Cardinal Sarah says of euthanasia that it 'is the most acute indication of a Godless, subhuman society that has lost hope'.[17] For it is true that euthanasia is an expression of sheer despair at the futility of existence: the organism writhes in agony and, although it may have a human face, ultimately it is just a sack of nerves having an experience that we call pain. There is something deeply melancholic and almost touching about the narrative that promotes this view: human society, having lost hope in anything beyond this world and knowing that there cannot be any such thing as morality, nevertheless clings to the belief that to euthanise a human being who is experiencing intense and irremediable suffering is an act of love and mercy.

And yet, for all these arguments in favour of mercy killings, the reality is far more disturbing. The true story is not about Western modernity discovering the exercise of compassion in the state-sponsored killing of the terminally ill but about the manifestation of a post-Christian culture of death directed towards the most vulnerable and the least convenient. As Danny Kruger observes:

It is an apparent irony that, through the long centuries during which death was often drawn-out and painful, and the old, the disabled and the weak were genuinely a burden on families and communities, state-sanctioned euthanasia was never thought of; yet now that medicine is rapidly diminishing suffering at the end of life and we provide support, and indeed legal protection against discrimination and ill-treatment, to infirm and disabled people, our culture is clamouring for the right for doctors to administer lethal drugs to people whom they judge to be better off dead.[18]

As with the killing of babies through abortion, so in euthanising the suffering we are caught between two worlds. In hospitals throughout the West, babies and the suffering are cared for by doctors and nurses and visited by friends and family members who offer assistance and support. This is the Christian world, the world that imagined the concepts of orphanages and hospitals. The fact that this is the Christian world is still vaguely attested to in the presence of hospital chaplains who exercise the ministry of pastoral care in such places and occasionally perform emergency baptisms for infants who have been born but are not long for this world.

And yet, in the same hospitals, another world has emerged. This is the post-Christian world of death for the innocent and the vulnerable. In this post-Christian world, babies are not cared for and baptised but destroyed through violence and their remains disposed of with the rest of the clinical waste.[*] In this post-Christian world, the suffering are seen not as people to be nursed and tended to but as inconveniences who are costing the taxpayer money and are wearing out their overburdened relatives.

The clamour for euthanasia is caused by nothing less than a

---

[*] 'It occurred to me that I had no idea what modern abortion clinics do with fetal remains. The answer, I've since discovered, is that the remains are usually burned, along with other "clinical waste".' – Louise Perry, 'We Are Repaganizing', *First Things*, 10.2023, [https://www.firstthings.com/article/2023/10/we-are-repaganizing].

radical shift in our view of humanity. As Kruger notes, our technological and medicinal advances point in completely the opposite direction of this apparent necessity. What we are asking for in these cases is precisely the reverse of compassion but killing for the sake of our own convenience. And this is why the Christian world did not countenance state-sanctioned euthanasia, but the modern world does: Man is no longer made in the image of God and destined for eternity in heaven or hell. He is an animal and, if he is in pain, he should be put to death like one.

It should be noted that the motivations of those who argue for, and act on, this ideology are complex. Advocates claim to be motivated by compassion and it is doubtless true that many of them are genuine about this. But, in participating in the state-funded killing of the weak and the vulnerable, they are supporting the post-Christian culture of death that conceives of man merely as a beast. And *this* viewpoint will lead to much darker places.

It is often said that the main argument against euthanasia is that of the slippery slope: once you allow for euthanasia in the most extreme cases, it will inevitably be broadened to include cases which are increasingly less extreme. While the slippery slope argument can be attested to empirically by plentiful evidence, it must nevertheless be added that the slippery slope is not the fundamental issue. The issue is, rather, the inherent sanctity of the human person. Once we have rejected that notion, it makes perfect sense that we might start to euthanise the terminally ill and suffering. And that puts us in the same world in which it makes perfect sense to euthanise other types of people also. After all, it is surely discriminatory to deny euthanasia to some people on the grounds of age or because their suffering is not imminently terminal. And why should euthanasia be restricted to those with *physical* illnesses? What about the terribly depressed or those with intractable problems such as addictions, personal failures and financial debt? These people must be considered also and there is no logical reason to rule them out.

This iron-clad logic has begun to be played out in real terms in the Western world, parts of which have legalised euthanasia and are now implementing its grim effects. In Canada, since the inauguration of the so-called MAiD (Medical Assistance in Dying) scheme in 2016, the number of people who have been killed with the authority of the Canadian state via euthanasia has increased by about a third each year. At the time of writing, over thirty thousand Canadians have been euthanised, with the latest annual figures released for 2021 showing that about ten thousand Canadians were euthanised in that year alone. This accounts for around 3 per cent of all deaths in Canada. For comparison, this is more than deaths from diabetes which accounted for about 2.5 per cent in 2020 and more than deaths from flu and pneumonia together which accounted for about 2 per cent in the same year.[19] And Canada has long since departed from the notion that only those who are in extreme agony and facing imminent death should be eligible for euthanasia. For example, those with serious disabilities,[20] those with mental health problems, and those who face dire financial circumstances also qualify.[21]

As an example of the Pandora's box-like quality of this practice, consider the case of a Canadian man from Toronto called Alan Nichols. Nichols was hospitalised with suicidal depression. Within a month of being hospitalised, he had submitted a request to be euthanised and was killed. This happened despite concerns being raised by his family. He listed a single health condition as the reason for his request and that health condition was hearing loss. His family subsequently said that hospital staff were not helping him to use the cochlear implant that assisted his hearing and that the staff assisted him in requesting euthanasia. His brother, Gary, said of this, 'Alan was basically put to death.'[22]

Again, there is a paradoxical and even contradictory quality in all this: on the one hand, doctors and nurses are trained to care for their patients, to help them to become well and to return to their ordinary lives. But in the cases of abortion and euthanasia, the role of doctors and nurses is reversed. Once a baby is no longer wanted, it is no longer the subject of care and concern but becomes a target of destruction. Once a suffering patient decides that he wants to die, there is no longer any obligation to do anything for him but to arrange the lethal injection. Care has turned to killing. Two contradictory and opposite approaches are now met in the same profession: doctors are those who bring life *and* health and they are those who administer death and destruction. They have, in this sense, acquired a god-like quality over their patients. Again, many will say that they are motivated by compassion in carrying out these actions. Many others, it is hoped, look upon the transformation of their profession with abject horror.

But the most disturbing trend of all here is surely the extension of this practice to children. In 2005, the Netherlands became the first country since Nazi Germany to legalise the euthanising of children, followed by Belgium nine years later. At the time of writing, it is legal in Holland to euthanise children between the ages of one and twelve if they have 'such a serious illness or disorder that death is inevitable, and the death of these children is expected in the foreseeable future'. In Canada, the MAiD scheme has extended euthanasia to 'mature minors', stipulating that the deaths of these children should be 'reasonably foreseeable'. Writing in the *Spectator* magazine, Madeleine Teahan comments:

> Isn't everyone's death 'reasonably foreseeable'? The committee emphasised that 'MAiD should not be denied on the basis of age alone' and therefore, it should be accessible to any child whom doctors believe has 'requisite decision-making capacity' which is ominously vague, given the child is making a life-or-death decision.[23]

She goes on to point out that anyone who has lived with teenage children will know that their hormones and mental processes are a chaotic farrago of shifting emotions and opinions. And yet the parents of the children in question will not have their views about the killing of their own offspring considered but 'the will of the minor . . . will ultimately take priority'. Teahan writes with great insight that the logic of the case for euthanasia, once applied to adults in extreme pain and facing imminent death, can easily be widened and applied to anyone else, for, as a quotation from the Collège des médecins du Québec (which appears in Canada's report on the euthanising of minors) says, 'Suffering is independent of age and that suffering experienced by minors can be as intolerable as it is for adults.'[24]

Where is this trend heading? It is one of those areas in which we desperately need to abandon the notion of liberal progress and to view development in the same direction as leading to a hell on Earth in which the governments of the Western world have absolute power over the life and death of their citizens. If we continue in this way, it is surely an inevitability that not only will the state occasionally be involved in the killing of its citizens in the name of mercy but this will become routine and even mandatory. Again, as Danny Kruger writes on this, '. . . the logic of the first step, the decision that some people should be killed with the help of the state, has an irresistible force'.[25] Nor is this fanciful. The journalist Matthew Parris has argued with great candour that, once euthanasia is legalised in the UK (as, at the time of writing, appears imminent), the terminally ill, due to their alleged economic parasitism, would be pressured into taking their own lives. He comments: 'I believe this will indeed come to pass. And I would welcome it.'[26]

Child Pornography, Sex Trafficking and Pederasty

The logic of the culture of death always concerns children. Abortion is, of course, about the termination of children. And the rationale of euthanasia finds its culmination in the state-sponsored killing of children. The cult of climate activism insists that humanity is a cancer upon the planet and implies that the propagation of children is simply to spread the disease.

We saw earlier that Christianity did away with the social acceptability of pederasty and paedophilia which was socially common in the Greco-Roman world. This fact was well known to the French existentialists and postmodernists of the second half of the twentieth century. One of those was Michel Foucault, who wrote a four-volume history of sexuality, the purpose of which was to critique and deconstruct the Christian view of sexual ethics and to justify his own paedophilic inclinations. Foucault was quite explicit about this, actually harking back to ancient Greeks in his view that pederasty was the highest form of love. He signed a petition to the Assemblée Nationale in 1977 calling for the decriminalisation of acts of 'consensual' sexual relations between adults and children.* Also in 1977, sixty-seven signatories including Jean-Paul Sartre, Roland Barthes, Jacques Derrida and Simone de Beauvoir wrote to *Le Monde* demanding legislation that would entitle adults to have sex with minors. This was in protest to the jailing of three men for sex offences against children aged twelve and thirteen.†

The call for greater levels of leniency towards paedophiles in the present day is reflected in the increasingly common use of the term 'minor attracted person'. For example, the Scottish police were forced to issue an apology when it emerged that they had used this term instead of 'paedophile' in their 2022

---

* On this, see Daniel Johnson's review of the fourth volume of Foucault's *History of Sexuality*: Daniel Johnson, 'Michel Foucault: the prophet of pederasty', 04.2021, *Critic*, [https://thecritic.co.uk/issues/april-2021/michel -foucault-the-prophet-of-pederasty/].

† On this, see Louise Perry, 'France faces a reckoning over historic child sex abuse', *New Statesman*, [https://www.newstatesman.com/world/2021 /02/france-faces-reckoning-over-historic-child-sex-abuse]. As is usually the case with this sort of thing, it seems that Foucault's academic work and political activism were merely an attempt to justify the crimes he had perpetrated against children in the service of his own perverse desires. An article from *The Times* in 2021 alleges that Foucault was in fact an active paedophile who raped children between the ages of eight and ten when he lived in Tunisia in the late 1960s: Matthew Campbell, 'French philosopher Michel Foucault "abused boys in Tunisia"', *The Times*, 28.03.2021, [https: //www.thetimes.co.uk/article/french-philosopher-michel-foucault-abused- boys-in-tunisia-6t5sj7jvw].

year-end report. They claimed that they were simply attempting to use terminology that was consistent with the European Union's 'Horizon Europe Project', a research and innovation programme with a multi-billion euro budget, and tried to distance themselves from its use.[27] Additionally, Paul Dirks writes the following about so-called 'sexologists' like James Cantor and Michael Seto:

> [Cantor and Seto] have provided the 'expert' basis for the acceptance of pedophiles or increasingly in the language of the literature, 'minor-attracted persons'. They argue that based on peer-reviewed evidence and research, pedophilia is an innate 'orientation' just like being gay or lesbian, that it is highly resistant to change, and that the best we can do for pedophiles is to de-stigmatize their orientation and keep them 'virtuous' and from actually abusing children.[28]

In 2023, the ire of the corporate media in the US and the UK was directed towards the release of the film *Sound of Freedom*. This was ostensibly because the film depicted the beliefs of 'conspiracy theorists' who say that child trafficking and sex slavery is widely practised among the US elite. In fact, *Sound of Freedom* is based on the real-life experiences of special agent Tim Ballard, who spent sixteen years working to identify and release children who had been abducted and forced into sex slavery. Ballard notes that globally there are around six million children who are victims of sex slavery, labour slavery and organ harvesting, with the United States being the number one consumer of child rape material and close to the number one in production of that material.* The internet has, of course, provided the means by

---

* Ballard cites these statistics in Jordan B. Peterson, 'The Fight Against Worldwide Child Slavery & the Sex Trade', accessed 15.04.2024, [https://www.youtube.com/watch?v=rTBGNEliczc&t=1258s]. For more specific details on forced labour and forced marriage from a global perspective, encompassing the dimensions of forced child labour and sexual

which this disgusting industry is enabled to flourish, though it is only because of the degradation of the moral fabric of the West that such a thing is possible and that it is not more widely known or cared about. The attempt to suppress and discredit *Sound of Freedom* by the Western machine on both the left and the right suggests something deeply disturbing about the nature of this industry, which is that elites and opinion formers on both ends of the political spectrum would prefer that the truth is not known.

To speak of this trend heading somewhere darker is to be in danger of missing the point. It has already arrived at a point of absolute darkness: the mass enslavement, rape and exploitation of infants, the silence and cover-up of the elites, the widespread engagement with child pornography, and the forced prostitution of children. Currently this is all illegal but calls for legalised pederasty by the French existentialists and postmodernists might prove to be a harbinger of the return of legalised child abuse and the sexual exploitation of minors.

Post-Christian Patriarchy

The killing and abuse of children is inextricably linked with the abuse and subjugation of women. This is one of the saddest ironies of the pro-choice movement. For, in arguing in the name of feminism for the rights of women to kill their own children through abortion, women who support this view are in effect arguing for their own inevitable submersion into a post-Christian patriarchy. They do not recognise that the logic protecting the lives of the unborn is the very one that confers to women the same social status as that of men.

This observation is made powerfully by journalist and author

---

exploitation, cf. International Labour Organization, 'Global Estimates of Modern Slavery: Forced Labour and Forced Marriage', accessed 24.06.2024, [https://www.ilo.org/wcmsp5/groups/public/---ed_norm/---[ro]ipec/documents/publication/wcms_854733.pdf].

Louise Perry. In an article from 2023, Perry argues that it is the image of God suffering upon the cross that changed human perceptions of weakness and vulnerability. In the pre-Christian, pagan world, the weak and vulnerable were simply objects of contempt, whereas in the Christian world that followed they became associated with the suffering Christ and therefore were deemed especially worthy of care and respect. This argument is taken from Tom Holland's *Dominion* and is similar to that of this chapter so far: namely, that it was Christianity that introduced to the world the notion that all people, regardless of social status, class, sex, age, or anything else, were made in the image of God and so should be treated with dignity and respect.

The particular emphasis upon weakness, however, is helpful because it indicates why the cases of women and children are so closely tied together. This is because it is women and children who, in a world dominated by the notion that might is right, will be treated as socially inferior by men. This is why it was the case that, as Perry writes, 'Roman men enjoyed unrestricted sexual access to the bodies of their social inferiors, including children, and murdered infants were understood as an acceptable consequence of the need for frequent male sexual release.' In other words, the rape of women and the forced abortion or 'exposure' of their children was the price that the Roman world willingly paid for freeborn male citizens to be able to have sex with whomever they wanted. Only certain women were protected from rape, yet this was nothing to do with the women themselves but depended upon the men to whom they were related or married.

In the Christian era, violence against women (or indeed anybody else, including children and the unborn) became a violation of the *individual person*, who was seen as intrinsically valuable. The same logic protected the weak whoever they were. Christianity, in contrast to the prevailing culture, taught men to control their sexual lusts through the cultivation of chastity and to see that it was the protection of women and the vulnerable – and not their exploitation – that was virtuous. This is why Perry is correct to say, 'Feminism is not opposed to Christianity: it is its descendant.'[29] This is why feminism cannot survive the era of abortion: once the Christian protection of the vulnerable *child* is forgotten, it will not be long before the protection of the vulnerable *more generally* is forgotten. And this includes the physically weaker sex, women.

Indeed, the whole practice of abortion is hedged about by the notion that individual women operate in a fully autonomous space, that individual women choose with absolutely no coercion whatsoever who to have sex with and, if they become pregnant, whether or not to have an abortion. Louise Perry has done a service to women everywhere with her book *The Case Against the Sexual Revolution* by making it clear that young women are routinely subjected to social pressure to have sex with aggressive and predatory men and that, perhaps in the majority of cases, they would choose not to if they felt it was a viable option. She writes that 'the sexual revolution has not freed *all* of us, but it has freed *some* of us, and selectively, and at a price'.*

---

* Perry, *Revolution*, p. 7. Perry's book is a salutary riposte to the ideology of the sexual revolution; however, the book is deeply unconvincing in certain ways. For example, Perry frequently contrasts evolutionary biology and psychology with religion and specifically Christianity: 'We could instead understand human beings to be animals . . . As a consequence of these many different (evolutionary) legacies, coupled with evolutionary selection pressures favouring these traits, we sometimes demonstrate kindness, gentleness and friendliness. At other times we kill, torture and rape' (ibid., pp. 26, 27). The clear logical implication of this evolutionary anthropology is that there is no such thing as objectively existing morality or even free will and therefore to write a book about the way human beings *should* behave is somewhat pointless. Nevertheless, Perry's book is full of the notion that there is a certain ethical code that *ought* to be observed by human beings. At one point, she dismisses 'traditionalism' upon the grounds that the social and technological conditions of the present are different from those of the past (which is, really, a complete irrelevance to the question of ethics). In the place of the great religious traditions of the past that 'cannot teach us how to live in the twenty-first century', she posits an appeal to

Indeed, the people who have been truly freed by the sexual revolution are immature and irresponsible young men who do not have the social, cultural or financial capacity to marry and raise children and so are unwilling to accept the natural consequences of having sex. The cultural moment in which they live gives them almost unlimited opportunity to seduce young women into having sex with no strings attached. In the unfortunate scenario in which a young woman becomes pregnant, the man responsible can simply pressurise her to kill the child and then leave her to deal on her own with the physical, emotional, psychological, financial and spiritual consequences. We call this women's liberation but it is in fact a deception that is predicated upon the idea that anybody can make decisions about sexual conduct in isolation of the social factors that undoubtedly affect them. That is not how human society works, in this or any other scenario.

'moral intuition' (ibid., p. 65). Moral intuition now having been discovered, we can say that 'Sexual liberalism is misguided in not only disregarding but *actively resisting* our moral intuition' (ibid., p. 66). But at no point does Perry tell us what the source of our moral intuitions are or how we discover their content. Again, she writes, '. . . we should treat our sexual partners with dignity. We should not regard other people as merely body parts to be enjoyed. We should aspire to love and mutuality in all our sexual relationships, regardless of whether they are gay or straight. We should prioritise virtue over desire. We should not assume that any given feeling we discover in our hearts (or our loins) ought to be acted upon' (ibid., pp. 66–7). This is extremely wishful thinking on Perry's part: to imagine that she can reject the metaphysical framework that has clearly formed her moral intuitions and replace it with an evolutionary anthropology that makes literally no distinction between human beings and other animals, and yet, at the same time, to hold forth on a creed of sexual ethics that is blatantly drawn (albeit with some deviation) from a Christian worldview. Animals cannot be said to treat their sexual partners with dignity or aspire to love and mutuality. They do not prioritise virtue over desire. And they most certainly *do* act upon their most primitive instincts. To say that we ought to be different is to elevate human conduct far above that of the animals, and, upon an atheistic and evolutionary schema, there is absolutely no reason that anybody *should* do so.

In any single abortion, there are numerous familial, financial and social factors involved, both in terms of the decision to have an abortion, and in terms of the consequences that follow afterwards. In other words, what we do with our bodies has a far greater and wider effect than any physical actions in isolation. It is not only the mother and her baby who are affected by abortion, but the mother and father's family and friends also. There is also a more general, cumulative social impact that goes along with the practice which is less tangible but nevertheless real and far-reaching. It arrives in the sense that the life of the unborn is less valuable and proceeds to the implication that the life of children and vulnerable people in general is also less valuable. To recall the language used earlier, over time these intuitions become part of our social imaginary, and we find it hard to conceive of things in any other way.

Louise Perry's book goes into much greater detail than is possible here. Suffice it to say that she demonstrates that the culture of promiscuity and pornographic saturation is creating generations of young men who are addicted to pornography and masturbation, impotent in real-life sexual encounters, and frequently incapable of sustaining habits such as holding down regular work and maintaining personal health and hygiene that would help them to develop into mature and responsible adults. The culture of porn and casual sex does not promote virulent, attractive, responsible, strong young men but a generation of males who are trapped in permanent physical and psychological immaturity. In the past, a young man had to prove himself worthy of a woman's love through having a good job, maintaining his physical appearance, developing social skills, and thus demonstrating a capacity to take responsibility for her and her future offspring. Only after the man had proved his worth and committed his whole life to the woman in marriage would the *act* of marital union be consummated. In today's world, men have to do none of this. They simply pressurise young women into casual sex upon pain of insult and ostracisation.

Perry also demonstrates that this innovation is not, on the whole, something that women enjoy. Casual sex and the various forms of sadomasochism that frequently accompany it are favoured by men and not by women. And pornography is overwhelmingly used by men and has little audience among the opposite sex. Indeed, the porn industry is essentially the industrial exploitation of women by men. Perry gives the shocking example of the star of the famous porn film *Deep Throat*, Linda Lovelace, whose real name is Linda Boreman. Boreman was systematically abused and coerced into prostitution and pornography by her first husband, Chuck Taylor. Although Lovelace, at the height of her fame, defended the porn industry and her role within it, her subsequent writings tell a very different story:

> They treated me like an inflatable plastic doll, picking me up and moving me here and there. They spread my legs this way and that, shoving their things at me and into me, they were playing musical chairs with parts of my body. I have never been so frightened and disgraced and humiliated in my life. I felt like garbage. I engaged in sex acts in pornography against my will to avoid being killed.[30]

This was a woman who some years before had been making the case for porn by saying that children need to be taught that sex is good and this would ensure fewer neurotics in the world. On Linda Boreman, Perry comments, 'This is a consistent pattern: women who have worked in porn will conform to the liberation narrative while they're still a part of the industry and share the dark side of their experience once they've left.'[31]

The permissive and porn-saturated culture has played a remarkable psychological trick. It has, on the one hand, told us that it is indicative of a culture that has liberated women from their historic oppression by men. And yet, on the other, it has shamefully and graphically exposed women to public male lust and abuse on a scale never previously imaginable. This, we are told, is how women can be free, by submitting themselves to the basest desires of the other sex. It is hard to disagree with the words of Cardinal Sarah:

> Today, so many organizations and groups advocate women's liberation so that they can be in control of their own bodies and destinies ... In fact, women's bodies are exploited, utilized in many circumstances, often for publicity and commercial purposes, so that they become a mere merchandise and sex object ... The West is the continent that most shamefully humiliates and despises women by publicly stripping them naked and utilizing them for hedonistic and commercial purposes ... How can anyone pretend that free access to pornography through the new means of communication, which is spreading a despicable view of sexuality – something sacred in itself, however – throughout society and even among very young people, is an example of progress in the world? How are we to understand the fact that the major UN agencies that claim to champion human rights do not fight vigorously against the powerful European and America sex industry?[32]

Indeed, the reason is that the UN and other organisations that claim to care about women's liberation are in the thrall of a post-Christian ideology that is committed to the absolute breakdown of the previous order in which women were differentiated from men and were thus far more protected socially and legally from sexual exploitation. Sarah is surely correct when he concludes: 'All of these dark clouds are signs of a world that lives far from Christ. Without the Son of God, man is lost and humanity has no future.'[33]

Once again, the post-Christian patriarchy will simply intensify as we move further and further away from our Christian moorings. It may go on under the pretence that it is in fact liberating women from their bondage or it may simply remove the mask and reveal what it has been all along: namely, just another way for the strong to exploit the weak and the vulnerable.

Some of the claims surrounding transgenderism illustrate where the post-Christian patriarchal ideology is heading. Notably this involves the inclusion within women's spaces of men who claim to be women and therefore argue that they have a right to compete in women's sports, use women's changing rooms and toilets, or to be accommodated in women's prisons. Such a position was not even thought of until the recent past and yet now this viewpoint has become so widely and passionately promoted that, in some cases, to speak against it is punishable by law.*

There are various disturbing examples of this phenomenon. Lia Thomas is the name of a US swimmer who identifies as a 'transwoman' but who is in fact a six-foot-two, fully endowed man. Riley Gaines (a female swimmer) tied against Thomas in the American National Collegiate Athletic Association (NCAA) championships and is now an outspoken advocate for keeping men out of women's sports. She claimed that being forced to change in the same locker room as Thomas was 'like a bad car wreck' and that some of the women opted instead to get changed in the janitor's closet.[34] In April 2023, Gaines was ambushed and attacked at San Francisco State University by a group of transgender rights protestors, one of whom was a man wearing a dress who hit her twice. She was called a 'f***ing transphobic bitch' and had to be evacuated by police and barricaded in a safe place for three hours.[35]

Meanwhile Lia Thomas managed to improve his ranking at

---

* At the time of writing, the most troubling legal development in the Western world is surely the Scottish Hate Crime and Public Order Act, which makes various types of 'threatening or abusive' behaviours illegal such as those which are intended to 'stir up hatred' against people with transgender identities. Critics of the Act have noted the vagueness of the language involved and that it is not entirely clear what constitutes stirring up hatred against those with transgender identities. But it is surely possible that claims such as the ones made in this chapter and similar might constitute falling foul of this new law. Cf. Scottish Government, 'New Hate Crime laws come into Force', 01.04.2024, [https://www.gov.scot/news/new-hate-crime-laws-come-into-force/].

UPenn in 2022 from sixty-fifth in the 500-yard freestyle, when he was competing as a man, to first now that he was in the women's competition, and from a rather disappointing 554th in the men's 200-yard freestyle to fifth in the equivalent women's event.[36] This was a miraculous improvement, especially seeing as we are still told by a well-known UK newspaper that 'the data' show that Thomas did not have an unfair advantage in the women's events. The main piece of data appears to be the observation that, although Thomas achieved 'impressive results . . . they weren't record breaking', and that some women involved performed better than he did.[37] The author of the article does not seem to consider the possibility that Thomas is, in reality, a mediocre male athlete who is able to beat most women by virtue of his being a different biological sex.

Even worse is the same trend manifested in the world of Mixed Martial Arts (MMA). Fallon Fox is the name of a man who 'came out' as transgender in 2013 and then proceeded the following year to fight a woman called Tamikka Brents. This forty-five-year-old man beat his female opponent so badly that she suffered concussion, had seven staples applied to her head, and sustained a fracture of the skull.[38] Fox is five-foot-seven inches and has visibly muscular arms. His shoulders are broad and are clearly those of a biological man. His physique contrasts significantly with the slender frames and smaller arms of the women he fights. After having her skull broken by Fox, Tamikka Brents said of him, 'I've fought a lot of women and have never felt the strength that I felt in a fight as I did that night. I can't answer whether it's because she was born a man or not because I'm not a doctor. I can only say, I've never felt so overpowered ever in my life and I am an abnormally strong female in my own right. Her grip was different, I could usually move around in a clinch against other females but couldn't move at all in Fox's clinch.'[39] Brents' evaluation is extremely sympathetic since this is another area of the culture in which inappropriate language is used to denote terrible realities. Fallon Fox is not a 'transgender athlete' but a male mediocrity and the women he fights are not his 'opponents' but his victims.

The referees taking charge of these encounters are not presiding over sporting contests but facilitating the public beating and injuring of women.

There is a passage in the Bible which is regularly denounced as patriarchal and patronising. It is taken from the first letter of Peter. There Peter tells husbands to 'be considerate as you live with your wives, and treat them with respect as the weaker partner and as heirs with you of the gracious gift of life' (1 Peter 3:7). The Christian ethic of relations between men and women, husbands and wives, is that of mutual understanding and service. It takes into account the biological differences between the sexes, including the differentiation in physical strength. Men are called to tame their lustful and aggressive instincts and to harness them so that they might protect those who are weaker and more vulnerable. In our post-Christian age, we have jettisoned such moral wisdom and now attempt to convince ourselves that there is not any significant biological difference between men and women. The result is Fallon Fox, sitting astride Tamikka Brents on the floor of the MMA Octagon, beating her incessantly about the head and the face until her skull breaks. Which vision is more appealing?

This analysis could go on, but perhaps the most extreme example of this trend is found in the placement of male sex offenders in women's prisons. Many women who find themselves in prison are from difficult backgrounds themselves and have been violently assaulted, raped or otherwise abused by men in the outside world. It is surely an act of barbarous inhumanity to introduce aggressive and predatory males into this literally inescapable arena. And yet that is exactly what has been happening under the auspices of transgender 'inclusion'. Karen White was a fifty-two-year-old man who bore absolutely no physical resemblance to a woman when he was introduced into a female prison in 2017. His mugshot is that of a grey and balding overweight male with a double chin and comprehensive stubble. He was a convicted paedophile and was on remand for grievous bodily harm, burglary, multiple rapes, and other sexual offences against women. This was all known to the authorities when he was transferred to New Hall prison in West Yorkshire. It comes as no surprise that during this time he sexually assaulted two of the women prisoners.[40]

In an article for the *Spectator*, Julie Bindel relates the case of Amy, a woman who was sexually assaulted in prison by another man identifying as a woman who had been convicted of sexual offences against women and children. Amy brought a legal challenge against the Ministry of Justice over the policy that allowed this, but the judge ruled that banning men from women's prisons would be unfair and would infringe on their right to live as their chosen gender. The Ministry of Justice said at the time that the policy is about 'protecting transgender people's mental and physical health'.*

Pushed to its most logical extreme, the transgender ideology will mean the complete erasure of women from public spaces and the total subjugation of women to male lusts. All a man will have to do to preclude interrogation and to give himself maximal opportunity to rape and assault will be to claim that he is, in fact, a woman. This ideology is deeply confused and damaging, but it seems that there is something even more pernicious than that beneath it. In addition to the denial of biological reality, it is also a denial of the Christian ethic of male and female: specifically that of men's duty to use what strength they may have to love, respect, care for and protect those who are weaker and more vulnerable. Perhaps many men would simply rather not fulfil this role and would prefer the situation to revert to that of ancient Rome with

---

* On the plight of staff in women's prisons, Julie Bindel writes, 'Female prison officers are forced to encounter these men in the course of their work, being subject to verbal threats, sexual harassment or even having to carry out intimate searches on male-bodied people. One female prison officer told me about walking into a cell occupied by a transwoman who was masturbating and refused to stop when told to.' Julie Bindel, 'No man should ever be sent to a women's prison again', *Spectator*, 04.02.2023, [https://www.spectator.co.uk/article/no-man-should-ever-be-sent-to-a-womens-prison-again/].

themselves in the place of the freeborn, male citizen. They would like to beat and rape women and children with impunity and to be protected by their social status. Transgenderism is the gift that gives them that opportunity.

Recognising This

The moral arc of the universe does not bend towards justice. Moral progress is a myth that is frequently invoked in Western culture to disguise a most disturbing fact; namely that we have no shared moral framework but are borrowing fragments of older belief systems and living off their intellectual capital. Chief among these is a belief in the dignity of humanity and this belief is dependent upon our Christian inheritance. And yet that borrowed intellectual capital will inevitably be spent before long. The conclusions of Christian morality are drawn from the premises of Christian belief. Once people stop believing in the Christian view in the broadest sense, it will only be a matter of time before they realise that there is no longer any binding reason to retain inconvenient moral hangovers that also derive from Christianity.

This realisation has already manifested itself in the widespread proliferation of the practice of abortion and it is continuing to metastasise in the increasing acceptance of euthanasia. In his encyclical *Evangelium Vitae*, Pope John Paul II described the late modern West as promoting a 'culture of death', and he was surely right to do so.[41] Coupled with our growing desire to kill the young and the weak is our reluctance to have children of our own. Here the apocalyptic climate narrative surely has a part to play as our young people are told that to have children is to populate the planet with a cancer that is killing it. But there is also a sense in which the nihilistic emptiness and individualism that permeates the experiences of younger people profoundly discourages them from committing to long-term relationships and reproducing from them. They have been taught that life is all about self-expression and that hindrances to self-expression are to be shunned and deconstructed. Why then would they take upon themselves one of the most extreme limitations possible in the form of becoming parents to demanding children?

This is all borne out by the evidence as the UK faces the fact that, by 2025, for the first time in recorded history, more people will die than are born here. And yet, immigration to the UK will continue, mostly from Islamic and other non-Western cultures.[42] It may be the case that our late modern Western populations will simply be replaced by other peoples who have a different ethic of reproduction from us. This is by no means a fantasy when we consider the statistics. In 2021, birth rates in France were lower than the rate of reproduction at 1.83 children per woman. In Spain they were even lower at 1.19 – a 29 per cent fall compared with a decade earlier. In South Korea in 2020, birth rates were as low as 0.84 children per woman, less than half the number needed to keep the population at a stable rate.[43] A report by the UN predicts that, by 2100, more than twenty developed countries will see their *populations* halve. These include Italy, Japan, Portugal, South Korea and Spain.[44] If these trends continue, it is a certainty that Western culture will be eclipsed by cultures that have stable and growing rates of reproduction, especially if immigration to Western nations like the United Kingdom continues at something like the present rate. This is a statistical inevitability. This is indicative of the fact that our culture is not only one of death but one of non-life.

In the absence of a replacement by foreign peoples, the culture of death will be joined with the rule of the strong, for it is only Christianity that has acted as a bulwark preventing the domination of the weak by the powerful. Even if Christianity is respected as a cultural phenomenon, metaphorical myths cannot withstand genuine belief in the reality of an alternative moral order. And the alternative moral order we are coming to believe in is that of individualistic ethical nihilism. The true outworking of that belief system is ultimately the subjection of the weak to the strong. We are already seeing the manifestation of this order in the practice of abortion and are likely to witness it further in that of euthanasia. We will see it ever more in the post-Christian patriarchy which is now emerging, with many of the claims of transgenderism acting as the thin end of the wedge.

There are various intellectuals and public thinkers who recognise much of this. The popular historian Tom Holland has pointed this out in great detail, acknowledging, for example, that the concept of human rights derives from medieval scholastic legal disputes and was not known outside a Christian framework; that the idea of secularism as a separation of religious and civic powers comes to us from a dispute between a medieval Pope and the head of the Holy Roman Empire; that the notion of humanism derives 'from claims made in the Bible: that humans are made in God's image; that his Son died equally for everyone; that there is neither Jew nor Greek, slave nor free, male nor female',[45] and many other things besides. At the end of his major survey, Holland asks the crucial question:

> If secular humanism derives not from reason or from science, but from the distinctive course of Christianity's evolution – a course that, in the opinion of growing numbers in Europe and America, has left God dead – then how are its values anything more than the shadow of a corpse? What are the foundations of its morality, if not a myth?[46]

The answer is, of course – if we have the courage to face it – that the values of Christianity are nothing but the shadow of a corpse and a myth *if* we persist in the belief that God is indeed dead. And it will follow from there, inexorably, that the gifts the Christian religion has bestowed upon the world and the moral precepts that we still cling to (albeit altered and incoherent) will fade away like a dream. Human rights, protection of the weak, equality of the sexes and, more broadly, Western civilisation itself as the birth rate declines and as we are eclipsed by Islamic and other foreign cultures: all of this will disappear. We may be left with a secular post-Christian patriarchy or with a state dominated by Sharia law. Either way, it will not resemble what we have now.

The alternative is a return – a *real* return – to Christianity, whether that is in terms of fully fledged belief or in support of the religion as a necessity to civilisational survival. And yet, support alone is not enough. To have a Christian civilisation, there must be many who genuinely believe that it is true and live as though it is. The two types of pro-Christian stance (belief and support) might be likened to a medieval cathedral. Those who are supportive but are not Christians themselves are like flying buttresses that hold some of the weight of the building. The Christian believers, however, are like the enormous interior pillars that hold up the ceiling. Both are necessary but the pillars are always vital. Without them, the edifice will crumble before long.[47]

It is an odd way to approach things in some respects, but perhaps for many of us real belief in Christianity might start with a hope that it *might* be true, and with a realisation that, if it is not true, everything we hold dear is lost. A person hoping it might be true might find confirmation in the manifold goods bestowed upon us by Christianity, and might see that no other belief system in the history of humanity has so blessed and dignified the world nor contributed so greatly to its beautification. Such a person might observe that the intellectual tradition of Christianity – the oldest and most powerful intellectual tradition in the Western world – is far more robust and serious than they had been led to believe previously. And that person might, as a result, begin to hope that there is, in fact, a real light that will overcome the looming darkness.

There is no middle path. It is salutary to have public intellectuals like Tom Holland, Louise Perry, Jordan Peterson and Douglas Murray give significant credence to the cultural importance of Christianity. But we must go further – much further – into the realms of real belief and practice. Without this, the night comes, and it may be coming more quickly than at present we imagine.

VI

The Church: Defence and Offence

... you must remember that Humanitarianism, contrary to all persons' expectations, is becoming an actual religion itself, though anti-supernatural. It is Pantheism; it is developing a ritual under Freemasonry: it has a creed, 'God is Man,' and the rest. It has therefore a real food of sorts to offer religious cravings; it idealises, and yet it makes no demand upon spiritual faculties. Then, they have the use of all the churches ... and all the Cathedrals; and they are beginning at last to encourage the sentiment. Then, they may display their symbols and we may not ...

Robert Hugh Benson, *Lord of the World*

Where We Are Now

My goal so far has been to outline some of the most serious consequences for the Western world of the decline of Christianity and to make the point that these consequences are coming about because the gifts that we most cherish and take for granted originated in the Christian past and are dependent upon the belief in, and practice of, the Christian religion. In the introduction to this chapter, I intend to describe in more general terms the trajectories that look likely as a result of the decline of Western culture. My argument, again, is that these things will happen because of the decline of Christianity. The reason this chapter is about the Church is because, ultimately, the Church is the only human institution (albeit divinely graced and inspired) that can hold out against the onslaught which is in all likelihood coming upon humanity. It is absolutely imperative that the Church in the West recovers its authentic Christian identity, therefore, in order that it might resist the coming

243

darkness. But, before I address the Church directly, more on the darkness itself.

As the Christian religion fades, so do its benefits. We cannot have the fruit without the root. I have so far argued that we have been propagandised into believing that the modern world is a break from the darkness of the Christian past, an escape from Christianity. This is the polar opposite of the truth, however, because the Western world is dependent upon Christianity for almost everything it values. Chief among these are surely the notions of reason and scientific progress, both of which first took hold not in the early modern and Enlightenment period as people bravely threw off the shackles of religious ignorance (as we have been told) but in the Christian medieval period, when the first organised institutions of higher learning were set up in major religious centres in Europe. We have examined how the materialist secularism that we have attempted to use to replace Christianity has cut us off from the aesthetic dimensions of existence, by which I mean those moments in life that help us transcend the mundaneness of everyday experience and put us in touch with something above us in a truly meaningful and spiritual sense. In place of these encounters, we have substituted crass displays of artistic self-expression, soul-destroying architecture, and a million other cultural expressions of nihilistic emptiness.

Perhaps the most serious and central claim of this book, however, is that we are fast losing our conception of humanity itself. In the Christian period, we believed in the image of God in humankind and therefore that all people should be treated as sacred beings and therefore afforded a significant degree of respect, care, dignity and fairness. These beliefs would eventually become deeply embedded in the political and legal systems of Christianised countries, albeit imperfectly and to different degrees. As we abandon belief in the Christian religion, it is becoming clearer that we are abandoning too the notion of the image of God in humankind with increasingly distressing results. We are disposing of the unborn in their millions with the justification of personal autonomy and we are doing away with the sick and the elderly under the inauthentic rhetoric of compassion. We have also seen that the equality of the sexes is an idea that is completely incomprehensible outside a Christian framework which will not long survive the collapse of the Christian belief system and that a more obvious manifestation of a post-Christian patriarchy is soon to follow.

In addition to what we might call 'ideological' problems related to the decline of Christianity, there are also more practical concerns. I have spoken of the declining birth rate in post-Christian countries and observed that this, coupled with high levels of immigration, will inevitably (from a statistical perspective) result in the replacement of those Westernised populations with non-Westernised populations and could result in these nations becoming Islamic both culturally and politically.

This scenario has been imagined in some detail by the contemporary novelist Michel Houellebecq, whose 2015 work *Submission* portrays an Islamic party winning the 2022 French presidential election with the help of the Socialist Party. Upon election the Islamic party immediately implement Sharia law which involves, among other things, the wearing of the hijab in public for all women, the Islamification of all educational establishments including universities, and the introduction of polygamy. During the novel, the new Muslim president announces plans to expand the European Union to include parts of Northern Africa, the Levant and Turkey. With an Islamic France at its head and with several Islamic countries incorporated into it, the EU looks set to become a new Islamic empire for the twenty-first century. One of the most interesting aspects of the novel is that the male, Parisian academic who is its protagonist decides at the end of the story to convert to Islam because he sees the material and social benefits of the patriarchal culture with its social and sexual hierarchies. Far from being an 'Islamophobic' novel as it was called by the (real) French Prime Minister Manuel Valls, *Submission* suggests that Western people, particularly Western men, might actually enjoy living under Sharia law and becoming Muslims more than they do living as isolated, porn-addicted loners in a socially atom-ised liberal democracy.

Whether the West is captivated by Islam or not, there is a statistical demographic reality that makes Muslim-majority populations in Western nations such as the UK an inevitability. Islam will have no sentimental gratitude to Western liberals for allowing Muslims to emigrate to their countries.

In 2023, the formerly atheistic thinker Ayaan Hirsi Ali declared herself to be a Christian. The principal reason she gave for her conversion was that she believed that only Christianity could provide a substantive defence against the three major threats that she saw gathering against Western civilisation. Ali, having previously embraced the new atheism of Richard Dawkins *et al.* as a reaction to her strict Islamic upbringing, admitted that the atheism she was embracing was 'too weak and divisive to fortify us against our menacing foes'.[1] She elaborates:

> Western civilisation is under threat from three different but related forces: the resurgence of great-power authoritarianism and expansionism in the forms of the Chinese Communist Party and Vladimir Putin's Russia; the rise of global Islamism, which threatens to mobilise a vast population against the West; and the viral spread of woke ideology, which is eating into the moral fibre of the next generation.[2]

I have already mentioned two of these forces: namely, Islam and woke ideology. And Ali might be correct about the third foe she mentions, namely the alliance of Russia and the Chinese Communist Party. But it seems to me that a far more insidious and serious threat is posed by globalist forces within Western democracies themselves that clearly desire to subvert those democracies in the creation of both a European and a global super state run by a cadre of elite technocrats. Such concerns may have seemed outlandish only ten years ago but, after the events of March 2020 and onwards, they cannot be dismissed as a paranoid fantasy.

I speak here of the global shutdown brought about by the fear of Covid-19. This was a phenomenon of immense complexity, but the forces of global technocracy have never been more clearly revealed to the general public. It was apparent that the main drivers behind the so-called 'non-pharmaceutical interventions' and the associated ideology that went along with them were globalist organisations such as the World Health Organisation who, in concert with the power of the pharmaceutical industry and government regulatory agencies, applied pressure upon national governments with the assistance of the corporate media.

Whatever else all this was, it amounted to a profound denial of the legal, political and cultural inheritance that was given to the West by Christianity over a period of hundreds and even thousands of years. In her essay, Ali says that the only thing that can unite the West now is 'the legacy of our Judeo-Christian tradition', and yet almost everything she mentions in that regard was either ignored during the Covid shutdowns or altogether opposed. On the Judeo-Christian tradition, she writes:

> That legacy consists of an elaborate set of ideas and institutions designed to safeguard human life, freedom and dignity – from the nation state and the rule of law to the institutions of science, health and learning . . . all sorts of apparently secular freedoms – of the market, of conscience and of the press – find their roots in Christianity.[3]

The globalist forces pushing Covid shutdowns could not have been more opposed in spirit to this legacy. Freedom was, of course, the first casualty, as literally billions of people were forcibly locked in their homes. In Britain, breaking the so-called 'lockdown' could have resulted in fines and arrests, while in other countries people were brutalised and murdered by the police for leaving their houses.[4] The dignity of the citizens of these nations was transgressed, as the elderly, children, adults with developmental disabilities such as autism, and many other types of people suffered terribly as a result of being deprived of their normal routines and sources of sociality. One of the most awful aspects of the response was the banning of family and friends from the bedsides of those who were dying. People died alone in NHS hospitals in Britain, attended to only by doctors and nurses anonymised as a result of their personal protection equipment. The rule of law, that precious legacy of the English Constitution, was simply discarded as the UK Government cynically used the 1984 Public Health Act to justify its manifold transgressions of the legal rights of its citizens. 'Science' was brandished as an excuse for governments not to take responsibility for their actions. It was politicised in a cynical and manipulative way to give the impression that science as a discipline could offer up simple and comprehensive answers to the questions of what exactly was going on and, more egregiously, what should be done about it. Businesses – mostly small and medium-sized, including a multitude of family-owned enterprises – were mercilessly destroyed. Those who questioned the ideology were labelled refuseniks and told that they were anti-social and inhumane. And the media, last of all, delivered to the nations of the world a unified narrative free from all nuance and scrutiny. In the UK, the number of dissenting journalists in mainstream corporate publications could be counted on a single hand. And yet, the political measures in question were the most significant and catastrophic in the history of Western nations. The logic upon which they were based was clearly questionable and would obviously damage millions of lives, but dissent was stifled and the media were content to be turned into propagandists in the pay of governments and globalist organisations.

The hand of the globalist technocrats was revealed both in its intent and in the scope of its power during the Covid period. It reconfigured our society, and it pushed us towards a globalist mindset in which we gladly and willingly laid down our personal liberties in an ostensibly heroic struggle against an abstract enemy. This is why we might consider the globalist forces at work within and above Western democracies to pose more of a threat than

obvious outsiders such as Russia and China. The globalists operate with a subtle though powerful ideological approach which
has been extremely effective. It begins with a global threat that is
discovered and understood by 'science'. 'Science', we are told, can
only be comprehended by scientists and, indeed, only by those
scientists with specialities in the relevant areas. Therefore, there
is only a small group of people with sufficient expertise to understand what is going on *and* what must be done.[*] Those who are
not a part of this small group of experts are told that they are not
allowed to comment (and certainly not to dissent) because they
cannot possibly understand the issues at hand.

We are then told, upon the basis of the expert advice, how the
threat must be dealt with. Because the threat is global, it must be
addressed using a global solution. Anyone who dissents from this
line is said, first, to be anti-science. This is because the dissenter
is objecting to the expert advice issuing from the ostensibly
unanimous scientific consensus. Second, the dissenter is accused
of being anti-social and dangerous. Not only does the dissenter's opinion endanger himself but it endangers the entirety of
the global community. It is therefore possible that the dissenter
should be suppressed or censored.

This playbook was manifested at the time of Covid-19. It is now
at large again on a potentially even greater scale, this time in the

---

* Where there are dissenting scientists with specialities in the relevant
areas, they are simply ignored and often silenced through censorship. This
happened during the Covid period as was revealed in the infamous 'Twitter
Files' which showed that successive US administrations had put pressure
upon Twitter to 'de-amplify' the accounts of certain people whose output
did not match the official narrative. When identified, these individuals were
put on a so-called 'trends blacklist', which included the names of world
experts in relevant scientific fields such as Dr Jay Bhattacharya of Stanford
University. Cf. Investigations Team, 'Twitter files reveal allegations site
blocked stories at US government's request', *Telegraph*, 03.06.2023, [https:
//www.telegraph.co.uk/news/2023/06/03/twitter-files-site-blocked-stories-
us-government/].

name of saving the world from what is referred to as the 'climate emergency'. The steps are the same: we are told that 'the science' agrees about man-made global warming that is causing extreme weather events and poses a significant threat to the future of life on planet Earth.* We are told that if only we can reduce the amount of carbon emissions into our atmosphere, then we can slow down global warming sufficiently to prevent the mass extinction of human and animal life. We must, therefore, reduce how much we travel using cars and aeroplanes. We must get rid of heating systems that use gas and oil. We must stop eating meat and dairy and subsist upon a plant-based diet. In addition, we must do various other things like stop buying clothes and renewing our laptops.

Disturbingly, the present Mayor of London, Sadiq Khan, is the chair of a group called C40, a global gathering of city mayors who have developed a vision for the inhabitants of their cities that they want realised by the year 2030. The targets include significant privations of the ordinary lives of citizens. The 'ambitious targets' of these mayors include the limiting of air travel to one short-haul return flight (less than 1,500 km) every two years per person, the complete banning of meat consumption, the complete banning of dairy consumption (cheese, yoghurt, milk,

---

* It is not true that scientists are unanimous about the threat posed by anthropogenic climate change. The World Climate Declaration, for example, signed by more than 1,800 eminent scientists and professionals with relevant expertise, states that there is no climate emergency and that the relevant claims made by the mainstream narrative are either overblown or false (cf. Clintel, 'World Climate Declaration: There Is No Climate Emergency', accessed 22.04.2024, [https://clintel.org/world-climate-declaration/]). There are also many prominent scientists with relevant expertise who have gone to great lengths (often to considerable personal cost) to critique the central claims of the narrative. These include genuine experts such as Steve Koonin, Bjorn Lomborg, Michael Shellenberger and Patrick Moore. Many of these scientists and some others were interviewed for the devastating documentary *Climate: The Movie (The Cold Truth)*. Cf. Clintel, *Climate: The Movie (The Cold Truth)*, accessed 22.04.2024, [https://www.youtube.com/watch?v=zmfRG8-RHEI&t=9s].

eggs), a maximum of three new items of clothing per person per year, and zero private vehicles. In other words, Sadiq Khan and his globalist cadre want inhabitants of their cities almost never to use a plane, never to eat meat or dairy, to buy hardly any new clothes and to own no private vehicles, including, of course, cars, motorbikes and vans.* No citizen of London or of the UK has voted for such radical and immiserating proposals and yet this is what is deemed to be justifiable because of the apparent scientific consensus about man-made climate change. If anyone argues with this, they are simply called 'climate deniers' and written off as anti-scientific lunatics. The logic is powerful and convincing. It plays upon people's respect for science, their belief in its objectivity, and their fear of being socially ostracised.

As a result of this globalist manipulation, all the benefits bequeathed to us by Christianity, spoken of by Hirsi Ali, are under threat: freedom of the individual, the nation state, the rule of law, freedom of the market, freedom of the press, freedom of conscience, and (real) science itself included. If the globalist technocracy becomes ascendent then the citizens of the West could face a bleak future of totalitarian control and surveillance.

It may be that liberal democracies have the power to resist this globalist technocracy, but, like the threat to liberalism from Islam, a globalist technocracy only needs to establish a foothold. Once that is done, democratic privileges can simply be confiscated

---

* Tim Sigsworth, 'No meat, no dairy and three outfits a year: Welcome to Sadiq Khan's plan for London', *Telegraph*, 15.09.2023, [https://www. telegraph.co.uk/news/2023/09/15/sadiq-khan-green-london-net-zero-ulez -c40-mayors-2030/]. At the time of writing, there is considerable speculation that Khan intends to begin charging road users in London by the mile. Khan has publicly denied this possibility (presumably because it would be too unpopular with the electorate), but a policy document which has yet to be disavowed appears to commit Khan to the strategy. Cf. Will Hazell, 'London drivers "could pay per mile" so that Sadiq Khan can hit net zero target', *Telegraph*, 20.04.2024, [https://www.telegraph.co.uk/news/2024/04 /20/london-drivers-pay-per-mile-sadiq-khan-net-zero-targets/].

permanently. This is one of the essential flaws in pluralistic political visions: once a non-pluralistic faction is allowed to take over then it can simply assume absolute power, never to offer the possibility of return.

The Coming of the Antichrist

It would be a serious mistake, however, to allow this book to become a political tract. One of the most emphatic points I want to make is that genuine belief is needed and not just a principled implementation of Christian values in the political and social spheres.

To press this point more strongly, it is worthwhile considering the scriptural symbolism of the Antichrist and how this concept is becoming ever more relevant as events progress. To put it in concise form, the Christian Scriptures seem to speak *both* of a spirit of Antichrist that manifests itself throughout human history and a literal figure who will appear at the very end of time. Much of this imagery is drawn from the book of Revelation, but it also finds expression in Paul's and John's letters as well as in the teaching of Christ himself in the Gospels. In those teachings, Jesus warns believers, throughout the generations, to be on guard against the belief that the Christ has returned to Earth before the signs predicted by Jesus have come to pass: 'See that no one leads you astray. Many will come in my name, saying, "I am he!" and they will lead many astray' (Mark 13:5–6). The significant point here is that the Antichrist and antichrists through history will not come openly proclaiming their wickedness. But they will claim to be doing good. In their most extreme form, they will claim a kind of messianic status. They will claim to be able to deliver the world from all affliction. Indeed, this is what the word 'Antichrist' literally means: not 'against Christ' but 'another Christ' – an alternative to the real thing.

Christ also predicts that these false christs will perform great signs and wonders and will lead astray both non-believers and believers (Mark 13:22). They will exert a very great power over people's minds. This will happen via a combination of an appealing ideology and a seemingly miraculous power.

At least three fictionalised modern accounts of the final days of humanity frame the Antichrist in these terms. These stories help us, I believe, to understand how the spirit of the Antichrist is manifesting itself in our days. The three accounts are Vladimir Soloviev's *A Short Tale About the Antichrist*, Robert Benson's *Lord of the World* and Michael D. O'Brien's more recent novels *Father Elijah* and *Elijah in Jerusalem*. In all three of these accounts, the Antichrist is depicted as an intensely gifted and charming man who rises to global prominence and becomes a unifying figure for all humanity, offering to the world solutions for seemingly unsolvable political problems. In *A Short Tale About the Antichrist*, for example, the Antichrist figure has a mysterious encounter with a demonic presence and is inspired to write a book called *The Open Path to Universal Peace and Prosperity*. This book goes on to become the greatest-selling book in human history and many millions come to believe that, within its pages, lies the solution to all of humanity's ills. In *Father Elijah* and *Elijah in Jerusalem*, the Antichrist character is similarly portrayed as a humanitarian philanthropist who rises to the very top of the global political pyramid. In *Elijah in Jerusalem*, the Antichrist's crowning achievement is the unification of the peoples of Israel and Palestine in a feat of diplomatic genius that is tantamount to a secular political miracle. And this is the point: all these Antichrists offer solutions to the world, but they are solutions not founded in the presence and purposes of God but in the worship of a secular political messiah who will ultimately demand worship and undeviating loyalty.

On *A Short Tale About the Antichrist*, the philosopher Daniel J. Mahoney comments on the Antichrist's book *The Open Path to Universal Peace and Prosperity*:

One is reminded once again of Matthew 4, where Christ rebukes Satan by saying, 'Man shall not live by bread alone,' and where the Devil took him up to a mountain and showed him all the 'kingdoms of the world' in a moment of time and offered Christ all the power in the world. This is *the* powerful allure of the Antichrist's book. Willing to succumb to the temptations of Christ in the desert, the Superman offers a universal, humanitarian utopia, the Kingdom of God, or rather, the Kingdom of Satan on Earth. He will convince men that they essentially live by bread alone . . . Possessed by the power of Satan, this man embodies the falsification of the good. Yet he is praised by nearly all, including most Christians. Few see the Antichrist's message for what it really is, a satanic falsification of the good.[5]

Every account differs and yet the broad outlines are the same. There are global problems that must be faced urgently. There is a powerful and charismatic and seemingly very generous and good man who stands at the head of a unified humanity, who is advocating a simple and straightforward solution to the difficulties. The only condition is that all must be unified in their unswerving devotion to him. And this is the key: unity, or rather uniformity of will. This uniformity involves submission, including *religious* submission. For, in order for the peoples of the Earth to be united in this saving humanitarian cause, they must put aside religious differences and consider them adiaphora. They must agree that saving the world is more important than the question of the lordship of Jesus Christ, which must be considered a somewhat esoteric and indulgent speculation. Mahoney continues:

Many Christians begin to notice that Christ is never mentioned in the pages of *The Open Path*. But most dismiss this, saying that religious writers in the past hadn't been sufficiently discreet. They had made too many references to God and had been too zealous in promoting the faith. A truly Christian spirit, we often hear, demands 'active love and all-embracing goodwill'. For far too many Christians, Soloviev suggests, what truly seems to matter is a humanitarianism that vigilantly makes no mention of Christ at all.[6]

There is something eerily prescient about all these predictions, particularly in the case of *Lord of the World*, which was first published in 1907. As with the other works mentioned, this story predicts that the spirit of the Antichrist will co-opt Christianity and the Church itself into its diabolical agenda, in this case literally by commandeering the churches and employing apostate clergy in the construction of a bespoke and novel religion of humanity. The story is set in the future and imagines that Western civilisation has been taken over almost completely by this religion of humanitarianism. In this scenario, the only opposition that remains is the fledgling Roman Catholic Church, which is severely weakened and represents a tiny minority in almost every country.

The quotation that begins this chapter is taken from a conversation between an elderly man and two younger Catholic priests who are trying to understand the world that they inhabit. The words are spoken by the older man, who has seen clearly how various political, social and religious currents have led to the present situation. The features of humanitarianism that are mentioned are that it is pantheistic, meaning that it sees the natural order as divine. In that sense, it is a return to an immanent pagan religion that rejects the possibility of a transcendent realm and a God who rules over all things. The apex of this pantheistic religion is man himself, who is set up as God. The subtle deception consists in the blurring of the line between philanthropy and idolatry. 'Philanthropy' means 'the love of mankind'. The religion of humanitarianism carries this notion beyond simple works of charity and says that mankind *is* in fact God and is the highest priority, above which nothing else must be considered. This is why, in the Gospels, the devil offers Christ bread in the wilderness and the worship of the Earth's kingdoms. After all, what could be more important than bread and the saving of human life?

Benson's character tells us that this pagan humanitarian religion offers real food for religious cravings, and indeed it does. Like the 'subtler languages' mentioned earlier, this immanent religion supplies human beings with an outlet for their spiritual desires without demanding anything too significant from them in terms of belief and practice. There are no strange claims that need to be believed about God or the afterlife. There are no pleasures that must be denied. There are no creeds which must divide.

But perhaps most prescient of all is this prophetic statement: ' "Then, they have the use of all the churches . . . and all the Cathedrals . . . Then, they may display their symbols and we may not".'[7] Benson's insight was that this new religion, in displacing the old religion of Christianity, would not only occupy people's minds and hearts but would also manifest itself symbolically at the sacred sites of the former faith. Just as the Christians of old built their churches upon pagan temples, so the new religion sets up its shrines upon the remains of the conquered ideology of Christianity.

We have already mentioned one of these major symbolic conquests, which is the pantheistic installation of images of the Earth and the moon within Christian churches and cathedrals in the UK. As with the fictional work *The Open Path to Universal Peace and Prosperity*, it seems an almost scrupulous effort has been made with the marketing of these objects, *not* to mention their status as creatures of God. Also in common with that book, their presence is justified by humanitarian concerns. In the case of the Earth and the moon, the objects are continually and specifically linked with environmentalism and climate change. In an installation of the moon in Winchester Cathedral in 2024, for example, among the events planned there is no mention at all of God, Jesus Christ, the Bible or creation. But we are told that the 'famous science broadcaster and author' Mark Thompson gave a talk entitled 'Climate change, the planets and us' in which he spoke, of course, about the 'climate crisis'. The artist Luke Jerram is specifically said to be interested in drawing people's attention to 'planetary health' and to prompting 'difficult discussions we all need to have about climate change and what we, as individuals and wider society, can do to make our lifestyles more sustainable'. Alongside these concerns, the general public is also invited to 'visit' the moon, to listen to choral music and to watch inspiring dance, to attend a date night under its light, to participate in silent discos for families and adults, and to practise Pilates.[8]

Another external symbol that has come to displace the traditional tokens of the Christian religion is the LGBT 'Pride' flag which has been installed across churches in the Western world. A significant recent example would be the use of a Pride flag as an altar frontal at St Nicholas Church in Leicester. This church has architectural features that date back an astonishingly long way and the present church is among the ten oldest in Britain.[9] Justification for the Pride flag's presence in Christian churches is, once again, that the Pride flag *is* fundamentally Christian and that it is a mistake on the part of other Christians to question its absolute compatibility with the values of Christ and the teaching of the Scriptures.

The final example of the co-opting of the churches into the religion of humanitarianism is that of their transformation into centres dedicated to the administration of the Covid-19 vaccine. Part of the significance of this move was the fact that it happened during the period in which the Church of England acquiesced to the government's insistence that places of worship be completely closed for worship because of the fear of contagion. Churches could remain open, however, to run food banks *and*, in this case, to administer Covid vaccines. In her work on the weaponisation of fear during the Covid crisis, Laura Dodsworth likens this to 'a modern biosecurity incarnation of transubstantiation – especially when delivered in cathedrals with organ music playing, in an intersection of the old religion and the new religion'.[10] The point Dodsworth makes is that the old religion that believed in miracles such as transubstantiation is being replaced by the new religion that shuns supernatural fantasy and instead focuses on real-world solutions to tangible problems such as pandemics and disease. In light of the seriousness of the latter, the Church's worship can cease without any significant consequence. And, in the very place in which that worship has ceased, devotion to more pressing concerns –namely, the alleviation of physical danger – is offered. The fact that the vaccines were administered to the sound of organ music only serves to underline the quasi-religious and ritualistic aspect of this phenomenon.

Perhaps the image that embodies most this post-Christian religion manifested itself during the Covid crisis in May 2021. The hundred-foot-high, hundred-year-old image of Christ the Redeemer that dominates the skyline of Rio de Janeiro, with arms outstretched in an invitation to the world to respond to the love of God, was lit up with an alternative message. This one simply said 'Vaccine Saves, United for vaccines'. The fact that the word 'Vaccine' was used as a singular noun almost serves to underline the religious component of this statement: it is no longer Jesus Christ that saves, but the new deity, 'Vaccine'. And it is no longer the Christian religion that unites those who will worship the one, true God, but we will unite 'for vaccines', as though the literal coming together of humanity in centres of vaccination will engender a more abstract but nevertheless powerful sense of fraternal and global solidarity.

The spirit of the Antichrist manifests itself in the name of the good of humanity. It tells us that God is irrelevant and that what is of the most critical importance is the alleviation of human need and suffering. Sometimes it does this by implication, as when the words 'God' and 'Jesus Christ' are underemphasised or simply unused. At other times, it is implied by those involved drawing an equivalence between Christianity and other religions, and by saying that all religions (and worldviews that are not religions) agree on the basic tenets of ethical reality: that we should love our neighbour, that we should do good to one another, that we should strive to safeguard our common home, and so on. In this sense, our religious commitments are only a means to an end: the amelioration of social and environmental conditions. The latter is the priority; the former is simply the motivation. And the motivation is interchangeable.

And yet this is a deep deception and it is hard to say where it is leading. At the very least, though, the Covid situation has given us an indication of the kind of technocratic, globalist and totalitarian society that many at the elite level of power would like to create. When vaccine passports were introduced in many countries, it seemed for a moment as though a precursor to the mark of the beast, mentioned in the book of Revelation, was on trial. In Revelation, a mysterious beast rises out of the Earth and causes all mankind to be marked upon the right hand or the forehead 'so that they could not buy or sell unless they had the mark' (Revelation 13:17(a). This might sound fantastic, and yet there were many calling for those who refused the Covid-19 vaccine for any reason to be locked out of the economic system by being banned from shops and fired from their jobs. In the UK, for example, around 19,000 members of staff in care homes were fired or left their jobs because of a mandatory vaccination policy.[11] This is an example of a societal impulse that clearly exists and has real-world consequences: the impulse to control, in the name of compassion, the population of the Earth using advanced surveillance technology. If a final mark of the beast ever arises, it seems plausible that it may indeed emerge along these sorts of lines.

In addition to this, there is the worryingly anti-human depopulation agenda that is increasingly popular among elites and many others espousing the climate change narrative. It is worth mentioning here that self-styled prophet of the World Economic Forum, Yuval Noah Harari. Harari's rhetoric is so obnoxious that it is hard to take seriously and yet his books are amazingly popular, and it is not unusual to hear similar sentiments repeated in public debates on related issues. In one interview, Harari was asked about his new book *Homo Deus* and a comparison he makes therein with the proletariat class created by the Industrial Revolution. He says that we are now facing the different question of what we do with the people whose jobs will be replaced by machines and AI. He calls this group 'a massive class of useless people' and says that the big political and economic question of the twenty-first century will be, 'What do we need human beings for? Or, at least, what do we need *so many* humans for?' The interviewer then asks him what his answer to this problem is, and he responds that his best guess is to keep them happy with drugs and computer games.[12] The implication of Harari's rhetoric is that if your labour can be replaced by a machine, then you are a useless person and there is no need for you to exist. You may be allowed to continue existing, but it would be best if you were sedated and distracted by computer games and virtual reality.

The depopulation agenda is already clearly advocated by elites at a political and intellectual level. It has begun as a simple encouragement for people to have fewer children, but it will surely metastasise into something far more sinister. We already see this in the cases of abortion and euthanasia. After all, what is the 'use' of an elderly person suffering from a terminal illness? In these stark utilitarian terms, the answer is, of course, that there *is* no use, and all this person is doing is consuming resources that could be better spent elsewhere. What else will occur to people? A heavier taxation burden for having more than one child? An enforced one-child policy as has been implemented in China in the past? Forced sterilisation and abortion? Things ever darker and more sinister than these? We are yet to see. But the notion that humanity is essentially a growing plague, a cancer on a planet that is suffering because of an ongoing anthropic colonisation – where most people, as Harari says, are becoming useless as their jobs are replaced by machines – champions a logic that is undeniable. And we return once again to that phrase which seems to hold the most explanatory power for our time: the culture of death.

The Church: A Community of Defence and Offence

If my analysis is correct then the path that the Christian Church must follow is abundantly clear. It must divorce itself, absolutely

and without ambiguity, from the false religion of secular humanitarianism and from allowing Christianity to be diluted to the
equivalent status of 'all faiths and none'. Sadly, it is already the
case that, across much of the Western world, the Church is being
co-opted into this false religion, which is gradually hollowing it
out and destroying it. One does not have to be a Christian believer
to observe the statistical reality that churches allowing themselves to be inculcated into post-Christian ideologies are declining and dying. In the UK, this is clearly true of denominations
that have liberalised such as the United Reformed Church and
the Methodist Church. It is also true of the Church of England.
To put it very simply, the Church of England declined from
about 1.2 million Sunday worshippers in the early 1990s to just
under a million around the turn of the millennium. In 2019 the
number had declined further still to 680,000, and then to 549,000
in 2022. In the three years between 2019 and 2022 there was a
drop of about 130,000 attendees.[13] If that happens another four
times, the Church of England will be fully and finally dead. By
any metric, the established Church is in catastrophic decline, and
it is not difficult to see why. It is not an excuse to say that the
pervasive atmosphere of secularism guarantees the decline of the
Christian Church since there are many evangelical denominations that continue to flourish and multiply in the Global South
and in highly secularised Western countries such as the UK. Even
within the Church of England itself, those evangelical and Anglo-
Catholic congregations that pursue a more obviously orthodox
approach are bucking the trend of the critical decline that characterises the rest of the denomination.

The Christian Church, when it is functioning properly, is a
community of both defence and offence. It is defensive in the
sense that it must defend certain ideas, beliefs and practices that
are integral to its identity. And it is offensive in a double sense.
The first is that it proposes an entire worldview that often has
radical implications for the individual, for culture and society.
This transformative power and its manifestation in Western

civilisation has been one of the major themes of this book: the Western world, its values and, indeed, its successes are all based upon a Christian view of man and his relationship to God. In this sense, it is by far the most influential belief system that the world has ever known. But there is a second sense in which the Christian Church is offensive and that is, quite simply, that it often causes offence, on both an individual and a societal level. This is because Christianity is, and always has been, a worldview that is so universal and radical that it inevitably puts itself on a pathway to confrontation with the worldviews of other religions and philosophies. There is no getting away from this: in order to produce a world that is leavened by the truth and beauty of the Christian gospel, other worldviews must be challenged and, to a great extent, set aside.

Defence

What the Church must defend has already been indicated. Put simply, it relates to the question of God and humanity.

First, there *is* a God to whom human beings owe their allegiance and worship. In the rejection of this belief, the West is reverting to the type of pagan idolatry that was spoken of in the first century by the apostle Paul: 'Although they claimed to be wise, they became fools and exchanged the glory of the immortal God for images made to look like a mortal human being and birds and animals and reptiles' (Romans 1:22–3). The apostle's psychological insight here is very striking. He argues perceptively that, when we deny the existence of God and do not worship him as we should, we transfer our ultimate devotion to something else. It may be man himself and the religion of humanity: because we can see nothing greater than man in terms of his intellect, his power and his beauty, and, indeed, because we are so in love with ourselves, we worship him and come to believe that there is nothing higher. Or we make gods of animals and the natural environment. Again, we have seen how disbelief in the transcendent realm is resulting in a reversion to the worship of the Earth and the moon. The distinction between God and the things that he has made is arguably the one overarching theme of the whole of the Christian Bible, from the first chapter of the Hebrew Scriptures in Genesis 1 to the end of the book of Revelation. It is a distinction that has been insisted upon by orthodox Christian theologians and writers since the beginning. I have mentioned the clear articulation of this view in the Bible. But to take one other example from Christian history, the great fourth-century bishop of Alexandria, Athanasius, in his work *The Life of Antony*, records an exchange between the monk and ascetic Antony of Egypt and some Greek philosophers. In this excoriating demolition of the pagan Greek worldview, Antony says the following of the relationship between the Greek gods and aspects of the natural world such as Earth, water, sun and sea:

> Perhaps it was because of the creation's beauty that you composed such tales. Nevertheless it is fitting for you to go only so far as to admire, not to deify, the things created, lest you render the honour due the maker to the things made. Otherwise, the time has come for you to transfer honour due to the architect to the house he has made or that due the general to the soldier.[14]

A more formal way of putting this is that there is a *radical ontological separation* between God and his creation. Whereas God is self-sufficient and is reliant upon nothing at all for his existence, the creation is upheld at every moment by the power of God. Whereas God is timeless and eternal, the creation came into existence at a certain point and endures throughout time. Whereas God transcends space and is present everywhere at once, the creation exists in space and individual creatures only occupy one place at each moment.

Nor is this some kind of trivial theological abstraction. The notion that God created the universe and rules over it is an affront to every tyrant who has ever lived, from the emperors of the early centuries Anno Domini, who commanded their subjects to burn a pinch of incense in their honour as to a god, to the communist mass-murderers of the twentieth. It is an affront because it says that, however powerful the ruler, however powerful the government and the state, God is infinitely more powerful still and infinitely more due the worship of humanity. The Christian Church has always taught that Christians should be loyal subjects to those God has put in a place of civic honour and authority. But this is precisely the point and precisely the controversy: kings, emperors and presidents have all been put in the place of power by the providence of God. Therefore, Christians are to obey, but they are not to do so if the tyrant commands idolatry and sin. This is because there is a higher authority, to whom *all* will give an account. This is the final and ultimate rationale against totalitarianism. For totalitarianism attempts to take all things in human society – including the human soul – and to subject them to the power of the state. And yet, seen in the light of God's existence, this is revealed for the folly that it is. For man possesses no totalising power to subject the creator to the creation.

The existence of God relates most intimately to the doctrine of humanity. As has been argued extensively, perhaps the most influential legacy of the Judeo-Christian tradition is the notion that human beings – *all* human beings – are made in the image of God, given a measure of his sanctity, and therefore must be treated with dignity, kindness, love and justice. Where people are not treated in this way, this is an affront not just to an abstract notion of justice or truth but to God himself. From this simple yet tectonic conviction there has developed the entire Western civilisational project.

The Church, above all else, is the place in which the Image of God in humanity must be cherished and protected. Part of the reason for this is because it is only in places of tangible human relationships that genuine acts of human charity can be demonstrated. It is very good to defend abstract notions of humanity made in God's image, but ultimately it is the *practice* of this belief, in the context of a real human community, that truly brings it into tangible existence in the world. The New Testament frequently speaks about the Christian Church as a family, with each member given a role to play. Men and women are no longer objects of fear, lust or abuse but now, being made holy and subjugating their base instincts to the power of God, are brothers and sisters in Christ. Young men and women become sons and daughters of those who are older and can benefit from their wisdom, protection and provision. The elderly are not despised, rejected and outcast as they have become in the present Western world, but they are valued for their experience as wise patriarchs and matriarchs. Whereas the contemporary West sees individuals as radically separate and therefore alone in their search for meaning, the Christian Church values the dignity of the individual and places him within the context of a loving family in which he can play his own particular part, bringing to bear his own specific gifts and experience.

Again, it is the concern of this book to raise the question of what will happen now that the Christian era appears to be coming to a close in its present form, and to argue that we have seen and that we *are* seeing the consequences of the decline of Christianity in the disappearance of the view that every human being is made in the image of God and must be protected and cherished as such. The recovery of this notion is the only way to protect humanity from the inevitable consequences of the trends that could become the dominant forces in the Western world. The globalist totalitarianism that is embodied by thinkers such as Yuval Noah Harari and organisations such as the World Economic Forum and the World Health Organisation in their technocratic desire to depopulate the planet and transcend humanity through the religion of technology and Artificial Intelligence can only be countered by the absolute insistence upon the goodness of man as an end in himself and of the image of God as uniquely present in humanity among his creatures, not to be diminished through depopulation, nor to be transcended through technological evolution. Non-Christian religions that are ultimately extremely patriarchal in nature or are intimately bound up with caste systems can be met with the same critique. And the emergence of the progressive worldview and the increasingly absurd 'woke' beliefs that are associated with it can only find their true riposte in Christianity because it is not Diversity, Equity and Inclusion that will bring justice and unity upon Earth but the Christian gospel embodied by a renewed humanity in the Christian Church.

There are many aspects of the woke ideology that are frivolous and apt to be ignored, but there are others that are deeply disturbing and go hand in hand with the rise of the culture of death. The woke ideology seeks to reverse whatever progress was made in the twentieth century with regards to harmony between the races and to promote an ideology of racial aggression in a contest for absolute power. In doing this, the woke have created their own sacrosanct speech codes and are looking to have them enshrined in Western legal systems, such that even to discuss and to criticise these developments is becoming difficult and acquiring the status of a quite literal thought crime. Once again, unity between those of different nations is a uniquely Christian inheritance, articulated in the pages of the New Testament, which preaches a gospel of reconciliation between Jews, Gentiles and other nations that were at enmity with one another. We see it more recently in history in the abolitionism of the evangelical Clapham Sect of the nineteenth century and in the work of Martin Luther King, Jr who based his campaign for civil rights upon an explicitly biblical and Christian worldview. We are told now that we are to stop seeing our fellow men and women as individuals and to begin once again to treat them differently because of the colour of their skin. This is a terrible deviation from our Christian inheritance and is, again, something that can be resisted by the Christian Church. How? By embodying in our local communities the opposite spirit and by treating each individual member with the same love and compassion not because we see the colour of their skin but because we see the image of God within them.

Even more troubling, of course, are the other aspects of the culture of death that have been described extensively. Divorced from our belief in the providential love of God and his plan for each human life, cut off from the notion of the sacredness of humanity and the Imago Dei, we are, like our Greco-Roman forebears, eliminating those members of the human race whom we consider useless or inconvenient. This originates at the beginning and at the end of life under the rhetoric of compassion, but we have already seen in the proliferation of eligible candidates for euthanasia how death on demand is being applied so much more widely across the age spectrum and for a multitude of reasons, including depression and debt. What can the Christian Church do in the face of this but to refuse it and to act in the opposite spirit? The life of each human being, from the womb to the tomb, is sacred and must be protected, loved and cherished, as far as it depends upon us, until its course is truly run. In this way, we, the ones who are healthy and strong, grow into our own humanity, as we practise not mercy killing but long-suffering compassion and care for the weak and for the sick. Again, this is the calling of the Christian Church: to be this kind of community, as a sign to the rest of the world of the justice and love of God, manifested here upon the Earth.

The Church, then, is a community of defence: it is a defence against all thoughts of killing, of subjugating, of diminishing, of discarding the image of God as it manifests itself in humanity. This is the only place in which all are truly welcome, whether slave or free, Jew or Greek, black or white, young or old, healthy or sick, rich or poor, male or female. And yet this can only be a welcome extended to all because the Christian Church insists that every single human being is a sign of God's presence in this world. To those who destroy that image because it is an inconvenience or an offence, the Christian Church says, unequivocally and without ambiguity: 'No'.

Offence

I have already indicated that the word 'offence' here has a double meaning, part of which is that the Christian way of thinking may indeed prove a scandal to the post-Christian West. It is no virtue to cause offence on purpose but there is a certain amount of inevitability when we touch upon values that have come to be seen as sacred and practices that have been promoted vigorously for decades. To name just one, the idea is increasingly shocking to modern people that our choices as individuals are not only concerned with securing immediately positive consequences for ourselves but have significant effects upon those around us, which should be considered seriously. Applied to the subjects of abortion and euthanasia, these ideas are especially sensitive since they literally concern matters of life and death. We are asking those who have doubled down on modern ideas of freedom and individual autonomy to consider that they might have been making a terrible mistake in doing so. And this suggestion has the capacity to cause discomfort and offence.

As we move away from the Christian era, the Church is finding itself in a situation in which it has something genuinely different to offer. It makes the biggest mistake of all when it seeks to conform itself to its new surroundings such that it is indistinguishable from them. One example has already been mentioned, which is the bowing of the knee to the new religion of 'Science', epitomised in the mistaken reaction of the Church of England hierarchy to the outbreak of the Covid virus in the early months of 2020. As in much of the world, the country was forcibly shut down by the government and the Church was relegated to the status of a 'non-essential' service. For the first time in 800 years, since the days of King John, the doors of the parish churches in England were closed and corporate worship ceased. Contrary to the expectations of some, the bishops of the Church seemed quite enthusiastic about the idea. Parish priests were told that they should not enter their church buildings to use them for prayer, even if their homes were attached to them. They *were* given leave to enter to maintain the buildings and to run food banks, but worship of any sort was strictly forbidden. A large part of the justification for the cessation of corporate worship was the fact that it could easily be replaced with 'online church', which was heavily promoted as a ready-made substitute.

This was a serious mistake from a practical point of view as it ignored basic facts of human nature, namely that once people are out of the habit of doing something like going to church, it is quite difficult to get them to resume that habit. If you provide people with an easy alternative like watching a service on the internet and claim that it is essentially the equivalent of attending a church in person, it is likely that people will do that instead, not only for a while but in perpetuity. Or, as seems more and more to be the case, that they will do it for a time, find a certain amount of spiritual emptiness in it, and then cease to engage with the Church altogether. This observation has been borne out in the increasingly shocking statistics of church attendance for the Church of England, as we have already mentioned.

Aside from the practical consequences of this disastrous set of decisions, there is the additional ideological and pastoral complacency to set alongside it. It is well documented that the generation we know as Millennials, most affected by the proliferation of the internet and smartphones, are living increasingly sad and isolated lives. In her book on transgenderism, the American writer Abigail Shrier notes, for example, that the current generation of young people is significantly different from the so-called Generation X that preceded it. In the previous generation, teenage pregnancies and abortions were at an all-time high, whereas in the new generation they are the lowest they have been for decades. Shrier reports that between 2009 and 2017, the increase of high schoolers contemplating suicide rose by 25 per cent, and between 2005 and 2014 teens diagnosed with depression rose by 37 per cent with the worst hit being teenage girls. Additionally, since 2009 self-harming has increased by 62 per cent. Among pre-teen girls aged ten to fourteen, self-harm rates are up by 189 per cent compared to 2010. She writes: 'Today's adolescents spend far less time in person with their friends – up to an hour less per day – than did members of Gen X. And dear God, they are lonely. They report greater loneliness than any generation on record.'[15]

What has happened? Instead of being out with their friends,

getting drunk, hooking up, becoming pregnant and procuring abortions, the current generation of younger people cut far more solitary figures. They are at home, alone in their bedrooms with their iPhones, cursing their own personal, perceived inadequacies as they compare themselves with curated images of perfection on social media sites like Instagram and TikTok. This is poison to the human soul and is causing growing rates of depression and anxiety. As a result, they self-harm and contemplate worse.

This is a situation in which the Church *could*, if it so chose, speak with a loud and convincing voice, about the basic human need for the warmth of a loving community. It is an increasingly rare offer in a more and more atomised, lonely and individualistic society. Rather than encouraging people to spend more time staring at their phones and iPads, the Church could instead invite them to spend time with real, embodied people, in a tangible community. It is easy to underestimate just how significant a rebellion such a simple notion could be: of time spent together in the worship of God and in the affection of a familial community. And yet the rebellion, if it spread far and wide, could be enough to challenge technology's encroaching grasp upon the soul of humanity.

This tangible community gives to us not only the warmth of human contact but the opportunity to experience the reality of aesthetic beauty and holiness. I have spoken about the human need for beauty to lift the soul above the banality that so often surrounds it, particularly in the post-industrial West with its pervasive ugliness. The Christian Church – particularly our established Church in England – has an embarrassment of riches on this front. We are still surrounded, a thousand years after their construction, by cathedrals and parish churches built to the glory of God and inspired by human intellect and creativity. Could we not once again see a rebellion against ugliness, against utility, against individual self-expression, in the curation of beautiful spaces and buildings constructed to the glory of God?

I have made every effort in this book to be as ecumenical as possible and not to insist on one particular version of Christianity as the answer to the West's problems, but it does seem to me that a higher view of the Church is more helpful here than an equivalent 'low-church' view. Rather than meeting in bare warehouses or whitewashed chapels with little to no ceremony and an aping of contemporary means to entertain and communicate, the Church could once again discover the splendour and beauty of ritual and the tangibility of the sacraments. These are things that simply cannot be done online but instead necessitate a gathering. This is even better, in my view, when it is done locally in the context of a parish church because the parish necessarily draws in people from different generations and frequently different backgrounds and socio-economic groups. This is admittedly an idealised view of the Church but anything even remotely approaching it is far superior to the counterfeit and destructive forms of community offered to us by the religion of technology.

The Church must gather to worship, and, in this gathering, it must find also the ability to care for its members and for the world more broadly. I have written much about the need to defend the concept of humanity in the abstract, but the Church is the place at which the rubber must meet the road. As the saints did at the time of the Greco-Roman empire, so must we provide practical alternatives for desperate and lonely people. Christians do wonderful acts of service when they not only protest against the taking of life but consider how they might provide alternatives. Often these acts are done in individual moments of charity. Sometimes they are through organisations such as pregnancy crisis centres that offer desperate young women alternatives to aborting their babies. Or they are carried out in caring for the elderly and the terminally ill, or in families offering to adopt unwanted children. However the practical outworking might look, the point remains: the Christian Church should not only *speak* but it must also *do*, and at times this will be sacrificial.

Perhaps enough has now been said to give an idea of the kind of defence and offence the Christian Church might offer to a dying world. Perhaps enough has also been said about the Church's folly when, instead of challenging the culture of death and the degradation of human life, it chooses to participate enthusiastically in it. The Christian Church has come under sustained attack since its inception and some of this has been justified, having been brought upon the Church by itself. But much of it is post-Christian propaganda that seeks to paint gathered Christian communities and Christianity more abstractly as boring, desiccated and devoid of life. Those of us who have had – and continue to have – glimpses of the Church at its highest know something of the truth, which is that, although the Church frequently and consistently falls short of its ideal, nevertheless she possesses the grace to point towards something higher: through the common experiences of gathered worship and the warmth of human community, to orientate the soul to the transcendent realm and to God. And it is as the human heart in community is orientated towards the transcendent that it is inspired towards works of great artistic and cultural beauty and to acts of sacrificial and imaginative charity.

We return, then, to the crux and central argument of this book: that it is only because people contemplated the divine presence as revealed in Jesus Christ that the culture of Western civilisation as we know it was born; that this did not happen by mistake or through the ordinary processes of material and economic history, but because of a divine irruption in the middle of the normal course of things. The divine presence was tasted and, over a period of many centuries, instantiated in the world that we have until recent times largely taken for granted. We will soon have only a memory remaining. My intention, then, has been an act of retrieval, and to argue that the dream remembered thereby can once again be relived, albeit in a different way, in the days to come.

Remembering the Dream

> I call heaven and earth to record this day against you, that I have
> set before you life and death, blessing and cursing: therefore
> choose life, that both thou and thy seed may live.
>
> Deuteronomy 30:19 (KJV)

To repair the disastrous effects of a particular course of action is,
in some ways, quite straightforward. As was said at the beginning
of this book, all that needs to be done is to observe how things
were before, to compare them with the detritus of the modern
day, and to work out what factors have changed and are therefore in need of restoration. The central argument of this book is
that the main factor to have changed is the widespread loss of the
Christian religion and that the consequences of this loss are so
deeply entrenched that most people are only dimly aware of them.

Harder to say, however, is what things would be like if this
argument were both correct *and* heeded. How would life change
if a great return came about? What might that world look like?
The question is so difficult to answer not least because, when
we look back at the great medieval civilisation brought about
by Christianity, it is exactly that: a civilisation. It was an entire
world that was built up during many centuries, and even millennia, through the endeavour, skill, artistry, courage, sacrifice and
vision of generations. It was worked out in meticulous detail in
every field of human knowledge, not least science, but the arts,
philosophy, law, politics, architecture, music, geometry, rhetoric
and the study of ancient tongues. In order to give any real account
of what a great return would look like, every area of such a civilisation would need to be described, and clearly this is far beyond
the scope of a single book or the ability of a single author.

But there is a second part to this challenge which is to say
that there is a sense in which a genuine return is impossible. We
cannot go back behind modernity and restore the conditions that
were present before it any more than a person can return to their

mother's womb and be born a second time (John 3:4). The fact is that the modern world *has* happened. The momentous shifts of thinking and living that have been examined cannot simply be erased from our memories as though they never occurred. So, since we cannot go back to the past to retrieve the faith, we must go forward, *through* the present age, and imagine what a return would look like *given* that modernity cannot be erased. And so the question must be: how do we both return and retain? Return to the faith once delivered and accepted, but retain that which is genuinely good in the present age, that which we have learned and that which has helped us, even though developed and discovered in part in an age of true post-Christian darkness?

In a sense we will be like the Patristic Fathers of the early Church. At that time there was a commonly employed metaphor for pagan learning and its relationship to the Christian faith. That metaphor took the Israelites' flight from Egypt and their despoilation of the wealth of the Egyptians for the Christian use of pagan philosophy. St Augustine famously used this image, as did the fourth-century Cappadocian Father, Gregory of Nyssa. On this, Gregory writes:

> It commands those participating through virtue in the free life also to equip themselves with the wealth of pagan learning by which foreigners to the faith beautify themselves. Our guide in virtue commands someone who 'borrows' from wealthy Egyptians to receive such things as moral and natural philosophy, geometry, astronomy, dialectic, and whatever else is sought by those outside the Church, since these things will be useful when in time the divine sanctuary of mystery must be beautified with the riches of reason.[16]

The Christian Church has always held that reason is accessible and useful for all of humanity. This was true of pagan learning in the form of Greek thinkers such as Plato and Aristotle, and it is still true today. The world cannot be swept away by a great return, but it can be transfigured, as the burning bush in the vision of Moses was both illuminated and yet unconsumed.

Given these difficulties, we can still ask ourselves what a world that was reconnected with the vision of God would look like in broad outline. The medieval period inherited a tradition of thought that saw God as coterminous with the so-called 'transcendentals' – qualities held to be both valuable in and of themselves and to be names, as it were, of God. Thus, beauty is an end for which there is nothing further. To gaze upon the majesty of a Gothic cathedral is, in and of itself, sufficient. There is nothing to be done but simply encounter the form of beauty. Conversely, an encounter with ugliness and chaos disturbs the soul and leaves it with a desire and a longing for that which is truly beautiful. Goodness is a transcendental end without which we simply cannot live. This is seen, for example, in the excellence of human skill and knowledge, and in the pursuit of virtue, which can be observed with particular clarity in certain saintly individuals. We also experience the longing for goodness in our own hearts when we take a wrong course, when we choose what is opposed to the good and instead embrace wickedness. We will know no rest until we return to that which is good for its own sake. We will be like the murderer who, though he has got away scot-free, nevertheless hands himself in because he knows, deep within his own soul, that he has stepped away from goodness and must be restored to it, even if that restoration involves his physical incarceration. Finally, truth is not a means to something further beyond itself but is valuable for its own sake. It is simply good to know the truth about a matter. And we see this in mankind's perpetual pursuit of knowledge and information about the world. Why does this matter? For utilitarian ends on many occasions, but it is always good just to know.

Beauty, Goodness, Truth: these are the names of God. And if we were to return in a significant way *to* God, we would find beauty, goodness and truth restored to our world as a result.

Beauty

We have spoken of the decline of Western aesthetic sensibility, and how the Western world, though undoubtedly equipped with vastly superior technology, nevertheless produces ugliness, particularly in the urban environments in which we live. We have noted that medieval cities all around Britain, once graced with exclusively uplifting architecture, are now spoiled by concrete and steel monstrosities, by squat, square or otherwise deadened architectural forms, that do not inspire but rather weigh down the soul. Observing his beloved Oxford going the way of all this, the poet Gerard Manley Hopkins wrote:

> Generations have trod, have trod, have trod;
> And all is seared with trade; bleared, smeared with toil;
> And wears man's smudge and shares man's smell; the soil
> Is bare now, nor can foot feel, being shod.[17]

It must be the case that a rediscovery of him who is Beauty would inspire us once again to create beautiful forms both to live within and to gaze upon. That inspiration can be the only explanation of how, without modern equipment, people managed to build, often over periods of centuries, the medieval cathedrals and churches that effortlessly overpower their modern equivalents with their transcendent majesty.

There is perhaps an example of what a return in this area might look like in the form of the Neo-Gothic revival of the nineteenth century, spearheaded by such eccentric but nevertheless deeply Christian practitioners as Augustus Pugin. The Neo-Gothic revival was a return to a certain architectural style, an architectural style that was deeply embedded within a Christian vision of reality. The principles of that style were passionately held by people like Pugin and included the notion that there actually exist rules that govern the laws of aesthetics and that the extent to which these rules were observed was the extent to which the works themselves were properly Christian or not. At the end of his book *Contrasts*,

Pugin literally draws a number of contrasts between churches and other buildings constructed during the medieval period and their equivalents of the modern day (which was, for him, the nineteenth century). Over and over again, the post-Christian, contemporary forms are shown to be manifestly inferior to those constructed centuries before. There are various examples, but maybe the most striking is that of the contrast between residences for the poor. The lower image on the page of the book is of an ancient poor house, not named but clearly a pencil sketch of the Hospital of St Cross in Winchester, which comprises a courtyard entrance and a larger quad, with the resplendent chapel at the far end connected via a covered walkway and a series of conjoined almshouses on the other side. The very image of such a place lifts the soul and implies the superiority of a civilisation that treats its poor with such dignity as to house them in a place of sanctity and beauty. The modern almshouse, by contrast, is an eight-sided building with a single entrance. Within, it is unceremoniously divided into parts through protrusions from a central tower which looks like a guardhouse. It resembles more a prison than a place of charity and inspires contempt and loathing in the onlooker.[18] Pugin was not wrong in his critique of what architecture had become. He knew, however, that the problem was not primarily aesthetic but ultimately spiritual in nature.

Because of the Neo-Gothic revival, there are at least some buildings in Great Britain constructed in modern times that are less than repugnant and soul-crushing. Pugin's most famous building is London's Houses of Parliament.* This remains a crowning achievement of the Neo-Gothic revival and perhaps gives us some idea of what a more widespread return to Christianity would mean in aesthetic terms. It is not hard to imagine what would

---

* The official architect of Parliament is Charles Barry, but the historical facts are that Pugin designed almost all of it while working for Barry, and that Barry's name was simply attributed to it. On this, see Rosemary Hill, *God's Architect: Pugin and the Building of Romantic Britain* (London: Penguin Books, 2008)

happen if we decided that we had had enough of the ugly individualism of modern architecture and began to replace it stone by stone with structures that, like the Houses of Parliament, observe objectively existing rules of symmetry, proportion, congruence and order, and make use of thoroughly Christian features such as pointed arches for windows, ceilings and turrets. These features would not cost that much more money to utilise, nor would their construction be indicative of some kind of class snobbery. They are simply superior features that have been replaced with manifestly inferior ones. This is because we have lost our sense of ourselves as eternal beings destined for eternity with God and, as a result, we have decided to build for ourselves slums in which to dwell rather than real homes. This can all change, and it wouldn't take much in material terms.

Goodness

What might a return to goodness look like? Perhaps the area in which we have so lost the notion of an objective good is in that of the political arena which appears to most to be utterly dominated by a contemptible and pervasive sense of utility. Any contemporary crop of politicians manifests as a breed of self-seeking, soulless careerists who have almost no ability to appreciate the feelings and desires of ordinary people. The entire political scene is dominated by short-term attempts to win votes so that the people who carry elections can either obtain power or remain in power. It is a shameful spectacle and people are so tired of it that they can barely bother to turn out to vote in either local or general elections.

The problem is that we have lost the vision of the transcendent good. In most people's minds, society isn't *for* anything, and so it naturally follows that a political class rises up that is not *for* anything either, except, that is, its own pursuit of personal gain. And if society is not *for* anything then neither are the people who comprise it. Remember the assertions mentioned earlier upon the lips of the prophet of the transhuman age, Yuval Noah Harari:

because machines are replacing jobs there is an increasingly large swathe of 'useless people' and it is not clear what we need *so many* people for. This is a chilling statement of political nihilism, as though the only societal purpose for a human being is to contribute to the economy by being employed in a useful task (something which is obviously *not* true of Yuval Noah Harari incidentally).

As a riposte to the assertion that politics in the modern day is not *about* anything, it might be said that politics concerns economic prosperity. But really this is an utterly vacuous overall goal for a society in that the mere improvement of material conditions could never constitute a valuable telos for humanity. In both the Greco-Roman and Judeo-Christian eras, the goal of politics was thought to be the securing of the most propitious conditions for the pursuit of virtue in the citizenry. On a specifically Christian understanding, this would consist of the cultivation of holy souls in preparation for eternity with God. We must retrieve something of *that* vision, and order society according to it.

Perhaps a renewal of Christianity could simply entail a renewal of politics because the outlook of so many individual politicians would be different. But there is a deeper intellectual work that needs to be done: we need to understand that the secular liberal, multicultural outlook that we have imbibed is a thoroughly *religious* project that is leading us to total societal breakdown. Not only is it not a neutral framework, as the proponents of liberalism have always claimed, but it is a fundamentally anti-Christian political vision that seeks to subjugate Christianity to the status of a privately held belief system that should not be manifested in the public square and which cannot influence or affect political decisions. All this while the secular liberal outlook and various other modern-day political ideologies, such as that of progressive wokeism, are at total liberty to manifest themselves in every public forum, be that political, educational, or anywhere else. Christianity must not go on accepting this illegitimate demarcation of permitted territories.

Once again, nobody is suggesting a simple return to the days of King Alfred and Anglo-Saxon England. But what we can do is return to a vision of a Christian nation *given* the ways that things have changed. We must accept that many religions and alternative outlooks exist alongside Christianity in Western nations. As has been argued in various ways, it is in fact Christianity that has bequeathed to the world the legacies of freedom, equal treatment before the law, and the dignity of the individual. So any return to the Christian faith as a nation must be congruent with these principles that were drawn from Christianity. A return to Christianity, therefore, would mean that other religions and their adherents would need to be treated with respect and fairness. But this respect and fairness would not mean that our laws and customs would be shaped by other religions and perspectives alternative to Christianity. Our criminal laws, for example, should be based upon the morality of the Christian religion and not upon, say, that of Islam or secular humanism. And there are many other areas in which an assumption that Christianity is true would shape public policy and legislation.

On the broader ethical side, a return to Christianity would involve a retrieval of the notion that we have a transcendent end, which is to be transformed into the likeness of God and to live with him for ever. This is crucial to our understanding of the ubiquitous human experience of suffering and is the only justification for it: namely, that suffering is permitted by God and can be redemptive in so far as it can be accepted humbly as a purification of the soul as it makes progress towards God on the pilgrimage of life. Seen in this way, the suffering of individuals, particularly as they approach death, is not pointless and undignified but has the capacity to be sacred and noble. It is the duty of other people not simply to kill those who, in terrible ways, suffer, but to care for them and suffer alongside them. This is a truly holy vision of suffering and death which, in its radiant beauty, secures an eternal reward for those who undergo such trials in faith. This vision must be preferred to the ugly, utilitarian expediency of the culture of death as it manifests itself in the increasingly widespread practice of euthanasia.

Further, a return to Christianity would mean a pulling back from the slide towards the practice of abortion which is, sadly, already so widespread. In a Christian outlook, the sacrifice of the young for the comfort and expediency of those stronger than they are (however beleaguered themselves) is never a virtuous trade. Such a society would need to do at least two things: it would need to protect unborn children through laws safeguarding their well-being while also providing a charitable and compassionate infrastructure which could help women who find themselves pregnant in dire circumstances. In doing both things at once, it is possible that both women and children could be cared for and respected.

Perhaps one of the hardest suggestions for our modern ears to hear is that such a return would also involve the reintroduction of respect for, and promotion of, the traditional family unit. It is obvious that the widespread individualism of our culture is poisonous to family life, destroying marriages and turning children against their parents. A true return to Christianity would mean naturally stronger marriages and greater levels of commitment by parents to their children. It would also entail greater respect for the elderly and an expectation that children should care for their own parents in their dotage. Without wishing to impugn those who sacrificially care for the elderly in our current society, it is surely one of the marks of the selfishness and inhumanity of our age that so many older people are all but totally abandoned by their own children to the help of others in care homes. A true return to the faith would see a significant change to this practice and many more children caring for their own parents into old age and as they approach death. Such a dignified and noble path taken by these children would be an edifying and uplifting spectacle for all, superior in every way to the current widespread abdication of natural moral responsibility.

The broader principle in all this would be a rediscovery of the notion that man is created for a certain end and that end is the pursuit of the good. The culture of death manifests in the way it does because mankind has lost sight of his transcendent end. He considers that the only thing he was put upon this Earth to do was seek pleasure and avoid pain. Upon such an anaemic, individualistic and utilitarian compass, it is not surprising that he can see nothing redemptive in pain, sacrifice and struggle. After all, these things are simply the enemy of his limited purpose and outlook. If they overwhelm him and drain the pleasure from his existence, what is left but the sweet relief of oblivion and death?

The Christian faith gives us an eternal end for which to live. We are sanctified and propelled towards the good not only through our relationship to God as individuals but through our love and care for one another. What difference would it make if this Christian set of principles began to permeate our national consciousness once again? My guess is that it would mean a complete transformation of outlook and therefore a great change in our society. We would pull back from a complete descent into the jaws of death and begin once again to choose life and health. For a start, we would care properly for the elderly, the unborn, the terminally ill, and other vulnerable people, and not seek to discard, marginalise or euthanise them.

Truth

Truth is an end in itself. It is worth knowing about things and living in congruence with what is true, with what is objectively the case. Because of the advent of postmodern thought, we are gradually abandoning the notion that the world is something that must be accepted as objectively 'out there' and replacing it with the idea that we create reality with our own subjective feelings and imagination.

This shift in outlook creates the conditions in which ideologies such as transgenderism can take hold. Transgenderism is fundamentally postmodern in outlook. In its most simple form, it says that there is an objectively existing 'sexed' body and a subjectively existing 'gender identity'.* If the objectively existing body does not match the gender identity, then the body must be altered through drugs and surgery to achieve congruence between the two. Only in this way can the transgender individual find true peace. The reality of the situation is, of course, that there is only one objective and true component to this anthropology, which is that every human being has an objectively existing body with a biological sex. Whatever a gender identity is, it is not something that exists objectively, but is something that is imagined by the person who possesses it. But the gender identity is considered in this ideology to be the 'real' part of the person. The 'real' part must therefore take precedence over the body, which is seen to be somehow less real. What is effectively happening, however, is that the nebulous and ephemeral gender identity is being preferred in significance to the objectively existing, real human body that each person possesses. Biology is real. Sex is real. 'Male' and 'female' are categories that denote significant and objectively existing differences between both the members of our species and those of the beasts. In transgenderism, we have seen the triumph of the postmodern notion that 'my' truth should subjugate that of the objectively existing actual truth.

One of the saddest elements of the transgender ideology is the cult-like way that vulnerable young people are initiated into it through internet groomers who inculcate them into its ideological framework and encourage breast-binding, puberty blockers

---

* It is a common critique of transgender ideology that the phrase 'gender identity' is underdefined. For example, the 'Gender Identity' Wikipedia page begins with the definition: 'Gender identity is the personal sense of one's own gender'. This might help if the page went on to define the word 'gender', but it does not. All we are told is that some scientific evidence shows that gender identity might have a biological basis while 'social constructivists' argue that gender identity is dependent upon cultural and social influences. But nowhere are the terms 'gender identity' and 'gender' defined ('Gender Identity', Wikipedia, accessed 01.07.2024, [https://en.wikipedia.org/wiki/Gender_identity#cite_ref-Morrow Messinger_1-0]).

and, eventually, life-altering, mutilative surgery such as double mastectomies and genital castration. They are also told, during this process of grooming and inculcation, that if their parents are anything less than 100 per cent encouraging then those parents are transphobes and ought to be completely cut off as a result.*

This is but *one* of the damaging manifestations of a post-truth culture. More broadly, the truth possesses a higher authority than all the rulers of the Earth, no matter how resourceful or powerful. This is the meaning behind the political dissident and writer Aleksandr Solzhenitsyn's rallying cry, 'One word of truth shall outweigh the whole world.' It was as if Solzhenitsyn was standing against the entire machinery of the rapacious, murderous and extremely powerful Soviet Union, and saying, 'It does not matter if you send me to the Gulag. It does not matter if you murder my friends and my family. It does not matter if you torture me and slowly starve me to death. The truth is still the truth, and, eventually, your empire of lies will come crashing down about you.' The truth will prevail. Every Nero, every Henry VIII, every Louis XIV, every Napoleon, every Hitler, every Stalin, every Pol Pot and every Chairman Mao will find that they are not able to change the unalterable facts of reality, no matter how much political power they may wield, no matter how many people they imprison, torture or kill. In Orwell's *Nineteen Eighty-four*, Winston Smith is arrested and tormented within the euphemistically named 'Ministry of Love' until he finally admits that two and two equals five. But we know that such things are ephemeral and passing manifestations of political violence that cannot survive contact with the rising light of the dawn. Two and two equals four. Communism is an economically disastrous system that has been responsible for the deaths of millions. The emperor is not a God. Men are not

---

* I have already mentioned Abigail Shrier's illuminating work *Irreversible Damage: Teenage Girls and the Transgender Craze*. Given her extensive research and its shocking results, Shrier's analysis comes across as remarkably irenic and restrained..

women, and women are not men. It does not matter, from age to age, who says it or even who believes it: the truth is the truth and the lie – whatever lie it might be – will not endure.

If we were truly to return, we would recover from the nightmare of postmodern relativism in a post-truth world. We would once again arm ourselves against the despotism and caprice of rulers who cannot resist the temptation to tell us that two and two equals five. We would be able to tell them that it does not because the Truth is a higher authority than all others. And this because the Truth is another name for the ultimate reality behind all things, who is God himself.

In saying this, we are also talking about a return to reason. It has been one of the arguments of this book that the 'scientific' worldview that has apparently replaced Christianity is actually a horrible deviation from the Christian legacy that first promoted reason and science. Given our adoption of moral relativism and our embrace of the culture of death, it is only to be expected that science itself would be co-opted by these forces and pressed into their service. As I have already observed, science has become a politically expedient excuse for the machinations of the powerful. Debate and dialogue are silenced with the claim that 'science' has settled all important matters once and for all and that our lives and our world must be radically altered as a result. And yet, at the same time, we are told that it is a 'scientific' belief to accept that men can be turned into women and vice versa. We are also told that the widespread response to Covid-19 was a triumph of science, even though all the available evidence tells us that it was a generational disaster. Science is, in other words, like a helpless child caught in the midst of a stampeding mob, being pushed and pulled, now one way, now another, depending on what is expedient. Science is, on the one hand, completely objective and unquestionable. But, on the other, science has become a tool of irrationality for the purposes of political and cultural expediency. How can science be freed from this bondage?

My answer is that science must take its place within a broader, overarching view of all reality. The view of reality in which science came to be born was Christianity and it is only Christianity, with its monotheistic framework and its unique understanding of reason, that can provide the appropriate theoretical canopy for a rational, scientific enquiry into the workings of the natural world. A return to Christianity would mean that the various branches of science could take their place within that broader framework and would guard against the idea that 'science' is somehow that framework.

Once again, we would not want simply to return to medieval science. But what we would need to retrieve is the notion that both science and theology are legitimate fields of human enquiry; they both have their proper spheres of interest, which, at points, intersect with each other. The orthodox Christian approach to this question must be that genuine scientific truth and genuine theological truth cohere with each other even if it is not clear at times how this may be the case. We have moved from a society in which this was believed to one in which it is assumed that genuine science is true and that theology is a backward and erroneous field of study that has nothing to contribute to humanity. We have become, in other words, believers when it comes to 'science' and cynics when it comes to theology. If we were to return to the faith of our ancestors, we would see a promotion of both fields with free scientific enquiry in operation. That freedom would operate in two directions: first, science would be free to pursue conclusions that might seem to contradict theological assumptions and beliefs. Second, it would also be the case that the conflict between provisional scientific discoveries and Christianity would be taken seriously and not simply dismissed through recourse to the superiority of the science. All this could be done without anxiety (as it was most of the time in the medieval period) because of the basic assumption that the Christian worldview is true, albeit imperfectly understood by human beings. Alongside this, the truly Christian society of the future would acknowledge the technological and medical benefits of science while weighing their dangers and disadvantages from within its own moral and philosophical tradition. It would be understood that technology is not morally or spiritually neutral but that it must be subjugated to the genuine needs and benefits of humanity in its quest for God and the good life.

Conclusion: Two Paths

In this final section, I have attempted to sketch an alternative future to the one warned of in the rest of this book. Reality is complicated, and things are never as simple as to say that one of two very well-defined and specific futures lies in store for a civilisation. But it is nevertheless the case that the West faces a choice. We can abandon the relatively recent societal experiment with godless, post-human secularism and recognise the disaster that it has brought upon us. We can reassess the bogus intellectual history and philosophy that we have used to justify our decision to pursue this path. We can recognise our dependence upon the faith that has given us almost everything of value that we possess, and cleave to it once again. Or we can continue upon the path we're taking, with its trajectories that are becoming ever clearer and ever more horrifying with each passing year. And we will face the consequences that result either way. As the book of Deuteronomy says, life and death are set before us. Blessing and curse. The choice is ours.

Finally, what might we do if we are concerned by all this? The first and obvious answer is to be a Christian and to commit oneself to this way of life, to be part of the Christian Church and to be a sanctifying presence within it. There may be an issue here, though, for those who are indeed concerned about the decline of Western culture and who understand the link with the decline of Christianity, but who nevertheless find it hard to commit to the Christian religion personally. This is a logically feasible position – after all, the fact that Christianity has acted as a bulwark against the darkness does not necessarily make it true. My suggestion is that people who find themselves in such a position take a more generally supportive approach. Recall the earlier image of a flying buttress which helps to hold up the wall of a cathedral. This approach may include a commitment not necessarily to the Christian religion but to the broad metaphysical picture that this concluding chapter has been utilising: namely, the transcendental ends of Beauty, Goodness and Truth. You may not be able to bring yourself to believe in all the tenets of Christianity, but perhaps a first step might be to recognise the objective reality of these transcendental ends and to pursue them personally. Orientate yourself to what is objectively good and true and beautiful. Reject the culture of death, lies and ugliness. Commit yourself to life, truth and beauty. In doing so, you will place yourself firmly in the philosophical and cultural tradition that culminated historically in the flowering of Christianity, and you will be a natural ally of the Christian rebellion. It is to be observed also that belief is not something that is easily defined or apprehended; it does not all come at once nor does it stay at a consistent level and gradually increase. There are ebbs and flows and undulations. Concern for one's civilisation may be a way to begin such a journey towards faith. This is a perfectly legitimate place to start. And the central question must surely be: does Christianity's powerful civilising effect point merely to its utility or is it a sign that it really is the truth?

Beyond this, as the culture declines, it may be that the Christian Church finds itself in a position in which it must be much more intentional in creating a parallel culture to that of the world. This will be even more expedient if the mark of the beast is introduced in any form, as it could lock Christians out of the economic systems of the world. Therefore, schools, universities, hospitals, businesses, theatres, libraries and many other cultural institutions will need to be pioneered from a specifically Christian perspective. This will be necessary in order to allow the Christian Church to survive and the people within it to flourish. But it will also be necessary to preserve the treasures of Western civilisation itself. As the early medieval monasteries preserved the learning of ancient Greece and Rome after the fall of the great empire, so too it may be that the Christian Church must preserve all that has been so good, true and beautiful in our world before it fell to the vandal forces of secular materialism.

We conclude, therefore, with a final scriptural reference. Wherever we find ourselves in the days to come, regardless of what darkness the world may descend into, the light of Christ will not be put out. It may seem for a time all too faltering and fading. In one great swathe of the world, embers only may remain. But to those who look upon this age with the eyes of faith, we must always remember that the true authority is not a president, a prime minister, a globalist corporation or the Antichrist himself. The true King of kings is Jesus Christ. He lives. And his light will continue to shine, even in the midst of this present gloaming.

The light shines in the darkness, and the darkness has not overcome it.

John 1:5

Notes

Introduction: A World Without God?

1 Cf. Callum G. Brown, *The Death of Christian Britain* (London: Routledge, 2001), pp. 145–92.

2 Friedrich Nietzsche, *The Joyous Science* (London: Penguin Books, 2018), p. 121.

3 Ibid., p. 225.

4 Fyodor Dostoyevsky, *The Brothers Karamazov* (London: Penguin Books, 2003), p. 757.

5 Nietzsche, *Science*, p. 226.

6 Ibid., pp. 133–4.

7 Ibid.

8 Charles Taylor, trans. Yanette Shalter, *Avenues of Faith: Conversations with Jonathan Guilbault* (Waco: Baylor University Press, 2020), p. 82.

9 Ibid.

10 David Bentley Hart, *Atheist Delusions: The Christian Revolution and its Fashionable Enemies* (New Haven: Yale University Press, 2009), p. 230.

11 Cf. Freddie Sayers, 'Neil Ferguson interview: China changed what was possible', *UnHerd*, 26.12.2020, [https://unherd.com/newsroom/neil-ferguson-interview-china-changed-what-was-possible/].

12 Cf. J.A. Franklin, *Charles Taylor and Anglican Theology: Aesthetic Ecclesiology* (Cham, Switzerland: Palgrave Macmillan, 2021).

I – History: The Myth of Enlightenment

1 Mattias Desmet, *The Psychology of Totalitarianism* (Vermont: Chelsea Green Publishing, 2022), p. 11.

2 Ibid., pp. 12–13.

3 Ibid., p. 13.

4 On this, see Tertullian *et al.*, *Apology, De Spectaculis* (Cambridge, MA: Harvard University Press, 1931).

5 William Cavanaugh, ' "A Fire Strong Enough to Consume the House":

The Wars of Religion and the Rise of the State', *Modern Theology*, 11(4) (1995) 397–420 (p. 398).

6 Jason Baxter, *The Medieval Mind of C.S. Lewis: How Great Books Shaped a Great Mind* (Westmont: InterVarsity Press, 2022), p. 151.

7 Hart, *Delusions*, p. 65.

8 Ibid., p. 66.

9 Cf. Rodney Stark, *Bearing False Witness: Debunking Centuries of Anti-Catholic History* (West Conshohocken: Templeton Press, 2016), pp. 166–7.

10 Jeffrey Burton Russell, *Inventing the Flat Earth: Columbus and Modern Historians* (New York: Praeger, 1991), p. xii.

11 Allan Chapman, *Slaying the Dragons: Destroying Myths in the History of Science and Faith* (Oxford: Lion, 2013), pp. 60–1.

12 David Bentley Hart, *The Dream-Child's Progress and Other Essays* (New York: Angelico Press, 2017), p. 91.

13 Cf. David Hutchings and James C. Ungureanu, *Of Popes and Unicorns: Science, Christianity and How the Conflict Thesis Fooled the World* (New York: Oxford University Press, 2021), p. 109, fn. 20.

14 Hart, *Progress*, p. 95.

15 Hutchings, *Popes*, pp. 87–8.

16 Ibid., pp. 90–1.

17 Samuel Klumpenhouwer, 'Early Catholic Responses to Darwin's Theory of Evolution', accessed 06.03.2024, [www.saeculumjournal.com/index.php/saeculum/article/download/11311/1300].

18 For example, in 2014, Pope Francis said, 'Evolution in nature is not inconsistent with the notion of creation' and elaborated on the need for God to explain the Big Bang and evolution. Cf. Scott Nueman, 'Pope Says God Not "A Magician With A Magic Wand"', NPR, 09.01.2023, [https://www.npr.org/sections/thetwo-way/2014/10/28/359564982/pope-says-god-not-a-magician-with-a-magic-wand]. The Roman Catholic Catechism says nothing particularly explicit on the issue, although, in Paragraph 283, it pronounces, 'The question about the origins of the world and of man has been the object of many scientific studies which have splendidly enriched our knowledge of the age and dimensions of the cosmos, the development of lifeforms and the appearance of man. These discoveries invite us to even greater admiration for the greatness of the Creator' (Catechism of the Roman Catholic Church).

19 Cavanaugh, 'Fire', p. 401.

20 Stark, *Witness*, p. 144.

21 Ibid., p. 151.

22 Seb Falk, *The Light Ages: A Medieval Journey of Discovery* (London: Allen Lane, 2020), p. 8.

23 Quoted in ibid., p. 5.

24 Ibid., p. 4.

25 Edward Grant, *God and Reason in the Middle Ages* (Cambridge: Cambridge University Press, 2001), p. 14.

26 Ibid., p. 2.

27 Ibid., p. 3.

28 Rodney Stark, *The Victory of Reason: How Christianity Led to Freedom, Capitalism, and Western Success* (New York: Random House Trade Paperbacks, 2006), p. 10.

29 Ibid. pp. x–xi.

30 Ibid., p. 12.

31 Grant, *Reason*, p. 15.

32 Ibid.

33 Falk, *Ages*, p. 5.

34 Stark, *Reason*, p. 28.

35 Ibid., p.30.

36 Both Rodney Stark and Edward Grant have illuminating chapters on developments of these sorts during the Middle Ages. For more, see Stark, *Witness*, pp. 72–91; Stark, *Reason*, pp. 33–68; and Grant, *Reason*, pp. 17–30.

37 For more on this see Abbot Suger, *Abbot Suger on the Abbey Church of St Denis and Its Art Treasures:* Second Edition, Erwin Panofsky and Gerda Panofsky-Soergel (eds) (Princeton: Princeton University Press, 2021).

38 Stark, *Witness*, pp. 152–4.

39 Ibid., p. 155.

II – Science: Why It Can't Replace Christianity

1 Ken Wilbur, *Quantum Questions: Mystical Writings of the World's Greatest Physicists* (Boston: Shambhala Publications, 2001), p. 11.

2 Readers familiar with Charles Taylor will recognise here what he calls 'cross-pressure'. Cf. Taylor, *Secular*, pp. 594–618.

3 Rupert Sheldrake, *Science and Spiritual Practices* (London: Coronet, 2017), p. 75.

4 For an illuminating study on this topic, cf. Andrew Davidson, *Participation in God: A Study in Christian Doctrine and Metaphysics* (Cambridge: Cambridge University Press, 2019); also cf. Franklin, *Theology*, pp. 107–11.

5 Taylor, *Secular*, p. 26.

6 David Bentley Hart, *Roland in Moonlight* (Brooklyn: Angelico Press, 2021), pp. 185–6.

7 M. Scott Peck, *The Road Less Travelled* (London: Arrow Books, 2006), p. 214.

8 Hart, *Roland*, p. 328.

9 Cf. Lawrence M. Krauss, *A Universe from Nothing: Why There Is Something Rather than Nothing* (London: Simon & Schuster, 2012).

10 Ibid., p. 105.

11 Cf. Peck, *Road*, pp. 221–300.

12 Premier Unbelievable?, 'Paul Davies: What would it take for me to believe in God?', accessed 18.03.2024, [https://www.youtube.com/watch?v=5q-nK_3T57s].

13 Charles Darwin, *On the Origin of Species* (Oxford: Oxford University Press, 2008), p. 356.

14 Cf. Anushka Asthana, 'Tim Farron says he's pro-choice after 2007 interview emerges', *Guardian*, 16.05.2017, [https://www.theguardian.com/politics/2017/may/16/tim-farron-says-hes-pro-choice-after-2007-interview-emerges].

15 Richard Dawkins, *The Selfish Gene* (Oxford: Oxford University Press, 2016), p. 25.

16 Sheldrake, *Delusion*, pp. 7–8.

17 Peck, *Road*, p. 217.

18 Ibid.

19 Gallagher tells his remarkable story in Richard Gallagher, *Demonic Foes: My Twenty-Five Years as a Psychiatrist Investigating Possessions, Diabolic Attacks, and the Paranormal* (New York: HarperOne, 2022).

20 Cf. Tia Ghose, 'The Science of Miracles: How the Vatican Decides', *Live Science*, 09.07.2013, [https://www.livescience.com/38033-how-vatican-identifies-miracles.html].

21 Carlie Porterfield, 'Dr Fauci On GOP Criticism: "Attacks On Me, Quite Frankly, Are Attacks On Science"', *Forbes*, 09.06.2021, [https://www.forbes.com/sites/carlieporterfield/2021/06/09/fauci-on-gop-criticism-attacks-on-me-quite-frankly-are-attacks-on-science/].

22 Anna Mikhailova, 'Exclusive: Government scientist Neil Ferguson resigns after breaking lockdown rules to meet his married lover', *Telegraph*, 05.05.2020, [https://www.telegraph.co.uk/news/2020/05/05/exclusive-government-scientist-neil-ferguson-resigns-breaking/].

23 Andrew Woodcock, 'Dominic Cummings says he left Durham self-isolation to drive to Barnard Castle to "test his eyesight"', *Independent*, 25.05.2020, [https://www.independent.co.uk/news/uk/politics/dominic-cummings-statement-barnard-castle-durham-eyesight-press-briefing-speech-a9531766.html].

24 Cf. Carol Roth, 'The Greatest Transfer of Wealth From the Middle Class to the Elites in History', Brownstone Institute, 01.11.2021 [https://brownstone.org/articles/the-greatest-transfer-of-wealth-from-the-middle-class-to-the-elites-in-history/].

25 Cf. Arthur Allen, 'How Pfizer Won the Pandemic, Reaping Outsize Profit and Influence', 05.07.2022, [https://www.nytimes.com/2021/05/04/business/pfizer-covid-vaccine-profits.html], accessed February 09.02.22. It was also reported in 2021 that the CEOs of Moderna and BioNTech were then each worth around $4 billion – Hannah Ziady, 'Covid Vaccine profits mint 9 new pharma billionaires', 21.05.2021, [https://edition.cnn.com/2021/05/21/business/covid-vaccine-billionaires/index.html].

26 Cf. 'The Rich are Getting Richer During the Pandemic', *Forbes*, 22.07.2020, [https://www.forbes.com/sites/jackkelly/2020/07/22/the-rich-are-getting-richer-during-the-pandemic/].

27 Cf. 'Government spend more than £184m on Covid Comms in 2020', *Campaign*, 02.03.2021, [https://www.campaignlive.co.uk/article/govt-spent-184m-covid-comms-2020/1708695].

28 Cf. 'Vax fee to general practice increased as government sets huge target', HSJ, 30.11.2021, [https://www.hsj.co.uk/primary-care/vax-fee-to-general-practice-increased-as-government-sets-huge-target/7031439.article].

III – Aesthetics: Why Secularism Cannot Ground Transcendence

1 Taylor, *Secular*, p. 309.
2 Ibid., p. 7.
3 Friedrich Nietzsche, *The Antichrist* (Milton Keynes: Merchant Books, 2012), p. 37.
5 Ibid., p. 59.
6 The phrase is taken from Charles Taylor's *A Secular Age*. Cf. Taylor, *Secular*, pp. 353–61.
7 Louis Dupré, *Religion and the Rise of Modern Culture* (Notre Dame, Indiana: University of Notre Dame Press, 2008), p. 55.
8 Amazon Prime Video Sport, 'EXCLUSIVE CLIP: "St James' Park Is Our Church" | We Are Newcastle United', accessed 26.03.2024, [https://www.youtube.com/watch?v=xqakKUGbBAo].
9 Gallagher, *Foes*, p. 176.
10 Ibid., p. 177.

11 BBC News, 'The Satanic Temple: Think you know about Satanists? Maybe you don't', accessed 26.03.2024, [https://www.bbc.co.uk/news/world-us-canada-65549975].

12 Gallagher, *Foes*, p. 57.

13 Ibid., p. 56.

14 Ibid., pp. 57–8.

15 Jordan B. Peterson, *12 Rules for Life: An Antidote for Chaos* (London: Allen Lane, 2018), p. xxvii.

16 Ibid., p. 111.

17 PhilosophyInsights, 'JordanPeterson: WhatToDoToBeSuccessful', accessed 27.03.2024, [https://www.youtube.com/watch?v=CPcQ5ZojGw8].

18 Jordan B. Peterson, 'Lecture: Biblical Series II: Genesis 1: Chaos and Order', accessed 27.03.2024, [https://www.youtube.com/watch?v=hdrLQ7DpiWs&t=8814s].

19 C.S. Lewis, *Surprised by Joy* (London: Collins, 2012), p. 242.

20 Patrick J. Deneen, *Regime Change: Towards a Postliberal Future* (Croydon: Forum, 2023), p. 122.

IV – Ethics (1): The Myth of Moral Progress and the Christian Revolution

1 Alasdair MacIntyre, *After Virtue* (London: Bloomsbury, 2007), p. 1.

2 Ibid., pp. 2–3.

3 Cf. Larry Siedentop, *Inventing the Individual: The Origins of Western Liberalism* (London: Allen Lane, 2017).

4 Cf. Tom Holland, *Dominion: How the Christian Revolution Remade the World* (New York: Basic Books, 2021).

5 Cf. Louise Perry, *The Case Against the Sexual Revolution: A New Guide to Sex in the 21st Century* (Cambridge, Polity Press, 2022).

6 Yoram Hazony, *Conservatism: A Rediscovery* (London: Forum, 2022), p. 194.

7 Cf. John Milbank, *Theology and Social Theory* (Oxford: Blackwell, 2006), particularly Part IV, 'Theology and Difference'.

8 Ibid., p. 117.

9 For all this see Siedentop, *Individual*, particularly Chapter I, 'The Ancient Family', pp. 7–18.

10 J.M. Bakke, *When Children Became People: The Birth of Childhood in Early Christianity* (Minneapolis: Fortress Press, 2005), p. 27. Much of the material in this section is based on Bakke's very helpful work on this subject.

11 'You shall not murder a child by abortion or kill that which is born.' *The Didache*, Chapter 2. Cf. Early Christian Writings, 'The Didache', accessed 08.04.2024, [https://www.earlychristianwritings.com/text/didache-roberts.html].

12 Bakke, *Children*, p. 29.

13 Ibid.

14 Bakke notes that, 'The physician Soranus gives a long list of criteria (some of them rather strict) a child must satisfy in order to be considered healthy enough to be allowed to grow up' (ibid., p. 31).

15 Quoted in ibid., p. 32.

16 Athanasius of Alexandria, trans. Penelope Lawson, *On the Incarnation* (New York: St Vladimir's Seminary Press, 1998), p. 93.

17 Extract from Gregory's Fourth Homily on Ecclesiastes. Cf. Early Church Texts, 'Gregory of Nyssa – In Ecclesiasten Homiliae – The Start of Homily IV', accessed 08.04.2024, [https://earlychurchtexts.com/public/gregoryofnyss_ecclesiastes_slavery.htm].

V – Ethics (2):
Confused Ideas and Disturbing Trends

1 Hart, *Delusions*, p. 20.

2 Ibid., p. 21.

3 Jean-Paul Sartre, *Existentialism and Humanism* (New York: Haskell House, 1977), p. 28.

4 John Gray, *Straw Dogs: Thoughts on Humans and Other Animals* (London: Granta, 2003), p. xii.

5 Cf. Brian Cummings (ed.), *The Book of Common Prayer: The Texts of 1549, 1559, and 1662* (Oxford: Oxford University Press, 2011), p. 248.

6 Gray, *Dogs*, p. 7.

7 Ibid., p. 11.

8 Ibid., p. 6.

9 Exeter Cathedral, '*Gaia* by Luke Jerram', accessed 10.04.2024, [https://www.exeter-cathedral.org.uk/whats-on/events/gaia-by-luke-jerram/].

10 Durham Cathedral, '*Gaia* at Durham Cathedral', accessed 10.04.2024, [https://www.durhamcathedral.co.uk/visit-us/things-to-see-and-do/durham-cathedral-in-lego/gaia].

11 Cardinal Robert Sarah with Nicholas Diat, *God or Nothing: A Conversation on Faith*, trans. Michael J. Miller (San Francisco: Ignatius Press, 2015), p. 161.

12 Don't Screen Us Out, 'Creating a world where people with Down

syndrome are equally valued', accessed 12.04.2024, [https://dontscreenusout.org].

13 NHS, 'What happens: abortion', accessed 12.04.2024, [https://www.nhs. uk/conditions/abortion/what-happens/].

14 UK Parliament, 'Partial Birth Abortion', accessed 12.04.2024, [https:// edm.parliament.uk/early-day-motion/12245/partial-birth-abortion].

15 Statistics cited in Paul Dirks, *Deep Discipleship for Dark Days* (Grimsby, CA: Ezra Press, 2023), p. 148.

16 See, for example, Stella Creasey MP, 'No watering-down, no new red tape: it's time to fully decriminalise abortion in England and Wales', *Guardian*, 08.04.2024, [https://www.theguardian.com/commentisfree/ 2024/apr/08/decriminalise-abortion-in-england-and-wales-parliament-women-stella-[ro]creasy?utm_term=Autofeed&CMP=twt_gu&utm_ medium&utm_source=Twitter#Echobox=1712558438].

17 Sarah, *God*, p. 161.

18 Danny Kruger, *Covenant: The New Politics of Home, Neighbourhood and Nation* (Croydon: Forum, 2023), p. 76.

19 HART, 'A line in the sand for euthanasia: Canada is killing with kindness', HART's Substack, 06.06.2023, [https://hartuk.substack.com/p/ euthanasia?r=126y6j&utm_medium=ios&utm_campaign=post].

20 Maria Cheng, 'Disturbing: Experts troubled by Canada's euthanasia laws', Associated Press, 11.08.2022, [https://apnews.com/article/covid-science-health-toronto-[ro]7c631558a457188d2bd2b5cfd360a867].

21 Kevin J. Jones, 'Hungry, Poor, and Disabled Canadians Now Seeking Assisted Suicide', National Catholic Register, 13.12.2022, [https://www. ncregister.com/cna/hungry-poor-and-disabled-canadians-now-seeking-assisted-suicide].

22 Cheng, 'Disturbing'.

23 Madeleine Teahan, 'The alarming spread of child euthanasia', *Spectator*, 03.05.2023, [https://www.spectator.co.uk/article/the-alarming-spread-of -child-euthanasia/].

24 Referenced in Teahan's article.

25 Kruger, *Covenant*, p. 77.

26 Matthew Parris, 'We can't afford a taboo on assisted dying', *The Times*, 29.03.2024, [https://www.thetimes.co.uk/article/we-cant-afford-a-taboo -on-assisted-dying-n6p8bfg9k].

27 Mary Wright and George Mair, 'Anger as EU project sees Police Scotland rebrand paedophiles as "Minor-Attracted People"', *Scottish Daily Express*, 30.12.2022, [https://www.scottishdailyexpress.co.uk/ news/scottish-news/anger-eu-project-sees-police-[ro]28841534?utm_ source=twitter.com&utm_medium=social&utm_campaign=sharebar].

28 Dirks, *Discipleship*, p. 155.

29 Louise Perry, 'We Are Repaganizing', *First Things*, 10.2023, [https://www.firstthings.com/article/2023/10/we-are-repaganizing].

30 Linda Lovelace and Mike McGrady, *Ordeal: An Autobiography* (New York: Citadel Press, 1980), quoted in Perry, *Revolution*, p. 99.

31 Ibid.

32 Sarah, *God*, pp. 157–8.

33 Ibid.

34 Dana Kennedy, 'Lia Thomas so "well-endowed" I had to "refrain from looking": Riley Gaines' *New York Post*, 05.08.2023, [https://nypost.com/2023/08/05/lia-thomas-so-well-endowed-i-had-to-refrain-from-looking-riley-gaines/].

35 Lee Brown, 'Riley Gaines "ambushed and physically hit" after Saving Women's Sports speech at San Francisco State', *New York Post*, 07.04.2023, [https://nypost.com/2023/04/07/riley-gaines-ambushed-and-hit-after-womens-speech-at-sfsu/].

36 Kennedy, 'Lia Thomas'.

37 Io Dodds, 'Critics accuse trans swimming star Lia Thomas of having an unfair advantage. The data tells a different story', *Independent*, 31.05.2024, [https://www.independent.co.uk/news/world/americas/lia-thomas-trans-swimmer-ron-desantis-b2091218.html].

38 Bhavesh Purohit, 'When transgender fighter Fallon Fox broke opponent's skull in MMA fight', Sportskeeda, 30.09.2021, [https://www.sportskeeda.com/mma/news-when-transgender-fighter-fallon-fox-broke-opponent-s-skull-mma-fight].

39 Alan Murphy, 'Exclusive: Fallon Fox's Latest Opponent opens up to #whoatv', Whoa TV, 17.09.2014, [https://whoatv.com/exclusive-fallon-foxs-latest-opponent-opens-up-to-whoatv/].

40 Nazia Parveen, 'Karen White: how "manipulative" transgender inmate attacked again', *Guardian*, 11.10.2018, [https://www.theguardian.com/society/2018/oct/11/karen-white-how-manipulative-and-controlling-offender-attacked-again-transgender-prison].

41 Pope John Paul II, 'Evangelium Vitae', Vatican, 25.03.1995, [https://www.vatican.va/content/john-paul-ii/en/encyclicals/documents/hf_jp-ii_enc_25031995_evangelium-vitae.html].

42 Bethan Staton, 'UK natural population set to start to decline by 2025', 12.01.2022, *Financial Times*, [https://www.ft.com/content/7a558711-c1b8-4a41-8e72-8470cbd117e5].

43 Rosa Silverman, 'Child-free by choice: The birth rate crisis gripping the West', *Telegraph*, 22.10.2022, [https://www.telegraph.co.uk/family/parenting/child-free-choice-birth-rate-crisis-gripping-west/].

44 'Populations in more than 20 countries to halve by 2100: Study', Al Jazeera, 15.07.2020, [https://www.aljazeera.com/news/2020/7/15/population-in-more-than-20-countries-to-halve-by-2100-study].

45 Holland, *Dominion*, p. 523.

46 Ibid., p. 524.

47 My thanks to Dr James Orr for this illustration.

VI– *The Church: Defence and Offence*

1 Ayaan Hirsi Ali, 'Why I am now a Christian: Atheism can't equip us for civilisational war', *UnHerd*, 11.11.2023, [https://unherd.com/2023/11/why-i-am-now-a-christian/].

2 Ibid.

3 Ibid.

4 Jamie Micklethwaite, 'DEATH STATES: Thought Tier 4 was bad? Brutal countries where you can be KILLED for breaking Covid rules from China to Nigeria', *The Sun*, 30.12.2020, [https://www.thesun.co.uk/news/13548567/coronavirus-lockdown-breach-executions-north-korea-china/].

5 Daniel J. Mahoney, *The Idol of Our Age: How the Religion of Humanity Subverts Christianity* ((New York/London: Encounter Books, 2018), p. 56.

6 Ibid., p. 57.

7 Robert Hugh Benson, *Lord of the World* (South Bend: St Augustine's Press, 2001), p. 9.

8 Winchester Cathedral, 'Festival of the Moon', accessed 23.04.2024, [https://www.winchester-cathedral.org.uk/event/festival-of-the-moon/].

9 Ewan Somerville, 'Pride flag on altar of "church of woke" triggers almighty court battle', *Telegraph*, 28.01.2023, [https://www.telegraph.co.uk/news/2023/01/28/pride-flag-altar-church-woke-triggers-almighty-court-battle/].

10 Dodsworth, *Fear*, p. 180.

11 University of Nottingham, 'Mandatory Covid vaccines for care home workers caused reduction in staff, new research finds', 28.06.2023, [https://www.nottingham.ac.uk/news/mandatory-covid-vaccines-care-home-workers-reduction-in-staff].

12 Wednesday Warriors, 'Yuval Noah Harari – Useless People', accessed 23.04.2024, [https://www.youtube.com/watch?v=IU-6YCXj6j4].

13 Cf. Revd Dr David Goodhew, 'After Covid: The Deepening Decline of the Church of England', Covenant, 08.01.2024, [https://covenant.living-church.org/2024/01/08/after-covid-the-deepening-decline-of-the-church

-of-england/] and Dr Ken Eames, 'Statistics for Mission 2022', The Church of England, accessed 24.04.2024, [https://www.churchofengland.org/sites/default/files/2023-11/statisticsformission2022.pdf].

14 Athanasius of Alexandria, *The Life of Antony and the Letter to Marcellinus* (New Jersey: Paulist Press, 1980), p. 86. Spelling Anglicised.

15 Abigail Shrier, *Irreversible Damage: Teenage Girls and the Transgender Craze* (London: Swift Press, 2021), p. 3.

16 Gregory of Nyssa, trans. Abraham J. Malherbe, *The Life of Moses* (New York: Paulist Press, 1978), p. 81.

17 Gerard Manley Hopkins, 'God's Grandeur', *The Major Works* (Oxford: Oxford University Press, 2009), p. 128.

18 Augustus Pugin, *Contrasts: A Parallel between the Noble Edifices of the Fourteenth and Fifteenth Centuries and Similar Buildings of the Present Day* (South Carolina: Create Space Publishing, 2016), p. 75.

Selected Bibliography

Athanasius of Alexandria, *The Life of Antony and the Letter to Marcellinus* (New Jersey: Paulist Press, 1980)

— *On the Incarnation* (New York: St Vladimir's Seminary Press, 1998)

Bakke, J.M., *When Children Became People: The Birth of Childhood in Early Christianity* (Minneapolis: Fortress Press, 2005)

Baxter, Jason, *The Medieval Mind of C.S. Lewis: How Great Books Shaped a Great Mind* (Westmont: InterVarsity Press, 2022)

Benson, Robert Hugh, *Lord of the World* (South Bend: St Augustine's Press, 2001)

Brown, Callum G., *The Death of Christian Britain* (London: Routledge, 2001)

Buckley, Michael J., S.J., *At the Origins of Modern Atheism* (New Haven: Yale University Press, 1987)

Cavanaugh, William, "'A Fire Strong Enough to Consume the House": The Wars of Religion and the Rise of the State', *Modern Theology*, 11(4) (1995), pp. 397–420

Chapman, Allan, *Slaying the Dragons: Destroying Myths in the History of Science and Faith* (Oxford: Lion, 2013)

Cummings, Brian (ed.), *The Book of Common Prayer: The Texts of 1549, 1559, and 1662* (Oxford: Oxford University Press, 2011)

Darwin, Charles, *On the Origin of Species* (Oxford: Oxford University Press, 2008)

Dawkins, Richard, *The God Delusion* (London: Black Swan, 2016)

— *The Selfish Gene* (Oxford: Oxford University Press, 2016)

Deneen, Patrick J., *Regime Change: Towards a Postliberal Future* (Croydon: Forum, 2023)

Desmet, Mattias, *The Psychology of Totalitarianism* (Vermont: Chelsea Green Publishing, 2022)

DiAngelo, Robin, *White Fragility: Why It's so Hard for White People to Talk about Racism* (UK: Allen Lane, 2019)

Dirks, Paul, *Deep Discipleship for Dark Days* (Grimsby, CA: Ezra Press, 2023)

Dodsworth, Laura, *A State of Fear: How the UK Government Weaponised Fear During the Covid-19 Pandemic* (London: Pinter & Martin 2021)

Dostoyevsky, Fyodor, *The Brothers Karamazov* (London: Penguin Books, 2003)

Duffy, Eamon, *The Stripping of the Altars: Traditional Religion in England, 1400–1580* (New Haven: Yale University Press, 2022)

Dupré, Louis, *Religion and the Rise of Modern Culture* (Notre Dame, IN: University of Notre Dame Press, 2008)

Falk, Seb, *The Light Ages: A Medieval Journey of Discovery* (London: Allen Lane, 2020)

Franklin, J.A., *Charles Taylor and Anglican Theology: Aesthetic Ecclesiology* (Cham, Switzerland: Palgrave MacMillan, 2021)

Gallagher, Richard, *Demonic Foes: My Twenty-Five Years as a Psychiatrist Investigating Possessions, Diabolic Attacks, and the Paranormal* (New York: HarperOne, 2022)

Grant, Edward, *God and Reason in the Middle Ages* (Cambridge: Cambridge University Press, 2001)

Gray, John, *Straw Dogs: Thoughts on Humans and Other Animals* (London: Granta, 2003)

Grayling, A.C.,*The Age of Genius: The Seventeenth Century and the Birth of the Modern Mind* (London: Bloomsbury, 2016)

Green, Toby, *The Covid Consensus: The New Politics of Global Inequality* (London: Hurst and Company, 2021)

Gregory of Nyssa, trans. Abraham J. Malherbe, *The Life of Moses* (New York: Paulist Press, 1978)

Hart, David Bentley, *Atheist Delusions: The Christian Revolution and its Fashionable Enemies* (New Haven: Yale University Press, 2009)

— *The Experience of God: Being, Consciousness, Bliss* (New Haven: Yale University Press, 2013)

— *The New Testament: A Translation* (New Haven: Yale University Press, 2017)

— *The Dream-Child's Progress and Other Essays* (New York: Angelico Press, 2017)

— *Roland in Moonlight* (Brooklyn: Angelico Press, 2021)

Hazony, Yoram, *Conservatism: A Rediscovery* (London: Forum, 2022)

Heiser, Michael S., *The Unseen Realm: Recovering the Supernatural Worldview of the Bible* (Bellingham: Lexham Press, 2015)

Hobbes, Thomas, *Leviathan* (Oxford: Oxford University Press, 2008)

Hopkins, Gerard Manley, *The Major Works* (Oxford: Oxford University Press, 2009)

Hutchings, David and James C. Ungureanu, *Of Popes and Unicorns: Science, Christianity and How the Conflict Thesis Fooled the World* (New York: Oxford University Press, 2021)

King, Martin Luther, Jr, *The Power of Love* (London: Penguin Books, 2017)

Klumpenhouwer, Samuel, 'Early Catholic Responses to Darwin's Theory of Evolution', www.saeculumjournal.com/index.php/saeculum/article/download/11311/1300

Kruger, Danny, *Covenant: The New Politics of Home, Neighbourhood and Nation* (Croydon: Forum, 2023)

Lawrence M. Krauss, *A Universe from Nothing: Why There Is Something Rather than Nothing* (London: Simon & Schuster, 2012)

Lewis, C.S., *The Screwtape Letters* (New York: Bantam Books, 1995)

— *Surprised by Joy* (London: Collins 2012)

MacIntyre, Alasdair, *After Virtue* (London: Bloomsbury, 2007)

Mahoney, Daniel J., *The Idol of Our Age: How the Religion of Humanity Subverts Christianity* (New York/London: Encounter Books, London, 2018)

Marx, Karl and Friedrich Engels, trans. Samuel Moore, *The Communist Manifesto* (London: Penguin Books, 1888)

Milbank, John, *Theology and Social Theory* (Oxford: Blackwell, 2006)

Nietzsche, Friedrich, *The Joyous Science* (London: Penguin Books, 2018)

Pasulka, D.W., *American Cosmic: UFOs, Religion, Technology* (New York: Oxford University Press, 2019)

Peck, M. Scott, *The Road Less Travelled* (London: Arrow Books, 2006)

Perry, Louise, *The Case Against the Sexual Revolution: A New Guide to Sex in the 21st Century* (Cambridge: Polity Press, 2022)

Pugin, Augustus, *Contrasts: A Parallel between the Noble Edifices of the Fourteenth and Fifteenth Centuries and Similar Buildings of the Present Day* (South Carolina: Create Space Publishing, 2016)

Rose, Fr Seraphim, *Orthodoxy and the Religion of the Future* (Platina: Saint Herman of Alaska, 2004)

Russell, Jeffrey Burton, *Inventing the Flat Earth: Columbus and Modern Historians* (New York: Praeger, 1991)

Sarah, Cardinal Robert with Nicholas Diat, *God or Nothing: A Conversation on Faith*, trans. Michael J. Miller (San Francisco: Ignatius Press, 2015)

Sartre, Jean-Paul, *Existentialism and Humanism* (New York: Haskell House, 1977)

Sheldrake, Rupert, *The Science Delusion: Freeing the Spirit of Enquiry* (London: Coronet, 2012)

— *Science and Spiritual Practices* (London: Coronet, 2017)

Shrier, Abigail, *Irreversible Damage: Teenage Girls and the Transgender Craze* (London: Swift Press, 2021)

Smith, Steven D., *Pagans and Christians in the City: Culture Wars from the Tiber to the Potomac* (Grand Rapids: William B. Eerdmans Publishing Company, 2018)

Stark, Rodney, *The Victory of Reason: How Christianity Led to Freedom,*

Capitalism, and Western Success (New York: Random House Trade Paperbacks, 2006)

—— *Bearing False Witness: Debunking Centuries of Anti-Catholic History* (West Conshohocken: Templeton Press, 2016)

Suger, Abbot, *Abbot Suger on the Abbey Church of St Denis and Its Art Treasures*: Second Edition, Erwin Panofsky and Gerda Panofsky-Soergel (eds) (Princeton: Princeton University Press, 2021)

Taylor, Charles, *A Secular Age* (Cambridge, MA: Belknap Press, 2007)

—— trans. Yanette Shalter, *Avenues of Faith: Conversations with Jonathan Guilbault* (Waco: Baylor University Press, 2020)

Tertullian *et al.*, *Apology, De Spectaculis* (Cambridge, MA: Harvard University Press, 1931)

Wilbur, Ken, *Quantum Questions: Mystical Writings of the World's Greatest Physicists* (Boston: Shambhala Publications, 2001)

Williams, Richard N. and Daniel N. Robinson (eds), *Scientism: The New Orthodoxy* (London: Bloomsbury, 2016)

Index

Index